J. Samuel Preus

EXPLAINING RELIGION

CRITICISM AND THEORY
FROM BODIN TO FREUD

AMERICAN ACADEMY OF RELIGION
TEXTS AND TRANSLATIONS SERIES

Edited by

Terry Godlove
Hofstra University

Number 16

EXPLAINING RELIGION
CRITICISM AND THEORY FROM BODIN TO FREUD

J. Samuel Preus

J. Samuel Preus

EXPLAINING RELIGION

CRITICISM AND THEORY
FROM BODIN TO FREUD

Scholars Press
Atlanta, Georgia

EXPLAINING RELIGION

CRITICISM AND THEORY FROM BODIN TO FREUD

J. Samuel Preus

Library of Congress Cataloging in Publication Data
Preus, James A. (James Samuel), 1933–
    Explaining religion : criticism and theory from Bodin to Freud /
J. Samuel Preus.
        p.   cm. — (American Academy of Religion texts and
translations series ; no. 16)
    Originally published: New Haven : Yale University Press, c1987.
    Includes bibliographical references and index.
    ISBN 0-7885-0321-9 (pbk. : alk. paper)
    1. Religion—Study and teaching—History.   I. Title.   II. Series.
BL41.P69   1996
200'.7—dc20   96-46105
                                                        CIP

Printed in the United States of America
on acid-free paper

Contents

Acknowledgments

When my son was four and I was a theologian, I undertook to explain religion to him. I spoke of God, maker of heaven and earth. "Who made God?" he asked.

My answer (now long forgotten) did not satisfy either of us. He went on to other questions; I stayed with this one and eventually wrote this book.

It is impossible to recall, much less repay, all my intellectual debts, but most of them were incurred like the one above: through people who listened and then asked the right questions. I wish especially to thank Wayne Proudfoot, Robert Bellah, David Ede, and E. Thomas Lawson for timely interventions. The responses of my colleagues at Indiana University have also been invaluable; both they and my students have driven me in the direction of clarity. For the rest, the footnotes and bibliography are an attempt to give credit where it is due.

To my wife, special thanks; her loving support never quits.

Indiana University
January 1986

Note on References

For the most part, references to primary sources are given parenthetically in the text. The abbreviations used in the text are explained in footnotes at the first citation in each chapter.

Footnote references are abbreviated throughout. For full bibliographical information, see the Bibliography.

Introduction

This is a historical study, in which the question posed to each of nine authors is as follows: how is one to account for the origin of religion? ("Origin" here will embrace the notions of cause and source.) That is an endlessly interesting question in its own right, but this book was first motivated by two more narrowly academic questions. Historically, how did an approach to religion that was informed by naturalistic rather than theological assumptions or religious commitments come into being? And how might one best make a meaningful (and I think necessary) distinction between such a study of religion and theology? Historical investigation of early modern European theories about the origin of religion can throw light on both these questions, and such is my purpose.

My claim is that the work of the authors treated here made a coherent research tradition[1] that produced a new paradigm for studying religion. This paradigm treats religion as an element of culture and is inchoately present but departmentally fragmented in the contemporary university. I shall refer to it as "naturalistic" rather than using the more common but misleading label, "reductionistic."[2]

1. Larry Laudan has a good definition of "research tradition," a term which he prefers to "paradigm": "a research tradition is a set of general assumptions about the entities and processes in a domain of study, and about the appropriate methods to be used for investigating the problems and constructing the theories in that domain" (*Progress and Its Problems: Toward a Theory of Scientific Growth*, 81). The function of research traditions, Laudan adds, is "to provide us with the crucial tools we need for solving problems, both empirical and conceptual" (82). They also "define partially what the problems are, and what importance should be attached to them" (ibid.)

2. "Reductionistic" is almost invariably used as a derogatory term in much of the literature on religion, where it denotes those sorts of explanations that do not resort to transcendence. Such usage wrongly implies that *only* the "reductionists" have explanations for religion, while the antireductionists modestly do not. Such is not the case. Antireductionists, rather, have a *different* explanation. I understand reduction to mean reducing complex data or phenomena to simple terms. This covers the broadest application of the term, from its medieval usage (as in Saint Bonaventura's "*reductio* of all the arts to theology") to contemporary science, where it means a certain kind of explanation: cf. Hans H. Penner and Edward A. Yonan, "Is a Science of Religion Possible?" 117–18. In the natural sciences, cf. Marjorie Grene, ed., *Interpretations of Life and Mind: Essays Around the Problem of Reduction*, 22 *et passim*. The term *Religionswissenschaft*, as defined by Reinhard Pummer, comfortably accommodates the naturalistic approach:

The new paradigm's decisive assumption was (and is) that religion could be understood without benefit of clergy—that is, without the magisterial guidance of religious authorities—and, more radically, without "conversion" or confessional and/or metaphysical commitments about its causes *different* from the assumptions one might use to understand and explain other realms of culture. Contrary to the claim of classical Western theology, this new tradition claimed and claims that it is not necessary to believe in order to understand—indeed, that suspension of belief is probably a condition for understanding.

The above paragraph makes obvious reference to the language of Thomas S. Kuhn, whose *Structure of Scientific Revolutions* provides a suggestive historical schema for understanding the evolution of other disciplines. However, my book was not conceived as a test of the Kuhn thesis or of how well it might "fit" the emergence of the study of religion from Western religious thought. It accomplishes only a part of the research tasks that would be necessary for a full application of the Kuhn thesis. Furthermore, Kuhn's book is theoretically "light," from a historian's point of view, and extremely plastic: it makes no claim to explain historical development on the basis of a novel theory of historical change.[3] Thus, I have no stake in the degree of validity the reader attributes to Kuhn's work, because nothing in the present work depends on that.

But Kuhn's work does provide the most useful available vocabulary for a study such as this and brings a number of interesting questions into focus. I will therefore use Kuhn heuristically rather than trying to "apply" him in great detail. First, though, I admit to using his key term *paradigm* in a way to which he may now object, since he has taken pains in his later work to argue that the primary and proper meaning of *paradigm* is narrower than the sense I have used above. In the postscript to the second edition of his original essay, and elsewhere, he stresses that *paradigm* most properly refers to "shared examples of successful practice"; more precisely, paradigms are "accepted concrete examples of scientific achievement, actual problem solutions which scientists study with care and upon which they model their own work."[4] But I retain also the broader meaning, and thus use *paradigm* in both of the two

---

see Pummer, "*Religionswissenschaft* or Religiology?" esp. 102–03, for discussion and clarification of terms.

3. David Hollinger, "Thomas S. Kuhn's Theory of Science and Its Implications for History," 199f., 215–16: Were I to elaborate a close application of Kuhn, I would focus on the notion of paradigm shifts and explore the analogy between the one traced here (from theology to the study of religion) and shifts such as that from astrology to astronomy, where a change in basic intent is accompanied by survival of considerable overlap in relevant data. As with early critiques of theology, ethical preceded empirical critiques of astrology. See Ernst Cassirer, *The Individual and the Cosmos in Renaissance Philosophy*, esp. 115.

4. Thomas S. Kuhn, *The Essential Tension: Selected Studies in Scientific Tradition and Change*, 318, 351.

senses Kuhn accepts: (1) as the "disciplinary matrix" of a discipline, including its basic assumptions, beliefs, and models; and (2) as exemplars of concrete puzzles and their solutions.[5]

In the first sense, for example, "theology" and "study of religion" (or "religious" and "naturalistic" approaches to religion) designate two rival paradigms, and we are especially interested in where they become incommensurable; again, completion of a "paradigm-shift" will be credited to Hume, because of his thoroughgoing naturalism. But my book also draws on the second and narrower meaning of paradigms as exemplars: in that sense, *each* of my authors might be regarded as paradigmatically significant, to the degree that they solved discrete problems in ways to which later students might profitably attend.[6]

A number of "Kuhnian" notions suggest themselves as we survey the terrain before us. For example, Bodin (the subject of my first chapter) already constructed a new paradigm in the very way he objectified religions in his *Colloquium,* for he managed to transcend the accepted and contradictory confessional frameworks available to him. Hume's *Natural History of Religion* is an elegant exemplar, in that he shows how the origin and cause of religion can be construed without reference to an innate religious sense. Or, moving to the level of the disciplinary matrix of contemporary studies, we might decide that the study of religion itself is still living in a "pre-paradigmatic" state, given the ongoing competition between incommensurable approaches.[7] Or should we, as some historians advocate (rightly, I think), take care to

5. Thomas S. Kuhn, *The Structure of Scientific Revolutions,* 2d ed., 175, 187. Kuhn admits that it was partly his own fault that "paradigms" became all things to all people, due to the imprecision and plurality of his initial usage: cf. his remarks in n. 4 above, 294.

6. As noted below, with reference to Walter Capps, the study of religion has not yet developed any consensus about its historical paradigm-exemplars. Most of my authors (except Durkheim and Freud) are not typically used in training students of religion, not having attained the "canonical" status of scientific exemplars through which students are initiated into the practice of science. In *religious* history, however, especially in the Christian history of dogma, close parallels to scientific paradigms are to be found in the history of dogmatic formulations and decisions, where a licensed group approves a certain formulation of a problem and its solution, and then banishes the competition. An excellent example is the Nicene formula of 325 C.E., which defined orthodoxy on one particular point and attempted to banish its rivals, the Arians.

7. In Kuhn's scheme, a paradigm is established only when it succeeds in eliminating the competition (but see Laudan's criticism of Kuhn's too stringent view of the elimination of rival paradigms; Laudan, above, n. 1, 133–36). Kunn holds that only one paradigm at a time defines the legitimate or "normal" scientific community—those who are "doing science." In religion, different communities keep emerging and exist in permanent competition, a situation described as "pre-paradigmatic" when applied to science (Kuhn, above, n. 5, 163). In religion, the several religions of the world, and the denominations and sects within them, represent the permanent survival of competing paradigms (in the sense of exemplars), but within each tradition, share the same paradigm (in the sense of basic presuppositions—for example, the rival denominations within Christianity). On a cultural level (the focus of this book), we are looking at the emergence

protect the pluralism afforded by tolerance of competing paradigms, and a flexibility unavailable to natural scientists?[8]

Overall, I would put my account in Kuhnian terms as follows: I try to show how a naturalistic approach to religion achieved paradigmatic status as a new enterprise—not only in the sense of being articulated in thought (as in Hume's "science of man"), but by becoming institutionalized as well, as the careers of my final three authors illustrate—Tylor gaining a university post in anthropology, Durkheim a first university chair in sociology, and Freud founding the International Psychoanalytic Association.[9] Around the turn of the present century, then, the study of religion was positioned for the work of training students in specialized knowledge of the field, so that they would be able to elucidate and revise the "maps" provided by the paradigms of Tylor, Durkheim, and Freud. This group of trained practitioners all worked within a new "disciplinary matrix," acquiring and putting into practice "a time-tested and group-licensed way of seeing" religious phenomena.[10]

But new intellectual frameworks, or ways of seeing religion, preceded such institutionalization, and it is this earlier development that I trace here—before the stage in which the study of religions became the domain of "licensed" groups or communities of scientist-scholars. Prior to that we discover an extended and arduous intellectual effort in which individuals struggled to resolve particular problems or to overcome anomalies that the received paradigms could not resolve.[11] The appearance of institutionalized forms of the study of religion cannot be explained or understood without reference to that preceding intellectual history.

---

of a new naturalistic paradigm now situated in institutions having quite disparate aims from those of all religious institutions—namely, universities.

8. See the superb essay of Hollinger (above, n. 3), 213, for a discussion applicable to the study of religion as well as to his own field of history.

9. Kuhn, especially in the 1969 postscript to his original essay, emphasized the sociological dimension of paradigm-completion: paradigms are the property of communities of inquiry (above, n. 5, esp. 176–81). In Britain, Tylor became in 1884 the first "Reader in Anthropology" at Oxford (Eric J. Sharpe, *Comparative Religion: A History*, 54). In 1888, Durkheim received "the first official recognition in France of the new discipline of Sociology" when the government entrusted him with a course in social science at the University of Bordeaux, and in 1896 the first chair of social science was created there for him (H. Stuart Hughes, *Consciousness and Society: The Reorientation of European Social Thought, 1890–1930*, 279–80). Georges Gusdorf notes that the first chair of anthropology was already established at the Museum of Man in Paris in 1855, while Paul Broca founded the Society of Anthropology there in 1859. London, Moscow, Rome, and Berlin all modeled similar societies on Paris ("For a History of the Science of Man," 83). Meanwhile, between 1833 and 1910, chairs in the history of religions were established at Basel, Geneva, Lausanne, Zurich, Bern, the Netherlands (four chairs), France, Brussels and Berlin (Gerhardus van der Leeuw, *Religion in Essence and Manifestation*, 2:701).

10. Kuhn (above, n. 5), 182, 189.

11. The characteristic feature of anomalies "is their stubborn refusal to be assimilated to existing paradigms" (Kuhn, above, n. 5, 97).

The naturalistic mode of inquiry traced here was put on its present theoretical footing only in the last century by such authors as Durkheim, Freud, Weber, and Malinowski. They are the subject of a recent review and assessment of the scientific study of religion entitled *Beyond the Classics?*[12] In that book, the "classics" are identified as the works of those nineteenth- and twentieth-century authors who laid the main theoretical and methodological lines along which contemporary study of religion proceeds. While the recent provenance of these designated "classics" correctly indicates the youthfulness of the field and its rich variety of exemplars, its longer intellectual history remains to be written. As the historian of early anthropology Margaret Hodgen declared, "To fix casually upon any handful of recent scholars as 'founders' or 'originators' is always a disservice to intellectual history."[13] In religion, it took three centuries to negotiate successfully a series of specific problems in order to prepare the way for those modern "classics." Thus, a major aim of this book is to identify some of the minor "revolutions" of thought behind those classics to reveal the intellectual sources from which they came.[14]

Selection of pertinent sources presents obvious problems; the possibilities seem endless, and I am certain my own list can be improved. Walter Capps warned anyone undertaking such a project that "the background context" for this field "is disparate, disjointed, flexible, and accumulated or even created rather than discovered. Its sources lie here and there, and its ingredients are always arbitrarily assembled."[15] He follows this well-stated caveat with a challenge to the field: "It cannot hope to be instrumentally self-conscious without knowing how to arrange its second-order literature. It cannot pretend to find its way until it can place its past in narrative sequences."[16]

I have tried to impose some coherence and shape upon that disparate early modern era by focusing on the question of origins or causes of religion—in its parts and as a whole. All of my authors exemplify approaches and solutions to that question, and the cumulative effect of their works—when arranged in the present way—can be construed as producing the naturalistic paradigm.

In addition to the problem of origins as the central organizing question of this book, its order and progression are informed by the notion that the

12. Charles Y. Glock and Phillip E. Hammond, eds., *Beyond the Classics? Essays in the Scientific Study of Religion.* The work considers the contributions of Marx, Freud, Durkheim, Weber, James, Richard Niebuhr, and Malinowski. Accordingly, its time-span stretches from 1818 (birth of Marx) to 1962 (Niebuhr's death). Although their evaluations of religion differed, all (including the theologian Niebuhr) distinguished themselves, the editors assert, through "borrowing the deterministic mode of explanation of the natural sciences and applying it to structure and change in the human personality and social arrangements" (xiii).

13. Margaret T. Hodgen, *Early Anthropology in the Sixteenth and Seventeenth Centuries*, 7.

14. Addressing his colleagues in the field of religious studies, Walter H. Capps observed in 1974 that "religious studies has not yet learned to operate with effective awareness of what might be called a second-order scholarly tradition"; it is a field that "has nothing functionally equivalent to apostolic succession" ("On Religious Studies, In Lieu of an Overview," 730).

15. Ibid.

16. Ibid.

modern study of religion has its roots in criticism of religion. Progressively advancing criticism, accompanied by successive levels of detachment from presuppositions and commitments typical of their time, led finally through the absolutes of confessional and natural theology to the question of origins being posed from an altogether nonreligious point of view.

My account begins with the theological wars of the sixteenth century.[17] At its outset, the protestant reformers engaged in criticism from alternative religious perspectives within Christendom, and they in turn received as much as they gave. The result was an impasse—a European religious war of all against all. Bodin provides my point of entry, because in the midst of this turmoil he brought religion itself into intellectual focus as a problem (the problem of contradictory absolute claims without criteria for solution) which could be approached fruitfully only from a perspective that would transcend contemporary confessional norms. His criticism of confessionalism and Christian parochialism led him to pose the question of origins in the hope of resolving contradictions by identifying aboriginal "true" religion.

Over time, as the debate progressed, it broke out of its tradition-specific (Judeo-Christian-Muslim) frames of reference and sought the "higher" ground of allegedly universal and rational yet still religious premises (Herbert of Cherbury and deism). Subsequently, those premises themselves were undermined by a skeptical historical criticism (Fontenelle), and the way was open for completely nonreligious naturalistic explanations. Such explanations were at first ostensibly offered only to explain religions *outside* the Judeo-Christian tradition, the latter being prudently and arbitrarily exempted from the new explanations (for example, by Fontenelle and Vico). But these naturalistic ideas were bound finally to burst the traditional theological framework within which their authors claimed still to be working.

My first four chapters (on Bodin, Herbert, Fontenelle, and Vico) prepare us to understand the situation in the time of David Hume (1711–76), who self-consciously conducted his inquiries into religion as part of a thoroughly naturalistic "science of man" (his term).[18] If there is one person in my account whose achievement might be marked as the completion of a paradigm shift,

17. The sixteenth-century fragmentation of Western Christendom signaled the crisis and breakdown of the medieval paradigm, ending an era that closely resembles Kuhn's conception of periods of "normal science." The medieval magisterium constituted "a uniquely competent professional group and acceptance of its role as the exclusive arbiter of professional achievement"; its members were "seen as the sole possessors of the rules of the game" in the realm of religious thought and action (Kuhn, above, n. 5, 168). The most systematic attack on the paradigmatic authority of the magisterium in the Reformation period was formulated by Luther in his 1520 address *To the Christian Nobility of the German Nation concerning the Reform of the Christian Estate;* cf. esp. 126ff.

18. On Hume's "science of man" and its limitations, see Georges Gusdorf (above, n. 9), 74–97. On the Greek origins of such anthropological study, see Clyde Kluckhohn, *Anthropology and the Classics.* Eric J. Sharpe (above, n. 9), 3, notes an earlier link between criticism of religion and its systematic study in classical times.

it is Hume. When Karl Marx later observed that the intellectual criticism of religion was essentially complete, he might as well have been referring to Hume as to Feuerbach.[19] Hume produced a thoroughgoing naturalistic critique of all available theological explanations of religion, whether rationalistic or revelational. But only because he pursued the logical consequences of his critique in his *Natural History of Religion* (1757) can we claim for him the achievement of a paradigmatic moment. For Hume not only undercut all appeals to supernatural or transcendent causes of religion, but went on to propose alternative paths of explanation of the available data—paths that are traveled still by scholars of religion. From Hume, our study follows the progress of such explanatory efforts through the evolutionists Comte and Tylor and finds appropriate closure with Durkheim and Freud, because their theories—much revised and debated—endure as the grounds for explaining religion within the naturalistic paradigm.[20]

Our focus on the course of criticism should not, therefore, be mistaken for another rehearsal of the "case against religion." I am after something much more interesting—the relation of that critical tradition to what inevitably (logically) had to come next for those who took the implications of criticism seriously: if "God is not given," how is one to explain religions—that is, their universality, variety, and persistence until now? Without taking that next step, criticism would remain parasitic on established theological models—a mere exposure of old anomalies without providing alternatives. Alternative explanatory theories had to be constructed, and this is what the naturalistic program undertook to do; its specific agenda, insofar as it broke decisively with theology, unfolded as an address to that fundamental problem.

My title reflects one of the most striking features of the early modern period, including the Enlightenment: its aspiration to explain everything. When applied to religious presuppositions, this effort involved their being reduced piecemeal from their role as the given context of thought to an object of critical investigation.[21] From the sixteenth century on, the religious set of givens that had provided the presuppositions and norms for almost every area of inquiry came to be the target of critical thought, first from rival religious perspectives and finally from nonreligious ones. Intellectual developments, especially in "natural philosophy" (the sciences), vastly reduced the cosmic scale of theological modes of explaining nature. The discovery of non-European cultures put into sharp relief the parochialism of Christianity's universalist ambitions. For a while, religion (or at least Christianity) was

19. Marx, in Reinhold Niebuhr, ed., *Marx and Engels on Religion*, 41.

20. It is at this "turn" that my account diverges from the direction taken by Michel Despland in his magisterial study, *La Religion en Occident: évolution des idées et du vécu*. His terminus ad quem is modern philosophy of religion. See my review in *Religious Studies Review*.

21. See my "Machiavelli's Functional Analysis of Religion: Context and Object."

exempt from the expanding naturalism. The very last bastion of theology (or religious thought) was, and is, its claim to be able to explain *itself*, on "its own terms." As I shall try to show, the birth of the modern study of religion occurred at the point where that claim was effectively challenged—where the same procedures for explanation that seemed accurate and fruitful in the realms of nature and social institutions were now applied to religion itself. Only on such an assumption could the modern study of religion build.

The conviction that religion could be explained captivated the imagination of the Enlightenment. Charles Dupuis expressed its exuberant spirit when he exclaimed: "The genius of a man capable of explaining religion seems to me to be of a higher order than that of a founder of religion. And that is the glory to which I aspire."[22] Only when such an aspiration was fully operational was a really new enterprise under way, because only then was every aspect of religion regarded as amenable to nonreligious explanation, including its very cause(s). Put conversely, so long as a supernatural (or some objective, transcendent) ground of religion was assumed as the really existent referent and generative source of religious language, the study and criticism of religion was limited to some, but not all, of its aspects, and no decisive line of demarcation could be drawn between theology and the study of religion. One could (and can) investigate the functions of religion, engage in historical-critical studies, and argue about hermeneutical approaches to myths and behavior without any essential contradiction arising between theology and the study of religion. But with the question of origins and causes it is a different story; the ways part, as the tradition traced in this book will show.

To be sure, the scientific study of religion has far more than this single dimension, the issue of causal explanation, in view; what I am suggesting is that it first stood on its own feet when it finally "confronted the gods," in Manuel's phrase, and tried to explain religion as such.

Theories of the origin of religion abounded, of course, in pre-Christian times, and a critical approach to the so-called revealed religions of the West long preceded the seventeenth-century enterprise.[23] From the Renaissance on, classical theories were revived and again became well known, above all through the medium of a revived exemplar—Cicero's *De natura deorum*.[24] But it was not simply a matter of warming up old materials; the problem was immensely complicated by the political as well as intellectual constraints of Christendom. In contrast to the rather light-hearted spirit of Greek and Roman speculation, which could be carried on without the burden of deeply

22. Quoted by Frank E. Manuel, *The Eighteenth Century Confronts the Gods*, 243.

23. Cf., for example, Ibn Kammuna, *Examination of the Three Faiths* (Judaism, Christianity, and Islam). To someone who has read only the European literature, this work by a Jew living in Muslim Baghdad will seem astonishingly modern, befitting at least a seventeenth-century level of critical inquiry. It was written about 1280.

24. Kuhn provides a nice parallel from the history of science, in which elements of an old paradigm may reappear and become fruitful in solving a new problem (Kuhn, above, n. 5, 108).

thought-out philosophical and dogmatic commitments and their coercive political sanctions, the early modern discussion was in deadly earnest.[25] Christian assumptions were increasingly under siege, as the very foundations of
Western Christendom—political and institutional as well as intellectual—
were being undermined by religious conflict, by the discovery of non-European cultures, and by the early achievements of natural science. The deep-
ening debate about religion, then, was only part of that epochal seventeenth-
century turn which, in retrospect, we recognize as the transition from the
medieval to the modern era.

The very abundance of contemporary literature about how religions and
their study ought to be conceived and organized amounts to evidence of an
identity crisis in the field; yet there is little indication today that the question
of the cause and origin of religion is, or even should be, a topic of interest.
It is worth reflecting on this remarkable and unfortunate fact. For about a
hundred and fifty years, from David Hume to Emile Durkheim and Sigmund
Freud, the issue was pursued and debated with the greatest urgency. Now
it is virtually ignored, and even demeaned as a futile question or worse.
Evans-Pritchard, for example, banishes the question from scientific consideration, noting with relief that we have at last "turned our eyes away from
the vain pursuit of origins."[26]
    This pursuit would indeed have been "vain" if in fact its representatives
supposed they could fix a discrete first beginning of religion in human (pre-)
history scientifically. But what was actually at stake was the question of
causes. What was being asked was not "Exactly *when* did religion come into
being?" so much as the fundamental question "How are we to account for
its very existence—not only its rise, but its persistence?" This is what Hume
was about, and Durkheim and Freud understood that no point of origin
could ever be scientifically fixed in place and time.[27] Thus, Evans-Pritchard

25. Jan de Vries finds nothing before the nineteenth century that advances beyond the ancient
classical theories: *The Study of Religion: A Historical Approach*, 11. This judgment may be based
in part on his total misreading of Hume (34). On the classical attitude to religion, see Kluckhohn
(above, n. 18), esp. 53ff. On the agonistic context of the early modern discussion of religion,
see Michel Despland (above, n. 20). The contrast is also noted by Sharpe (above, n. 9), 7.
26. E. E. Evans-Pritchard, *Theories of Primitive Religion*, 104. Cf. Kuhn (above, n. 5), 148,
on how certain problems get banished from consideration in science. Similar banishment of the
question of causes on the basis of the futility of identifying origins is implicit in Ninian Smart's
observation: "The search for a tidy account of the genesis of religion in prehistory by reference
to primitive societies . . . was hardly likely to yield decisive results. Thus, the anthropologists
have been more concerned with functional and structural accounts of religion in society and
relinquished the apparently futile search for origins" ("Religion, Study of," 619).
27. On Hume, see chap. 5 below, and the remarks of Richard H. Popkin in "Hume:
Philosophical versus Prophetic Historian," 92. Durkheim writes, "To be sure, if by origin we
are to understand the very first beginning, the question has nothing scientific about it, and
should be resolutely discarded. There was no given moment when religion began to exist. . . ."

in no way disposes of the question of why there is religion at all, or what might explain its virtual universality, its persistence, its irreducible varieties, and its changes.

In the language of early modern Europe, explaining religion took the form of giving an account of its origins (rather than speaking of its "causes") for good historical reasons. The whole inquiry was framed with reference to reigning cultural assumptions of an aboriginal divine creation and self-revelation. These assumptions determined that the question of causes would be posed in temporal terms, since the traditional explanation of the presence and persistence of religion was set within the framework of the biblical story.[28] Religion began with Adam, or someone very much like him. As that assumption became eroded by criticism, alternative accounts sought to fill the temporal gap, or somehow to integrate a natural with the received supernatural primeval history (Vico's prodigious efforts on this score are described in chapter 4). But whatever form the discussion took, the problem of the ever-present causes of religion was never out of mind. As a matter of fact, from Comte on (among my authors), its *survival* rather than its origins was the predominant problem requiring explanation.

If the real issue was causes rather than first beginnings, however, such questions are still an indispensable component of the study of religion. For how can such an enterprise proceed without any theory of causes, especially when its primary data, provided by the representatives of specific religious traditions, are routinely authenticated by references to a divine origin of some sort—especially *when such references function as explanations that are mutually exclusive?*

It seems that lack of interest in explaining religion stems from a combination of personal commitments, apologetic interests, and political convenience as much as from the "scientific" modesty often expressed by religious writers. "Religious studies" as it is normally carried on seems comfortable with a quasi-theological or metaphysical "solution" (or paradigm), by which the origins or causes of religion are placed beyond investigation on the ground that the source of religion is "transcendent." From such a perspective it is both unnecessary and impossible to advance any further toward explaining religion.[29] The "sacred" is something that can only be illustrated by collecting and classifying examples; it cannot be defined, analyzed, or explained, else it would not *be* sacred! Moreover, it may then be asserted, as Eliade does, that "the 'sacred' is an element in the structure of consciousness, and not a stage in the history of consciousness."[30] But such an assertion becomes con-

---

Emile Durkheim, *The Elementary Forms of the Religious Life*, 20. Evans-Pritchard is thus merely echoing what was already known.

28. See my "Zwingli, Calvin and the Origin of Religion."

29. Essentially the same point is made by Penner and Yonan (above, n. 2), 131.

30. Mircea Eliade, *History of Religious Ideas*, I: xiii; also idem, "The Quest for the 'Origins' of Religion," preface.

troversial in an academic setting where other scholars are struggling with the evolutionary emergence of our species. From such a perspective one legitimately wants to know how Eliade's remarkable "element in the structure of consciousness" might have gotten there.

Here we are in a realm where basic values are at stake, just as in paradigm disputes in the sciences as Kuhn describes them: the question is, "Which problems is it more significant to have solved?"[31] Answering this involves deciding, in Kuhn's language, what is "the fittest way to practice future science."[32] On that score, his analysis is relevant to our own project. From the sixteenth century on, we see a divergence between religious orthodoxy and authors such as Bodin and Herbert about what questions are significant to have solved. For orthodoxy, it was to establish the boundaries of theological truth; for men of diplomatic background—trained to transcend single-party perspectives—the priority was to understand the causes of war and the way to religious and political peace (not to mention peace of conscience!).

In the present setting, similar sorts of questions arise. What is the fittest way to study religion? What are the most significant sorts of questions to be tackled? The stakes are enormous, because basic decisions are involved about how the next generation of scholar-teachers ought to be trained, and such decisions are in turn informed by fundamental ideas about what liberal education is about, as well as notions about the future of religion.[33]

The idea that religion might be explained in naturalistic categories as clearly and well as any other cultural artifact of course invites the larger question of whether "explanation" applies to culture at all.[34] That question is a fair one, but it is not dealt with here. Less ambitiously, I suggest only that religion and the study of religion enjoy no privileged status. Despite the claim that religion is sui generis (whatever meaning one attaches to that notion), it seems self-serving rather than rationally persuasive to argue that religion can therefore be understood only from within a religious perspective.

To approach religion from outside the context of religious commitment may suggest to some that the difference between theology and the study of religion is that the former is "normative" while the latter is merely "descrip-

---

31. Kuhn (above, n. 5), 110.

32. Ibid., 172, in the context of the argument that an essentially Darwinian process of selection characterizes scientific development.

33. Hollinger (above, n. 3, 215) deals wisely with such issues in his critique of the "whiggish" interpretation of history, which protests that "certain ethical and logical ideals are so important to our survival, and so precariously held, that they need reinforcement, not the more complete 'understanding' that risks the miring of these ideals in the swamps of human nature and history." Freud's *Future of an Illusion* is an exemplary naturalistic critique of similar protests on behalf of religion.

34. Wilhelm Dilthey declared that we explain nature but only interpret culture. See the discussion by Gusdorf (above, n. 9), 93.

tive." As a matter of practice in a state university this has indeed been a serviceable cliché. It not only applies to a large part of what is actually done (especially in history), but emphasizes that we teach "about" religion and seriously intend to avoid the appearance of advocacy, apologetics, or attack. But even when one only "describes" religious traditions, the self-understandings and self-justifications of these traditions are inevitably included in any adequate description. The result is that a subtle form of apologetic may result, since the message conveyed is that the (only) right and proper explanations of religions are of the sort given by believers.

At the literal and elementary level, these are simply the particular accounts that traditions (Jewish, Christian, Muslim, and so on) give of their own origins. At a more abstract and generalized level may come the explanation (rooted in the deist tradition and aimed at blunting unpleasant questions about contradictions) that *all* religions are manifestations of a universal religious sense, or more or less adequate "manifestations of the sacred."

It is important to note that already implicit in this reduction of religious motivation to the terms of natural theology is the notion that the *reasons* for belief and action provided by believers do not necessarily exhaust an appropriate account of *causes,* that it is possible to discern, behind the explicitly stated, conscious reasons and causes identified by believers, forces or impulses of which they may not be aware. But that raises another question: what *are* the nature and explanation of these forces? The naturalistic tradition claims that "transcendence" is not the only or the best answer, and that the task at hand is not to limit possible answers to those that support religion. The goal, after all, is not to legitimate religion but to explain it. Failure to pursue that objective avoids the path of critical inquiry that characterized the study of religion in its vital formative period—namely, the proposal of alternatives to the explanations that the *religious* offer for religion.

This "alternative tradition" (James Thrower's label),[35] as it developed in the early modern West, is what this book is about. And the writers it treats, whatever else they are doing, are not creating a merely descriptive tradition, or merely adding to the store of historical material available (as a matter of fact, a purely descriptive approach stems historically from nineteenth-century apologetic theology, exemplified by Schleiermacher's effort to describe the contents of the religious self-consciousness to its "cultured despisers"). The new paradigm whose roots I discover is in its own right normative in the sense that it does not aspire merely to describe religious ideas and practices, but to render rationally supportable judgments about how these items (claims, beliefs, rituals) connect with the external realities to which religious language constantly refers and which ritual represents, as well as with the extramental reality generally and publicly available to everyone else.

---

35. James Thrower, *The Alternative Tradition: Religion and the Rejection of Religion in the Ancient World.*

Students of religion sometimes have difficulty appreciating theories such as we shall deal with here because they discover at some point that all the theories are wrong. The difficulty may lie in a misunderstanding of one difference between a religious tradition and a scientific one. Unreflective representatives of religious traditions do not routinely admit to the provisional character of their knowledge or to the method of trial and error in their investigations. Granted, my authors were all "wrong" about some things— just as Galileo, Newton, and Einstein were—in that their theories failed to resolve all old problems, or raised new ones that their own theories could not solve. But they all advanced the inquiry in some productive way. Their work was progressive because it identified and solved crucial problems of their times and generated new criticism and research. Their successors learned increasingly to treat their subject matter through questions that could be answered and theses that could be tested and corrected.

Considering my extended time-frame, the number of authors treated here is very small, and obviously some greater minds than, say, Herbert or Fontenelle have been omitted—Hobbes, Spinoza, Rousseau, Marx. But my authors seemed especially appropriate because they focused on what for me is the key issue—that of origins; because they were especially adept at formulating and addressing the particular problems of their times, and because, when read in the order presented, they can be observed as creating a coherent and progressive tradition of study. In their several ways, all tried to comprehend the sources of religion as such, and all pushed the discussion beyond where they found it.

I hope this book does as much. It tries to identify a coherent intellectual tradition running alongside and then breaking out of received theological and religious paradigms; it challenges the popular notion that the only proper approach to religions is "from inside," and the implicit corollary that the only proper comprehensive explanation of religions is that they are "manifestations of the sacred" or responses to "transcendence"; it argues that a clear distinction between a naturalistic approach—with its own explanatory apparatus—and religious approaches is necessary to achieve a coherent conception of what the study of religion is about; and, negatively, that such a distinction is needed in order to clarify the difference between study of religion in the framework of humanities and human sciences and often hidden apologetic intentions that inform much contemporary writing and teaching about religion.[36]

---

36. Ivan Strenski, "Our Very Own 'Contras': A Response to the 'St. Louis Project' Report," reflects my own view of what the study of religion is about.

PART I

RELIGION AS A PROBLEM

Chapter 1

Conflict, Contradiction, and Impasse: Jean Bodin

Jean Bodin (1530–96) treats at length the question that links together the writers examined in this book—the origin of religion. At the same time, he provides a vivid example of the context out of which the question arose and helps explain the paths of inquiry that the study of religion would subsequently follow.

It hardly exaggerates the case to state that the context generated, even required, the question. Given the situation, it was bound to come up. The context to which I refer has two salient features: religious conflict in Europe (nowhere worse than in France during Bodin's lifetime)[1] and the disturbing reality of the vast religious world being discovered outside of Christendom. The pressure of both these elements of context are amply evident in the work with which we shall primarily be concerned, the *Colloquium Heptaplomeres de rerum sublimium arcanis abditis* (in its English translation, *Colloquium of the Seven about Secrets of the Sublime*), written by 1593 but not published until 1857.[2]

The exploration of the world had raised the ante on the Reformation question of which version of Christianity was authentic and true; now the question was not merely what form of Christianity but which *religion* is true? Repeatedly, the *Colloquium* states the painful and global state of affairs: "omnes ab omnibus refelluntur—all are refuted by all" (V, 256/196). And when one participant naively asks, "Who can doubt that the Christian religion is the true religion or rather the only one?" the answer is brutal and short: "Almost all the world" (IV, 163/125).

Bodin realized that making intellectual headway in such a situation required going radically beyond the mutually contradictory claims, credentials, and paradigms of the religious traditions; it required a new criterion for assessing

---

1. Cf. Preston T. King, *The Ideology of Order*, especially 47–55.
2. Joannis Bodini, *Colloquium Heptaplomeres de rerum sublimium arcanis abditis*, ed. Ludovicus Noack (hereafter, *Colloquium*). Usually I follow the translation of M. L. D. Kuntz, *Colloquium of the Seven about Secrets of the Sublime*. References in my text are to book number, page in Kuntz translation/page in Noack (e.g., V. 256/196).

religious claims, an Archimedian point outside the conflict. This search led, in Bodin's logic, to the idea that the key to making a rational judgment about true religion depends on uncovering its first origin.

But there was more to the problem than that. Bad enough that the theoretical question of mutually exclusive religious claims presented itself in a world where there was no one to arbitrate such disputes (cf. IV, 170/131). Worse, the European religious conflict was simultaneously a sociopolitical crisis, which involved not only intellectual disagreement but powerful public officials making decisions about religion in the public realm (toleration? coercion?). And that, in turn, faced conscientious individuals with choices that frequently pitted conscience against interests of survival. Since this was a world of coercion, persecution, and compulsion in religion, one had not merely to reflect upon abstract matters of truth but upon a course of action, for "if there are laws contrary to laws, and lawgivers hostile to lawgivers, religion opposed to religion, priests warring with priests, what will the poor subjects do when they are pulled here and there into the sects?" (IV, 163/125).

Already, then, existed three problems of immense gravity: religious truth, religious policy, and the religious conscience. These issues, all addressed in the *Colloquium*, were excruciatingly exemplified in France during the lifetime of Jean Bodin and reflected in the perilous course of his own biography.

Bodin's identification and discussion of these issues merit for him an important place in the modern study of religion. Simply, he was one of the first to identify religion itself as a problem requiring a new and comprehensive kind of analysis. Adopting a perspective decidedly outside each of the rival traditions, he proceeded on the assumption that their insoluble conflicts and endless variety belied their claims to exclusive possession of true religion and divine approval. His very invention of the format of the colloquium signals a paradigm-shift by setting up a confrontation, on equal ground, of contradictory paradigms, in the attempt to find a new common ground. Bodin was confident that the problem could be fruitfully investigated in all its dimensions by men of goodwill whose criterion for judgment would be reasoned argument alone, operating in a detached setting where no authority should prevail except their own consensus or, lacking that, harmony in their agreement to disagree.

The complexity of Bodin's *Colloquium* results in part because he approaches religion from so many different angles and tries to grasp it as a whole rather than reducing it to one problem. An important principle for ordering and interpreting the material is to realize that Bodin has succeeded in differentiating his inquiry into three related but distinguishable realms—intellectual, political, and attitudinal.

In the first sphere one asks: what is true religion and how, if at all, are we to identify it? Second, what is religion's role in society, and what obligation and right (if any) does the government have to regulate it? Third, what are people to do when they are simply confused by the rival claims, or when they find themselves in situations in which their private views are at odds with public religious obligations?

For Bodin, all these questions are entailed in the problem of religion as he begins to sort it out, and what he tackled all at once later students would treat in more specialized pursuits, as the study of religion differentiated and fragmented itself into the disciplines of philosophy, sociology, and psychology of religion. Stated a little more broadly, Bodin's questions anticipate everything to be dealt with in this book: the relation between religion and reason, between religion and society, and between religion and personality. In that respect, his work displays the spectrum of religion as a problem of study, raising the curtain on a new tradition of research that only later divided into the several disciplines that comprise the study of religion today.[3]

Jean Bodin was born in the year of the Augsburg Confession (1530) and died two years before the Edict of Nantes of 1598. His life, then, is appropriately bracketed by two of many temporary and tenuous attempts to establish peace in an age of religious warfare, settlements testifying to the power of protestant arms to carve territory out of Catholic Europe, but indicative also of the permanent impasse created by rival forms of Christianity. A lawyer and diplomat, he was perhaps the most learned man of his century and the most able European political writer between Machiavelli and Hobbes.

It is perhaps no accident that the first class of "professionals" that broke ranks in the religious wars and focused on religion itself as a problem—of truth, of conscience, and of social order—were outsiders, not theologians but diplomats. Prior to Bodin one thinks of Machiavelli[4] and Thomas More (the *Utopia*); after Bodin, Herbert of Cherbury and Thomas Hobbes. All of them made creative contributions to the analysis of religious motivation and behavior, and of the role of religion in society, and all for the sake of a tolerable postmedieval social order.[5] The skillful diplomat must cultivate detachment

3. The increasingly analytical approach to problems of religion in this period signals the revival of the style of inquiry into religion developed by the ancient Greeks, after a long "parenthesis" following upon the triumph of Christianity: see esp. Michel Despland, *La Religion en Occident*, 56–57.

4. Cf. my "Machiavelli's Functional Analysis of Religion: Context and Object." Thomas Kuhn appreciates the often decisive role of outsiders in bringing about paradigm shifts. He cites the revolutionary result of Dalton's application "to chemistry [of] a set of questions and concepts previously restricted to physics and meteorology," resulting in "a reorientation toward the field . . . that taught chemists to ask new questions about and to draw new conclusions from old data" (*The Structure of Scientific Revolutions*, 139). The field of religion is, of course, much more porous to nonprofessional intrusion than science, which is more thoroughly insulated from the public sphere of discourse and has no laity.

5. On Machiavelli, see further Isaiah Berlin, "The Originality of Machiavelli," in Myron P. Gilmore, ed., *Studies on Machiavelli;* on Bodin, George H. Sabine, "The Colloquium Heptaplomeres of Jean Bodin," in idem, *Persecution and Liberty;* on Hobbes, Sheldon Wolin, *Politics and Vision: Continuity and Innovation in Western Political Thought*, chap. 8.

and objectivity; he must have the imagination to put himself above the fray, to be able to identify with all sides of disputes without forgetting where his ultimate loyalties lie. However consistent and coherent his theories (and Bodin was a master theoretician), resolution of problems requires facing all the actualities of a real situation.

Bodin had all those skills; yet it would be a mistake to regard him as a religious skeptic or as someone for whom piety was of minor concern. His quest for true religion *(vera religio)* was existential. On the other hand, he made a clean intellectual break from Christianity and engaged in a heroic and presumptuous search for an outlook that was post-traditional but still truly religious and normative. Religiously, he has been an enigma to those who have studied his life and thought. The best sense of his development has been made by Paul Rose, who sees his religious biography in three phases but finally settles on a Judaized natural religion as the best way to characterize Bodin's final view.

Rose summarizes as follows:

> Bodin's religious biography on the surface is a chapter of accidents and reversals, sudden conversions and enthusiasms: a young Carmelite monk in the 1540's who left the order, a professed Catholic in 1562, imprisoned as a suspected Huguenot in 1569, outwardly a *politique* Catholic from 1576–89, then a Leaguer Catholic from 1589–93, followed by a reversion to the politiques, and finally his death as a reputed crypto-Jew or at least *Achriste* in 1596, a matter which did not, however, prevent his receiving a Catholic burial.[6]

Rose tries to make sense of all this by discovering a three-phase development: first, by 1559, "conversion away from Christianity to a sort of natural religion which nevertheless made allowance for theistic revelation; the second . . . characterised by his distinctly Judaised recognition of the crucial importance of revelation and prophecy for *vera religio;* the third . . . Bodin's own transformation into a prophet in 1567–69."[7]

So much at least is of importance for us, because it controls Rose's deeply grounded interpretation of the *Colloquium,* a matter to which we shall return. Rose is right in insisting that interpretation of this difficult document requires preliminary effort to establish, from earlier writings, Bodin's own vision of *vera religio.* The following elements are crucial before turning to the text.

First, Bodin as both religious virtuoso and diplomat conveys a clear sense that religion exists in two "guises," inner or personal and outward, and that the authentic core and essential definition of religion relates to the former, relying on a definition, often repeated, from Philo of Alexandria: "Religion is nothing other than the turning of a purified soul to the true God.[8] This suggests that where civil and compulsory forms of religion differ from one's

6. Paul L. Rose, *Bodin and the Great God of Nature,* 151.
7. Ibid., 151–52.
8. Ibid., 186. See, e.g., *Colloquium* V, 235/179.

inner conviction, one may conform, regarding as religiously indifferent any governmental requirements. But the issue is complicated by the fact that Bodin seems to believe that some publicly constituted consensus about religious behavior is necessary for viable public life, and that makes more serious the question of disagreement between what people actually believe in their hearts and what they are told to observe in the public realm. In an ideal world, the two should be at one, Bodin asserts:

> One thing in the state is to be sought above all from immortal God. It is that the will of the citizens in both spiritual and temporal matters [divinae ac humanae res] always be the same and in harmony [consentiens]. This is the end of human society and of all public life. The laws of all nations, the religions and cults of all peoples, all the duties of judges and magistrates, indeed all institutions, rites and customs relate and are directed to one instance—that men may live in affection and trust.[9]

But this ideal, in the context of sixteenth-century Europe, was utterly utopian, as the *Colloquium* clearly reflects: its whole fifth book is organized around the problem of the contradictions between private and public imperatives in *real* life, that is, "whether it is right for a good man to feel otherwise about religion than he confesses publicly" (IV, 232/177; cf. V, 235/179).

A second issue stressed by Rose, to be discussed further, is the extent of Bodin's attachment to Jewishness. Rose is completely convincing in his argument that Bodin was a learned and serious Judaizer, deeply informed by Philo, Maimonides, and the cabbalistic tradition, and that he found in Judaism a superior option to those offered by rival traditions. On the other hand, he was not about to "convert" to Judaism, or to "Judaize" in practice. Rose sees the *Colloquium* as essentially a restatement (albeit uncensored because unpublished) of views that can be derived from earlier writings; as will be spelled out below, however, I am convinced that Bodin's judaizing is so compromised as to be finally reduced to (or at least subordinated to) natural religion.

Bodin is in several ways a quintessential transitional figure in terms of some established scholarly landmarks interpreting this period. We have already noted that although still religious, he is no longer Christian. Although not accepting any sectarian label, he is not yet quite deist or skeptic. Furthermore, his plight approaches the situation aptly described by Richard Popkin[10] as the crisis of the criterion for truth: not yet, for Bodin, the full crisis of Pyrrhonism—of truth in general—of the next generation, but he is past hope of resolving the religious question within any of the accepted

---

9. Rose, 155, quoting Bodin's *Oratio de instituenda in Republica inventute ad Senatum Populumque Tolosatem*.

10. Richard H. Popkin, *History of Scepticism from Erasmus to Spinoza*, chap. 1.

boundaries of his day. Who, the *Colloquium* asks, can serve as arbiter in this bloody contest of religions (IV, 170/131)?

In trying to map a response to this dilemma, Bodin's *Colloquium* is fairly clear about what he thinks the options are, but there is deep ambiguity about his solution; it is not quite clear which of the characters in the dialogue speak(s) for Bodin, as we try to follow the ebb and flow between traditional and innovative answers.

Bodin is transitional also in his use of the Bible: he is completely revisionist in his interpretation; yet its framework is still normative in that it provides the overall world-picture for both history (at least primal history) and nature. In fact, what is most decisively premodern about him is his magical-religious cosmology, alive with angels and demons who really function and who are up to no good.[11] He is in the midst of the situation described by Hans Frei, according to which the biblical framework, for centuries the reality structure within which everything in human experience was understood, was breaking down as more and more accumulating knowledge of the world refused to accommodate itself to the narrow bounds of biblical chronology and cosmology.[12]

A final preliminary: Bodin recognized that he was treading new and dangerous ground in this book. Not only did he not publish it—a circumstance that allowed him, presumably, to speak his mind about what he really believed (if we can figure it out)—but he spends some time defending the very propriety of putting religion up for free-wheeling debate.[13] That in itself was commonly regarded as dangerous, doubt-raising, and subversive. Even more scandalously, he dared to put Christianity on the same level as its rivals, treating it as one among the world's religions. The *Colloquium* has frequently been called the first work of comparative religion,[14] but it is not that so much as a trial or contest, with the further novelty that Christianity is not treated as a privileged contestant. Quite the reverse. The three Christians express the very views, and reflect the very context, that make religion a problem: exclusivity, intolerance, obstinate certainty about their own points of view, willingness to use coercion against rivals, and finally, a set of beliefs most contrary to nature and reason (original sin, incarnation, and so on). Perhaps most profoundly unsettling is this: once it is admitted for debate that "God" may be at the source of religions *other than one's own*, then one must move from the explanation of true religion offered by one's own tradition and

11. Frances Yates, "The Mystery of Jean Bodin"; H. R. Trevor-Roper, *The European Witch-Craze of the 16th and 17th Centuries;* Horst Denzer, ed., *Jean Bodin*, 429ff., esp. the contribution of Christopher R. Baxter, "Jean Bodin's Daemon and his Conversion to Judaism" (in Denzer, 1–21).

12. Hans W. Frei, *The Eclipse of Biblical Narrative: A Study in Eighteenth- and Nineteenth-Century Hermeneutics;* the introduction lays out the problem in a broad way.

13. *Colloquium* III, 143/111; IV, 163/125.

14. E.g., Hiram C. Haydn, *The Counter-Renaissance*, 47; Paul L. Rose, *Bodin*, 8.

entertain the question of the origin of religion *as such*. (Not yet in question here is the belief that the one God is the originator of humankind, and that he instructed his creatures in knowledge of himself.)

As noted, the *Colloquium Heptaplomeres* was written by 1593 but not published until a Latin edition of 1857.[15] Meanwhile, it circulated widely and became an underground classic widely read by seventeenth-century free-thinkers.[16] At its heart was Bodin's attempt to locate—simply stated—the "best religion."

As befits a rational inquiry away from the conflict, Bodin sets his colloquy on neutral ground—Venice, a haven of political and religious calm. There he convenes a group of seven learned representatives of different religious viewpoints who enjoy the hospitality of a liberal Catholic host, Coronaeus, eating, drinking, praying, and talking about practically everything. Their religious perspectives divide basically in two: five of the participants belong to specific religious traditions that authenticate their claims by appeal to divine revelation; of these, three are Christian, (Coronaeus; Curtius, a Calvinist; and Fridericus, a Lutheran), one (Octavius) is Muslim; and one is Jewish (Salomon, who will emerge with a clear advantage in this group, as will be seen). The other two, Toralba and Senamus, represent Bodin's alternatives to the confessional traditions, both aiming beyond particularistic identification toward a universally authentic, generic religiousness.[17]

The pace is leisurely, but finally in the fourth book the issue of the "best religion" comes to the fore—the issue with which Bodin has begun the book and started the whole series of conversations.

That beginning is worth noting, because it marks one of the admirable characteristics of the *Colloquium*, the concreteness of its reference to "religion" throughout. Bodin's opening signals both the existential bite of the question of "best religion" and its essentially theological orientation. The question is posed through a hair-raising account (related by Octavius) of a near shipwreck, escaped at the last minute by the lifting of a deadly storm. The passengers have all been praying desperately to their several gods; now they give thanks for their miraculous deliverance.

The question is: "with such a variety of religions represented, whose prayers did God heed in bringing the ship safely into port?" (I, 14/10).[18] Did God heed the prayers of all? Some? Or did he save the ship for the sake of one? It is hard to resist seeing this story as an allegory of the religious condition

15. On the uncertainty of dating, see M. L. D. Kuntz, *Colloquium*, introduction, xxxvii and n.69. An abridged edition had been published in 1841 (ibid., lxx).

16. Ira O. Wade, *The Intellectual Origins of the French Enlightenment*, 113.

17. The gap between these two and the other five is wider than that between Toralba and Senamus; on this I disagree with Christopher R. Baxter, "Jean Bodin's Daemon," 20–21.

18. I omit the demonic and magical features with which the story is embroidered.

of Europe, or even of mankind: when things are going all to hell, whose prayers will God hear?

We have already encountered the more abstract statement of the problem, where Senamus has posed the possibility that none of the religions is true and the logical impossibility "that more than one of these is true" (IV, 154/119).[19] From this Ciceronian thought he advances the obvious solution in the realm of public policy: complete toleration (his agnosticism about which prayer God hears is the best defense for such a policy). Against Salomon's objection that the toleration of many religions entails impiety, Senamus replies by appealing to an exemplary Roman emperor:

> When, therefore, he [Alexander Severus] realized that Jews, pagans and Christians were divided on religious principles [de summa religionis dissidere], he chose to embrace all groups rather than, by repudiating one, to arouse any one to the contempt of divinity. With this reasoning he joined not only individual men but all men in the state to the greatest harmony [consensio] of piety and love. (IV, 159/122)[20]

Curtius (a Calvinist Christian), lining up with Salomon, agrees that the example speaks well for Severus's integrity and wisdom, but not for his piety. How can a truly pious government tolerate everything without incurring the wrath of God?

Senamus is ready with a reply, and it is an argument he will repeat: pulled every which way by religious claims and counterclaims, the common people do not know what to do (IV, 163/125). Senamus would relieve their conscientious plight with a bold theological suggestion: God excuses innocent error; no worship rendered with sincerity and purity of heart is displeasing to him. In unqualified support of this point, Senamus stands alone; his relativism with regard to the forms of religion is too liberal for all the others, including even Toralba (the other nonconfessional participant). It is Toralba, in fact, who now argues that the truth must be found out: "In such a variety of different laws and religions one must establish what is the true religion [statuendum est, quae sit vera religio] (IV, 163/125)."[21]

This statement brings the debate to its critical question, having shifted from what is socially sensible, liberal, and wise to what is true. But again, on the brink of this discussion, Senamus is ready with his critical question of a criterion for truth: "I think these arguments [disputations] about religion will come to nothing. For who will be the arbiter of such a controversy" (IV, 170/131)? It is easy enough, he adds, to agree that "true religion" is

---

19. This thought precisely echoes Cicero's dialogue: " . . . in this medley of conflicting opinions, one thing is certain. Though it is possible that they [the religions] are all of them false, it is impossible that more than one of them is true." *The Nature of the Gods*, 71.

20. As already seen, this idea is dear to Bodin himself: see the quotation from the *Oratio*, above, at n. 9.

21. The translation reads "decide"; "establish" better preserves the ambiguity of *statuendum*.

that which has God as its "author." The problem is "in discerning whether
He is the author of this law or that law" (IV, 172/132). (Bodin uses *lex* here
to indicate this or that institutionalized religious tradition or form.)

Senamus supports his doubts about Toralba's agenda by telling the story
of the oracle of Apollo: "When he was asked what was the best religion from
the countless variety of religions, he replied in one word: "the oldest" [an-
tiquissima]. When doubt was expressed about what might be the oldest, he
replied: "the best" [optima]" (IV, 173/133). But Toralba is not to be put
off. For him, antiquity is self-authenticating, especially in light of the dis-
ruptive social results of all the new religions that have appeared (ibid.).
Encouraged by Coronaeus,[22] Toralba insists that "the best religion is the
oldest," believing that this can be established.

Thus do we arrive finally at Bodin's consideration of the "origin of religion." Toralba constructs what may be Bodin's own view of the matter,[23] a
rationalistic gloss on Genesis 1:

> If we measure the best kind of religion by its antiquity, we must seek its origin
> from the parent of the whole human race [totius humani generis parente origo est
> petenda]. For he must have been supplied with the best habits, the best training,
> the best knowledge, and finally the best spiritual virtues [animi virtutibus] by God.
> ... It is consistent with his [God's] nature that he should endow his beloved sons
> with such unusual virtues and especially with true religion so that they would adore
> the eternal God and worship him [His tamen multis and praeclaris virtutibus filios
> sibi charissimos imbuisse consetaneum est atque inprimis vera religione, ut scil.
> Deum aeternum eique sacra facerent....] (IV, 182–83/140)

Thus, the oldest and best religion is that with which Adam was endowed
by his Creator. The verbs Bodin most often uses, usually in the mouth of
Toralba, for God's giving of religion are *imbuo* and *insero*. The first means
to train, educate, or instruct, with the added connotation of steeping, filling,
or infecting. *Insero* means to sow, plant, ingraft, or implant. That which is
ingrafted is *religio*, or "right reason" *(recta ratio)*, or the "law of nature" *(lex
naturae)*, which is in turn roughly equated with the Decalogue.[24] This first

22. Coronaeus's comment (*Colloquium* IV, 174/133) that this line of enquiry will support the
claims of the Roman church draws on ancient Christian tradition. Eusebius asserted that "the
Christian religion is 'none other than the first, most ancient, and most original of all religions,
discovered by Abraham and his followers, God's beloved.'.... What Christians teach and the
way they live are not recent 'inventions' but the 'natural concepts of those whom God loved in
the distant past' " (Robert L. Wilken, *The Myth of Christian Beginnings*, 61). Augustine held
that "what is now called the Christian religion has existed among the ancients, and was not
absent from the beginning of the human race, until Christ came in the flesh: from that time the
true religion, which existed already, began to be called Christian" (quoted by E. E. Evans-
Pritchard, *Theories of Primitive Religion*, 2–3).

23. Senamus, while not directly disputing Toralba's account, has already cast doubt on the
exclusive validity of the Hebrew or any other account of original religion.

24. *Imbuo*: IV, 192/147; 225/172. *Insero*: IV, 184/142; 185/142; 192/148; V, 243/186; VI,
325/248; 337/257; 462/351. *Recta ratio* and *lex naturae* used together, IV, 226/172, with ref. to

religion was of course monotheistic: "the best and most ancient religion of all was implanted [insita] in the human minds with right reason [recta ratio], by eternal God, and this sets forth the one eternal God as the object of man's worship" (IV, 185/142).

Reinforcement for this view is brought from Plato and the sixth-century Neoplatonist philosopher Simplicius who, according to Toralba, "states that as long as the human soul shall cling with deepest roots to its originator [autori], it shall easily safeguard this integrity in which it was created; but if the soul is torn away from him, it will languish and wither until it turns itself again to its origin and founder [originem et autorem]" (IV, 185–86/142–43).

Toralba is emphatic about the innateness—the external "untaughtness"—of the divine endowment, in the sense that "we have seized, drawn, elicited this law by [or from] nature [hanc enim a natura legem arripuimus, hausimus, expressimus]. We were not instructed, but made to this law; not educated, but imbued to it [non docti, sed facti, non instituti, sed imbuti.....]" (IV, 192/147).

This innatist doctrine is, of course, capable of complete detachment from the biblical setting in which Bodin leaves it in his revised version of the primal biblical history. By leaving it in its biblical framework, he is able to extend his subversive interpretation. From Adam comes a line of religious worthies: "...Adam and his son Abel had been imbued with the best religion [optima religione imbutos fuisse], and after that Seth, Enoch, Methuselah to Noah who worshipped in great holiness, to the exclusion of all others, that eternal and only true God" (IV, 183/141). This list is often repeated with variations that add Job, Abraham, Isaac, Jacob (for example, VI, 337/257 [Toralba]; IV, 226/172–73 [Salomon]). The list is always confined to Old Testament figures, although Bodin's view is not that they *alone* were endowed with true religion. Toralba, for instance, observes that several schools of the Greek philosophers knew how to speak properly about God, an ability that "seems to have been planted, as it were, by nature herself in the hearts and minds of all men" (in omnium hominum animis ac mentibus ipsa natura insitum esse videatur; VI, 325/248). Even Salomon, who will represent Israel's special claims, makes a decisive concession: despite the antiquity and divine favors to her, Israel "received nothing which has not been common knowledge to everyone of all languages, spread throughout the whole world and made commonly available to everyone [nihil accepimus, quod non sit omnibus omnium vocibus ac linguis toto terrarum orbe dissipatum ac pervulgatum]" (II, 89/70).

Should one conclude, then, that, according to Bodin, "original religion" (best, oldest) is revealed or natural? Bodin would not have understood the

---

Romans 2:12–15: cf. VI, 337/257. Decalogue as law of nature: IV, 192/147. *Lex naturae* joined with *religio;* VI, 337/257.

sharpness of the distinction, and would probably have said "both at once." God is the source, originator, creator of religion; but "nature" can also be so designated; thus, Bodin speaks of "the natural and God-implanted religion" (naturalem et insitam . . . a Deo religionem; IV, 184/142).[25] We are not far from Spinoza's "God, *or* Nature."

While there is virtually no distinction to be made between God and nature as the source of true religion, there *is* a clear distinction between that universal source and *revelation* in the sense of a specific, historical moment of divine intervention for purposes of instruction. This is seen in the role assigned to Moses, conspicuously absent from all the above-mentioned lists of Old Testament representatives of natural religion. Moses has a special status as prophet and founder through whom the specifically Jewish religious tradition was inaugurated. But his status is finally ambiguous. On the one hand, he is the founder of the specific tradition to which Bodin accords top honors. On the other hand, the "revelation" accorded him adds nothing essential to natural religion; it is described as nothing more than a merciful divine "recall" to or renewal of the purity of original religion. Thus, Bodin makes Salomon the Jew agree with Toralba's account of original religion but has him add the following interpretation of the role played by Moses when Israel, in Egypt, became infected with idolatry: "Then God took pity on his people . . . and inspired Moses to *call the people back* to their natural and God-inspired religion which had almost become obliterated from their souls [moysen excitavit, per quem naturalem et insitam animis hominum a Deo religionem ex animis hominum paene obliteratam ad usum revocavit]" (IV, 184/142; italics mine). At Sinai, Salomon describes a similar divine act of giving the Decalogue to renew the natural law:

> Since the latter [natural law] seemed to be obliterated and violated by the great sins and crimes of men, the best and greatest God, having pity on the ruin of men, *renewed* the laws and prohibitions of nature with solemn covenant in the greatest assemblies of his people [. . . solenni legislatione naturalie edicta et interdicta maximis sui populi comitiis renovavit. . . .] (IV, 191/147; italics mine).

At this point, a key assertion (for orthodoxy, a revolutionary one) is made: this original and natural religion is sufficient for salvation. On this, Salomon agrees with Toralba: "the law of nature is sufficient for salvation" (Toralba; IV, 225/172); "all the things which pertain to salvation are contained in the laws of nature" (Salomon; IV, 226/172).[26]

Obviously, this view undercuts the exclusive validity of Judaism, Christianity, and Islam equally, as they are self-understood. Indeed, Bodin produces a creative misreading of Saint Paul to further support his complete

25. Paul L. Rose, *Bodin*, 4, 179–80, shows that there is no paradox, for Bodin, between the revealed and the natural.

26. Rose's emphasis on the Jewish aspect of Bodin's thought thus has to be qualified by the drastic attenuation resulting from Salomon's concessions to Toralba.

subversion of the orthodox idea that some divine revelation beyond the "original" is necessary for salvation: in Romans 2:12–15, Bodin-Toralba argue, Paul "taught that right reason and the law of nature were sufficient for man's salvation" (IV, 226/172). The traditional Christian doctrine of the Fall—the entire premise of the Christian doctrine of salvation—is reinterpreted by Bodin to line up with his doctrine of the sufficiency of nature: the "fall," such as it was, occurred when original religion was abandoned: "Those who have departed from that most ancient and best religion have fallen into an irreconcilable labyrinth of errors" (IV, 183/141; cf. VI, 337/257).[27]

We can now see the whole structure of Bodin's way of explaining religion: ultimately, the explanation of religion *as such* (supposing there is such a thing) is the undisputed assumption that God is its author, source, origin, and cause. By his creative act, humans are naturally endowed with sufficient resources to achieve salvation. But what Bodin has done beyond that is to imply, at least, a thoroughly human and historical general theory to explain all the *actual* religions of the world (with the possible exception of Judaism—depending on whether Bodin thinks any of it beyond the Decalogue qualifies as divinely instituted). The immense variety of religions—everything *but* the abstract (nonexistent?) innate original religion—are all of human creation. In Bodin's view, they provide impressive evidence of "the fall," as he reinterprets it:

> I think men's destruction must be attributed to men themselves, because they, of their own accord, departed from the law of nature which contains the worship of one eternal God; and in knowing error did not allow themselves to be recalled to its service. Indeed, as I view the almost infinite variety of sects, Christians differing with Ismaelites and pagans differing among themselves, no standard [norma] of truth seems more certain than right reason. . . . (VI, 337/257).

The positing of a new and allegedly universal norm for solving the problem of religion indicates the beginning of a paradigm shift, or better, a new paradigm (since theology continues on its own traditional paths) for treating religion, grounded in a view that purports to explain both the existence of religion and its astonishing historical variety. Unlike traditional histories of salvation that legitimate revelatory founding events for specific groups, this approach envisions a universal history of religion(s) which treats all of them under a universal source and a universal norm detached from all of them. The biblical and monotheistic framework is still there, but orthodox readings of it are abandoned, and nothing is to prevent that framework being replaced by any other which can make a persuasive case that it is grounded in nature and reason.

But Bodin is far from finished with his subject. The quest for true religion has led beyond all confessional claims, and the rational alternatives have been

---

27. The traditional Christian doctrine of original sin is one of those rejected as "contrary to the divine laws and the laws of nature" (VI, 392/296).

finally reduced to two—Toralba, who knows objectively something he calls
vera religio, and Senamus, who denies that any such objective "oldest-best-
truest" can be identified and reified.

A new group of problems is now opened up with a question especially
relevant to Toralba's commitment to natural versus particular religious forms:
what is the place of observance through cult and law? Do they have any
essential place in the definition of "true religion"? Or does the interior life
wholly comprehend the meaning of that term?

Salomon, having registered agreement with Toralba on the lineaments of
"true religion," now offers an insightful opinion. Interestingly, he adopts
Toralba's universalist framework of argument by using a Roman rather than
a Hebrew example: "I am persuaded that no religion can exist completely
without rites and ceremonies. I believe the Roman religion has no greater
secret for its so great duration than every imaginable variety of rites and
ceremonies" (VI, 226–27/173). Cautiously, Toralba agrees: "Those who press
the people with a multitude of rites turn religion into superstition; however,
those who completely remove all rites overturn all religions from the
root. . . . " (IV, 228/174). For both, however, the reasons are more sociological
than philosophical, and Bodin does not pursue further the assertion that there
is no religion without cultic activity. For him, the question of cult is the way
to open up the second major phase of his discussion, that of government
policy with respect to religion.

Here, the criterion shifts from reason's quest for abstract truth to pragmatic
concern for the common good, expressed ideally by the notion of harmony.
Truth aside, is religion necessary for social order? Is one religion better than
another? Are religions that reason judges to be false, idolatrous, impious, or
even demonically inspired nevertheless acceptable if they meet the imperatives of social order, peace, and harmony? To examine these questions, we
leave for later the attendant questions that may be raised for individual
conscience as a consequence of government policies.

As a general principle, Bodin believed that religion was a necessary component of a commonwealth, and that the health of the society should be the
prime consideration in establishing policy on religion. Bodin had addressed
these principles in an earlier political writing, where he cited the Greek
historian Polybius as his favorite witness. Even that atheist recognized that
"there is nothing which doth more uphold and maintain the estates and
commonweals than religion; and that it is the principal foundation of the
power and strength of monarchies and seignories: as also for the execution
of justice, for the obedience of the subjects, the reverence of the magistrates,
for the fear of doing evil, and for the mutual love and amity of every one
towards others. . . . "[28] Polybius acknowledged that "Roman power increased
more through religion than through any other thing" (IV, 160/123).

---

28. *The Six Bookes of a Commonweale*, ed. Kenneth D. McRae (repr. 1606 translation by
Richard Knolles), IV.7; 536 I, K. Cf. III.1; 270 G, and the preface, appendix A, A70.

In accord with this, Bodin believes that superstition, despite its faults, imposes constraints, and therefore is not as bad as atheism, which is absolutely intolerable. At the least, "superstition . . . doth yet hold men in fear and awe, both of the laws and of the magistrates, and also in mutual duties and offices one of them towards another, whereas mere Atheism doth utterly root out of men's minds all the fear of doing evil."[29] Oddly, Bodin's detestation of atheism becomes an argument not only for government taking a role in religion but also for personal religious liberty, "for otherwise it shall come to pass, that they which are destitute of the exercise of their religion, and withal distasted of the religion of the others, shall become altogether atheists (as we daily see [!] . . .)."[30]

Europeans, we are told, should follow the example of Islam: "The great emperor of the Turks doth with . . . great devotion . . . honor and observe the religion . . . received from his ancestors, and yet detesteth he not the strange religions of others, but to the contrary permitteth every man to live according to his conscience. . . . "[31] Such a policy has the social effect of promoting the greatest harmony, but now the theological consideration (introduced earlier by Senamus) is brought to bear as well: "The people of ancient time were persuaded, as were the Turks, all sorts of religions which proceed from a pure mind, to be acceptable unto the gods."[32]

If Bodin thinks observance of religion is necessary as a social and political bond of the commonwealth, and if he thinks atheism is detestable and leads to anarchy, what, then, is the role of government in religion? He is not clear on this point. His abhorrence of atheism seems to argue *both* for some sort of government involvement and for toleration! He seems to have taken for granted (as most did in his time) government-regulated religion of some sort. He favors a government which, like that of the ancient Romans, attended to religious matters as a first priority, as a result of which "they established unto themselves the greatest monarchy in the world."[33] Baxter is generally right in saying that "it is the duty of all princes to maintain the traditional religion, even Christianity, and to punish backsliders"[34] —but not for the reason Baxter gives (that any sincere religion is pleasing to God).

On the other hand, the genuineness of Bodin's acceptance of plurality in religion pulls him away from the rational certainty of Toralba, with its implied consequence that some form of religion ought to be established (*statuenda*) and enforced, toward the ideas of Senamus which, I believe, make sense of what Bodin himself actually did in his own life. Perhaps Rousseau's proposal

---

29. Ibid., IV.7; 539 E. Witchcraft, for Bodin, does not fall under the category of superstition but of atheism.

30. Ibid., 539 C.

31. Ibid., IV.7; 537 E.

32. Ibid., 538 F.

33. Ibid., III.1; 270 G.

34. Christopher R. Baxter, "Jean Bodin's Daemon," 17.

of a nonsectarian civil religion would have appealed to him as a reasonable compromise.[35] This brings us to the third problem area: that of conscience, and to a third criterion for adjudicating the complex problem of religion: the pure mind, or sincerity.

Senamus from the beginning has been presented as an agnostic about original religion, as we have seen. Consistently, he calls for complete toleration and freedom of religion, and is never convinced by Toralba that there is an objectively knowable original religion rooted in "right reason" to be designated as the authentic core from which all the sects and varieties of religion (with the possible exception of Judaism) can be seen as deviations. He takes variety as a given and proposes an affective criterion of authenticity in place of Toralba's intellectual norm of truth. He suggests that because no certain set of true beliefs or right behaviors can be identified, one must take the world as it is and accept sincere religiousness, or piety—an inner quality of the heart—as sufficient where it ultimately counts—in the eyes of God.

In this respect, Senamus/Bodin is leaning toward the position to be taken by the "moderns" in the coming dispute between ancients and moderns—a dispute marking the abandonment of the Renaissance devotion to antiquity and its presumption that the oldest is best. Although voicing conservative sentiments (IV, 165/126), Senamus nicely illustrates the modern turn to subjectivity described by Hannah Arendt, wherein truthfulness makes do in the absence of certainty of truth, and reliability, in the absence of an absolute ethic.[36] This position shifts attention away from referential questions about the "religious object" (about which consensus is not possible and therefore not necessary) to subjective matters about what characterizes the authentically religious person, and from what is true to what is an appropriate response to the ultimate reality to which all religions bear witness.

Senamus is clever enough to discern that even Toralba's solution is not radical enough, for even his natural religion can turn into another sect, only adding another alternative to the variety of rival religions. This realization is implied as Senamus spells out the pluralistic implications of his single criterion of sincerity:

> I believe that all the religions of all people, the natural religion which Toralba loves, the religion of Jupiter and the gentile gods, whom the Indians of the Orient and the Tartars cherish, the religion of Moses, the religion of Christ, the religion of Mohammed, which everyone pursues with his own rite, not with faked pretense but with a pure mind, are not unpleasing to eternal God and are excused as just errors, even though that which is the best is the most pleasing of all [. . . quam suo quisque ritu non facata simulatione, sed integra mente prosequitur, aeterno

---

35. See Rousseau's chapter on civil religion, in *The Social Contract*, book 4, chap. 8
36. Hannah Arendt, *The Human Condition*, 253–54.

Deo non ingratos ac justos errores excusari confido, tametsi omnium gratissima est illa, quae optima]. (V, 251/192)[37]

Salomon the Jew can partially agree to this, that "an upright conscience (recta conscientia) is pleasing to God," so that even devotion "offered to clay gods in a just error and in good faith are not displeasing to God" (V, 242/184). Even Toralba agrees, although he is not sure that the learned have any excuse for such behavior, once they have been "instructed with a knowledge of natural things, from which they could have drawn the clearest ideas about the nature, power and goodness of one God, as Paul himself declares openly" (V, 243/186, referring to Romans 1:18ff.).

Only the Muslim, Octavius, agrees completely with Senamus: both suppose that the example of the Turks best accords with the freedom of conscience and with what God really requires. Thus, Senamus argues,

If all people could be persuaded as the Ismaelites, Octavius, and I are that all the prayers of all people which come from a pure mind are pleasing to God [omnia omnium vota, quae a pura mente profisciscuntur, Deo grata], or surely are not displeasing, it would be possible to live everywhere in the world in the same harmony [concordia] as those who live under the emperor of the Turks or Persians. (VI, 467/355)

I am inclined (with van Gelder),[38] to take the view of Senamus as Bodin's final statement, despite the greater amount of copy given to Toralba and Salomon. Toralba's learned rationalism and Salomon's fidelity to the Jewish law, for all their merits, do not solve the combined problem of the conscience of most people nor contribute to social harmony. The real world of religion and politics belongs to the pluralist Senamus,[39] who himself does homage at all shrines, depending on where he is. His view actually harmonizes best with Bodin's own last wish to be buried in the Catholic church—something Toralba would have had trouble with. Bodin-as-Senamus could be buried in that church whose religion prevailed in the place where he lived and died, as a final sincere and pious public gesture to the local deity. Toralba, after his thorough exposé of the absurdities of Catholic theology, could not have rested easily in a Catholic grave. Bodin died an unbeliever from any traditional Christian point of view; yet, like Senamus, he believed that the majority religion of any land was legitimate, could be presumed to be pleasing to God, and therefore made a moral and social claim on the person who was there.

---

37. Senamus also voices the negative implications of this same thought: " . . . it is clear what we have said before: even sacred rites of pagans performed carelessly were displeasing to immortal God, and brought death and destruction to the people" (VI, 320/244).

38. H. A. Enno van Gelder, *The Two Reformations of the Sixteenth Century,* 394.

39. Here I disagree with C. R. Baxter ("Jean Bodin's Daemon," 20–21) that Senamus represents only the "early Bodin" before he became convinced of the sacredness of revelation. The conclusion of the *Colloquium* does not support such a view, in light of the probability that Bodin had no need to clothe the work in more ambiguity than reflected his own actual thinking.

Therefore Bodin follows the practice of Senamus, who reports that he worshiped at all the shrines "of all religions, wherever they are, so as not to be considered an atheist by wicked example and also that others may hold in awe the divine" (V, 251/192).

Vigorously argued but finally unresolved, then, are three basic questions: Is true religion capable of formulation in terms of rationally objective knowledge? What are the responsibilities of public authorities in light of the necessity for religious constraints in every society? And what are the allowable limits within which the religious conscience might express itself in public behavior? In all three areas, Bodin is mindful of both theological and rational considerations—both of what is pleasing to God and what lies within the capacity and aspirations for human good.

The humanistic leaning is clear: reason, grounded in nature, can identify true religion if anything can; social utility and harmony govern public policy; and the autonomous (or perhaps theonomous) conscience is given free reign to settle its own religious accounts. Neither church nor revelation imposes any authority in such questions. Religion as a human attribute is left to the capable arbitration of man himself.

We chose Bodin as our starting point because he introduces us to an extended debate about religion as a problem. We have seen the complexity of the questions involved (and we have not dealt with all of them) and how his *Colloquium* tends to differentiate the problem of religion into three distinct realms. It is possible to see in Bodin's analysis an anticipation of the divisions of the modern study of religion into philosophy, sociology, and psychology of religion.

In the ensuing chapters, however, I have chosen the more concrete, if less tidy, route of selecting key authors and listening to their "colloquium," conducted seriatim, on religion. They will mark stages along the way of dealing with all three of the problem areas identified by Bodin.

The intellectual framework in which the seventeenth century went beyond Bodin is marked above all by the triumph of a naturalistic understanding of both nature and history; negatively stated, the demise of the biblical model for organizing perceptions of reality as a whole. The celebrated case of Galileo, and the epoch-making views of Bacon and Descartes, all occurred in the generation immediately after Bodin (all three were born before Bodin died).

Herbert of Cherbury will in some respects represent a continuation of Bodin's Toralba, though more clearly liberated from Bodin's magical-supernatural universe and more decisively distancing himself from the natural theology that characterizes seventeenth-century Christian orthodoxy. Whereas the orthodoxies used an innatist natural theology as a basis for revelation, Herbert used it as an argument that "revelation" is not necessary.

After Herbert, we find Fontenelle, more in the style of Senamus, reveling in the variety of religious forms and, agnostic about their credentials (the

Hebrew tradition prudently excepted), boldly proposing a demythologized, psychohistorical method of rewriting religious history and explaining the very origins of religious myths.

Together, they will prepare the way for Hume: against Herbert's tradition, he will reject the rationalism and innatism of the deist tradition (of which Herbert is often identified as the father). Like Fontenelle, Hume oriented his own theory of religion in a more historical direction, reinforcing the psychohistorical approach with theoretical proposals. Meanwhile, in the problem area of religion and society, we shall look into the thought of Vico, who with astonishing intuition proposed to treat the origin of religion *and of society* together as a single question. From there, Comte will link Hume with the rich sociological ideas developed by French thinkers and put them into an evolutionary framework.

All this will set the stage for the three final chapters, in which we reach a provisional terminus ad quem in that we shall have arrived within the contemporary framework of social-scientific study of religion. E. B. Tylor continues the focus on reason, explaining original religion as a way of organizing knowledge about the world. Emile Durkheim sees religion as a social product and as an original ingredient of social order, while Sigmund Freud continues the examination of the interior sources of religion in the psyche.

In all three realms, naturalistic answers to our focal question—that of the origin of religion—will provide the theoretical basis on which the modern study of religion is grounded. And the bedrock of that naturalistic ground will be history, articulated in practice first by Fontenelle and echoing a dictum of Sir Francis Bacon, that truth is the daughter of time. In our next chapter, Herbert will have grasped half—but only half—of that great truth. For him, *false* religion is the daughter of time, but "true religion" is unchanging.

PART II

RATIONALIST VERSUS HISTORICAL APPROACHES

Chapter 2

The Deist Option:
Herbert of Cherbury

Edward Herbert (1583–1648), diplomat, adventurer, and from 1629 Lord Herbert of Cherbury, embarked on a sea of religious conflict in search of "universal religion." The results have earned him the title of "father of deism." The best justification for this ill-defined honor is that, in his search, he made a clean break from the framework of biblical antiquity, revelation, and authority, approaching the problem instead from a world-historical perspective that was at once rationalistic and religious. Convinced (against Calvinist predestinarianism) that a universal providence has provided every person with the rational capacity to judge for himself essential religious questions, he rejected the stern logic that among rival religions either one or none of them had to be true. This logic derives from the original premise that the rise and course of authentic religion was determined by specific revelation, or primal divine instruction of some kind, positing in the world *vera religio* as a reference point and norm for all that followed. But when the first premise becomes the conviction that a universal providence exists, the logical outcome is the opposite: there is likely to be at least some remnant of worthiness in every religion.

That religion had its origin and object in God, Herbert never doubted; that its origin could be credited to any particular tradition he emphatically denied. Armed with his faith in providence as God's greatest attribute,[1] he faced the incredible variety of religions not with disdain but with a sense that all shared—beneath the accumulated "rubbish" of traditions—the same fundamental aim and intent, and could be reduced to the same essential meanings—meanings which corresponded to innate faculties of the mind. He exhibited a serene confidence that a merciful providence has endowed everyone with the necessary resources to make all essential religious judgments and to find the path to salvation. He tried to demonstrate this faith by showing that a factual consensus exists among the world's religions about what ultimately matters. This consensus could be summarized as five "common notions" (or "catholic truths") of religion, and this is the idea for which he is best known.

---

1. *De Religione Laici* (hereafter *RL;* see below, n. 10), 125.

Herbert's quest for a universal religion was an Englishman's[2] response, by a layman and amateur philosopher, to his environment of religion, politics, and war. A diplomat and soldier of fortune, he fought on the side of the duke of Orange against the Spaniards in 1610 and supported the cause of the Arminians against the orthodox Calvinists. As an able English ambassador to Paris from 1619 to 1624, he tried to persuade the duke of Guise to honor the Edict of Nantes, warning that persecution would lead to further civil war.[3] He also attempted to keep the French out of what turned out to be the Thirty Years' War. He numbered among his friends the great Arminian jurist and theologian Hugo Grotius; both he and Descartes read Herbert's work. At home, he was distinctly unfriendly to the Puritan cause. Coming to the House of Lords in 1642, he was committed briefly to the Tower by the Long Parliament for disagreeing with the majority over the conditions upon which the king might make war on Parliament. Two years later he reluctantly surrendered his castle at Montgomery to parliamentary forces.[4]

It is no wonder, then, that he perceived the great problem of his time, in the sphere of religion, to be the question of how to resolve contradiction and conflict and to establish religious peace, both in minds and in society. Integrally related to that problem was the one that preoccupied the philosophy of the time: the question of criteria for truth.[5]

The two questions are inextricably linked. Religious strife arose and continued on the presupposition that there was a single religious system of truth and that it was the duty of those in authority to impose it on all, for the glory of God and his church.[6] But the insoluble conflicts that arose with the clash of rival claims to truth forced the issue ever more to the fore: how can the impasse be broken in some way other than by force? If there is no way to choose between the rival claims, is there not some way to transcend them all? Is it not possible to promote both the glory of God *and* peace?[7]

2. Michel Despland, *La Religion en Occident*, provides an in-depth comparison of the situations in France and England, together with the impact of those contexts on the discussion of religion; see esp. 278–87.

3. H. R. Hutcheson, introduction to *RL* (below, n. 10), 19.

4. Sidney L. Lee, "Herbert, Edward," in *Dictionary of National Biography*, 9:628.

5. Discussing Herbert's motivation in his introduction to the *De Veritate*, (see below, n. 10), M. H. Carré quotes Montaigne to illustrate the general and urgent sense of need for the criterion of truth: "To judge of the appearances that we receive of subjects, we ought to have a judicatory instrument; to prove this instrument, we must have demonstration; to verify this demonstration, an instrument; and here we are upon the wheel" (14). Richard H. Popkin, *History of Scepticism from Erasmus to Spinoza*, reviews the whole seventeenth century, beginning with an analysis of the crisis of the criterion for truth created by the Reformation. See also R. D. Bedford, *The Defence of Truth: Herbert of Cherbury and the Seventeenth Century*, chap. 2: "The Problem of Certainty."

6. As H. R. Hutcheson puts it, "The seventeenth-century conscience felt an obligation to mould—ideally by persuasion, by force if necessary—differing consciences; Herbert, far in advance of his contemporaries, strenuously denied this obligation" (*RL*, Introduction, 49.

7. The last sentence of the *RL* reads: "God grant that what we here have written serve to increase His glory and to establish the common peace" (133).

Herbert thought it was. He diagnosed the root cause of religious conflict as the claim of each competing religious body to control exclusively the means of salvation. This is the claim that justifies persecution and war. And each such claim is based on the presumption of a "special revelation." Transcend that bit of arrogance, and one eliminates the problem at its root.

Herbert was not a great thinker but a man of great common sense. His ideas made little specific impact[8] but quietly intruded everywhere. Far less learned and academic than Bodin, and rarely profound, he is frequently original and almost always fresh. In Herbert the ordinary person finds his champion. Against the schoolmen, priests, and theologians he asserts: the problem with religion is not to *know* what is true, right, and good, but to *do* it—"hard to follow . . . yet not difficult to perceive."[9]

We draw on three major works for Herbert's views on religion: the *De Veritate* (1624, as revised 1645), the *De Religione Gentilium* (written by 1645; published in 1663) and the *De Religione Laici* (1645).[10] The full title of the first, in translation, reveals its full scope: *On Truth as It Is Distinguished from Revelation, Probability, Possibility and Falsehood*. It is devoted to the problem of discovering truth—not just religious but truth in general. Thus, it is as ambitious in scope as the work of Descartes that was completely to overshadow it. I shall analyze the text, however, only so far as is necessary to understand what it has to say about religion. An English translation of the second work appeared in 1705, under the title *The Ancient Religion of the Gentiles and Causes of their Errors Considered: the Mistakes and Failures of the Heathen Priests and Wise-Men, in their Notions of the Deity, and Matters of Divine Worship, are Examin'd; with Regard to their Being Altogether Destitute of Divine Revelation*. These titles already forewarn us that "divine revelation" will be considered but that the possibilities of knowing religious truth apart from it will be Herbert's major concern. *Of a Layman's Religion*, the remaining work, is the most straightforward treatment of the problems that concern us.

Herbert's great contemporaries, Francis Bacon and René Descartes, are much better known for their contributions to early modern approaches to knowledge in harmony with the budding scientific revolution. But Herbert contributed more than either of them to questions of interest to us, for his

---

8. Hutcheson, *RL*, Intro., 3, 72ff. Cf. R. D. Bedford, *The Defence of Truth*, 248ff.

9. *RL* 103.

10. I have used the London 1645 ed. of *De Veritate* (hereafter *DV*), reprint ed. Günter Gawlick; Eng. trans. Meyrick H. Carré. For *De Religione Gentilium* (hereafter *RG*), the 1663 ed., reprint ed. Günter Gawlick, 1967. Eng. transl. London, 1705. References to these works will be first to the English, then to the Latin editions, e.g., *DV* 310/228. *De Religione Laici* (hereafter *RL*), ed. H. R. Hutcheson, contains Latin and English on facing pages; only the page in English will be referenced.

primary concern was religion, while for both of them religion was a peripheral interest.[11]

Like Descartes, Herbert was deeply troubled by the crisis concerning the criteria for truth in general. That his *De Veritate* was soon forgotten does not detract from the boldness and freshness of his venture, though an amateur, into epistemology. As one of his interpreters and editors says:

> What counts is the attempt to formulate a rational method of discovering truth, for the very making of the attempt was an intellectual achievement. While most of his contemporaries were busy informing each other, none too gently, of the truth, Herbert was engaged in the less self-indulgent task of first inquiring how the fallible human mind might attain some reasonably accurate notion of what the truth actually was.[12]

As Herbert himself observed:

> It is indeed a matter for perpetual wonder that writers expect their doctrines to be received as the truth, while they display such misunderstanding as to what truth is, its quality, extent and diverse functions, its spheres of reference, its modes, the time and place of its occurrence, its origin and use, that they do not seem to have grasped even the meaning of their own assertions on the subject. (*DV*, 76/1–2)

The average observer, he says, is caught between complete despair of knowing anything and yielding to the dogmatism of those who claim to know everything.

Some resolution of this problem "has never been so necessary as now," he urges.

> It is extraordinary . . . how persistently weak mortals alternate between total acceptance of the theories of the authorities and total rejection of them. *They have no criterion* [nullo uti novit delectu], but dully immersing themselves in a naive credulity, they become incapable of using their own faculties; and not having the heart to confront the terrors with which they are threatened, they fall back on fear and hate. (*DV*, 117/39; my italics)

Perceiving the problem of religion as a war of mutually irreconcilable and absolute claims, Herbert echoes exactly the questions raised by Bodin through Senamus in the *Colloquium Heptaplomeres*. Herbert says: "What . . . shall the layman, encompassed by the terrors of divers churches militant throughout the world, decide as to the best religion [religio optima]? For there is no

---

11. On Bacon, see my essay, "Religion and Bacon's New Learning." Herbert's silence concerning Bacon (noted by Hutcheson, *RL*, 28) may be due in part to totally different approaches to religion, based on their opposing views regarding revelation. Bacon accepts it as an established and already perfected body of truth beyond criticism and wholly outside the scope of his vast inquiry. Indeed, for Bacon, revelation legitimates the whole scientific enterprise (see especially the *New Atlantis*). For Herbert, revelation is precisely the focus of much of his critical inquiry.

12. Hutcheson, *RL*, Intro., 31. Cf. R. D. Bedford, *The Defence of Truth*, 81.

church that does not breathe threats, none almost that does not deny the possibility of salvation outside its own pale" (*RL*, 86). And the accompanying question (also of Bodin's Senamus)—that of an arbiter for these disputes—is also raised by Herbert: "who will be the witnesses, who will be appointed judge [judex] of these controversies?" (*RL*, 101–02).

People lack that without which "it is impossible to establish any standard of discrimination in revelation or even in religion" (ut citra earum [i.e., common notions] opem nullus commode institui possit Revelationis, vel ipsius quidem Religionis delectus; *DV*, 289/208). The criteria that Herbert proposed aimed to provide a new platform for religious peace—both of mind and for society; at the same time, these criteria would provide a norm against which to test every claim to divine revelation and to undermine all such claims on the basis of which the competing sects busily damned one another. His solution was to discover a universal standard in the realm of religious truth, for "the wretched terror-stricken mass have no refuge, unless some immovable foundations of truth resting on *universal consent* [consensus universalis] are established, to which they can turn amid the doubts of theology or of philosophy. . . . " (*DV*, 117/39).

This consensus, once identified, would be the "*summa*" or "*unica veritatis norma*" (*DV*, 117/39, 118/40). Already we see a departure from the solution toward which Bodin (through Toralba and Salomon) moved: Herbert is not going to search out the "best" by finding the *oldest* but, rather, by discovering those fundamental matters on which the religions agree.

This strategy is derived from Herbert's first theological premise and religious conviction, that of universal providence, which implied, necessarily, that it must be possible to find evidences of that providence in the commonalities shared by all the religions of the world in all times and places.

As a statement of conviction and intent, the autobiographical note on which the *Ancient Religion of the Gentiles* opens is worth quoting in full:

> When, for a long time, I had employed my most serious thoughts, in considering whether any common means for obtaining eternal salvation, were so proposed to all mankind, that from thence we might necessarily conclude and infer the certainty of *universal divine providence* [providentia divina universalis], I met with many doubts and difficulties, not easy to be solved. I found that many fathers of the church had not only a mean and contemptible opinion of the ancient divulged religion of the heathens, but also absolutely and entirely condemned it. The divines of this last age pronounce as severe a sentence against all those that are without their pale, so that, according to their opinion, the far greatest part of mankind must be inevitably sentenced to eternal punishment. (*RG*, 1–2/1)

This long-term eccelesiastical posture seemed to Herbert "altogether incompatible with the dignity of an universal divine providence"; in fact, it led him to wonder whether the ancients even "meant the same by GOD as we now do" (*RG*, 2/1).

Such a question required a search of ancient texts and opened up the entire realm of human religiousness to sympathetic scrutiny. The need for some criterion resting on "universal consent" carried the same mandate: to find out what people in all times and places had in fact believed, in order to ferret out matters of universal assent, and to show from those findings that God is fair: "My design is to make it evident that an *universal providence* is extended to all mankind" (*RG*, 6/4, my italics). In Herbert, then, "we hear the voice of common humanity, refusing to be damned."[13]

Everyone with even a nodding acquaintance of Herbert of Cherbury already knows the outcome of his search: the notorious Five Common Notions concerning Religion.[14] I have been rather elaborate in posing the question, however, because it shows that neither the problem nor the solution is quite as simple as might first appear. On the surface, and with selected texts, one might simply conclude that Herbert's solution to religious conflict is that everyone is endowed with a stock of innate *ideas*, of which five are somehow immediately knowable as essential religion. He frequently describes the notions as "inscribed" (descripta) on the mind by God (for example, "the undoubted pronouncements of God, transcribed in the conscience: indubia Dei effata . . . in Foro interiori descripta"; *RL*, 101).

Much debate has gone on about the epistemologically important question of innate ideas, or faculties, and the extent to which Herbert really advocated their existence. Carré, like Herbert's first critic John Locke, quotes Herbert to the effect that certain *ideas* are inborn, and he agrees with Locke that Herbert fell into simple contradiction when he appealed to common consent as the necessary means of confirming them.[15] In the end Herbert is just not clear enough, or rigorous enough (as Hutcheson correctly observes).[16] A sensible interpretation is that rather than innate *ideas*, there is an innate religious *sense* that accounts for religion's very existence, in addition to which there are reliable critical faculties for identifying the true and discriminating it from the false, when it is experienced. Religion is universal because of *something* innate; its fundamental ideas emerge as experience is interpreted through innate but not predetermined faculties. Herbert writes:

13. Hutcheson, *RL* 5. Bedford, *The Defence of Truth*, 111ff., notes the ongoing debates about immortality of the soul as another dimension of the context in which Herbert wrote.

14. "*Notitiae communes.*" For the extensive classical background, see Maryanne Cline Horowitz, "The Stoic Synthesis of the Idea of Natural Law in Man." Maurice Wiles notes use by the early Christian apologists: *The Making of Christian Doctrine*, 25. Herbert's Five Common Notions of Religion are that there is one God, that he ought to be worshiped, that virtue is the principle part of religion, that we ought to repent of our sins, and that there are rewards and punishments in the next life.

15. Carré, *DV*, Intro., 33–34. Bedford, *The Defence of Truth*, 78, is correct in asserting that "it was not ideas as such that Herbert claimed to be innate . . . but modes of thought, the very processes of the mind." This is exactly Hutcheson's conclusion (*RL*, Intro., 37). Locke's criticism of Herbert is found in the *Essay Concerning Human Understanding*, I.3.15–19.

16. Hutcheson, *RL*, Intro., 5.

Religion is a common notion; no period or nation is without religion. We have, then, to search for what is by universal consent acknowledged in religion and compare these universal principles with each other; and what is universally acclaimed as religious truth must be recognized as Common Notions [quae...ab omnibus tanquam vera in Religione agnoscuntur, Communes Notitiae habendae sunt]. Such a proceeding may be deemed laborious, but there is no other way by which the truths of common notions can be ascertained. (*DV*, 121/43)

For our purposes, and for the study of religion, his attempt to establish such a consensus is equally important and perhaps more interesting than the idea of an innate religiousness; his own autobiographical testimony demonstrates that it was not by an introspective inventory alone that he made what he regarded as his great discovery; rather, it was what the comparative data seemed to reveal. Disturbed, he says, by conflicting religious claims and the "dissensions and bitter animosities" generated by them, he began

> seriously considering the various parts of that most ancient and generally divulged religion of the heathens, [and] began to collect those that were absolutely necessary, and grounded on common reason, esteeming them principally asserted and freed from the dirt and rubbish in which they lay; Thus, not without a frequent and accurate dissection of, and inspection into religions, I found those five articles I have so often mentioned. . . . (*RG*, 367/218)

The effect of this discovery was exhilirating: "I thought myself far more happy than Archimedes" (ibid.).

Ultimately, his argument is circular: the innate grounding of the common notions is proved by universal consensus (allegedly) derived from the data; the factual inevitability of consensus is guaranteed in advance by the innateness of a religious sense that issues in "the worship of the supreme God by means of every virtue, penitence when we fail therein, and reward or punishment after this life" (*RL*, 89).[17]

Since the problem which generated the whole research is that of the criterion for judging between rival views, it is as such that the common notions mainly function, rather than as an account of the very origin of religion—that is, an Archimedian lever rather than a font.

Many passages could be cited to show Herbert working inductively to arrive at his common notions, or at least to match what he is already inclined to regard as essential with sufficient data to support the theory. His procedure then involves a reduction of the data to a common core:

> To these truths . . . all the wonders of individual religions so reduce themselves when analysed [ita analytice reducuntur cuncta particularium Religionum magnalia], that he [the inquirer] will scarcely substitute anywhere a remoter purpose; and especially every eminently sane dogma of theology, or what holiest sacrament

17. Notice that here Herbert has given the Five Common Notions of Religion in summary form.

of the Church you will, tends nowhere else when resolved to its final elements [haut aliorsum tendat in resolutione sua ultima]. (*RL*, 121)

Herbert appeals to "right reason" as a reliable guide, but consensus is the final norm, because the evidence might contradict one's reason—an idea impossible to square with the notion that everything is *derivable* from pure reason: "If . . . there are some matters based on universal consent . . . which seem to be opposed to reason [a ratione aliena], it must be remembered that it is the nature of natural instinct to fulfill itself irrationally, that is to say without foresight. . . . The common saying is therefore justified which says that man must believe some things that surpass his understanding" (*DV*, 120/42).[18] In the context of this passage, Herbert has classified the common notions as a peculiarly *human* form of those instincts for self-preservation that man shares with animals. One instinct that manifests itself especially is the common notion that man survives death (a notion Herbert classifies as religious). The fact that some common notions might seem irrational, or beyond reason, makes all the more pressing the demand for evidence: "I maintain that universal consent (which has not been established without the aid of divine providence) is in the last resort the sole test of truth" (unica veritatis norma; *DV*, 118/40). Universal consent, then, may not offer a logical guarantee of truth, but it will support an article of faith that God "has bestowed common notions upon men in all ages as media of his divine universal providence" (media providentiae suae divinae universalis; ibid.). We are brought again to Herbert's most fundamental aim: to write a theodicy of universal providence.

Herbert's lack of precision about whether religion is innate or acquired is evident when we address the question of the origin of religion, for we see him bumping up against data that do not seem to support the hypothesis of an innate stock of ideas. The idea of a universal providence seemed, in Herbert's mind, to guarantee that some form of religion would be found everywhere. But it committed him to no theological account of exactly *how* it began. Unlike Bodin, Herbert had no stake in presenting an account of the *origin* of religion that was at the same time religiously normative. It will be recalled that, for Bodin, discovery of the oldest would be, ipso facto, discovery of the best, the "true" religion. For Bodin, then, original religion must be the rational monotheism of Toralba, rooted in original revelation. For Herbert, the question of first beginnings was of less importance, not being attached to the constraints of the biblical framework. The question of origins was completely open to discovery and speculation on the basis of whatever evidence came to hand.

18. Cf. *DV* 123/45: an instinct is "an immediate emanation of the mind, co-extensive with the dictates of nature, so that it directly supports the doctrine of self-preservation; and it is so essential that even in death it cannot be destroyed."

This has considerable significance for the development of the study of religion. For even though Herbert's motivation for inquiry was every bit as religious as Bodin's, his flexible providence paradigm set few limits on what sorts of data might be relevant; *any* evidence of religion could serve to support so general a theory, even though it required interpretive manipulation to show some at least implicit connection to the monotheism of the five common notions. In a complete departure from Bodin's procedure, Herbert ignored the biblical primeval history, deriving his evidence elsewhere when considering how religion might have started.

He did in fact conceive a sort of golden age of primeval religion, that period before religion was (to use our own term) institutionalized. Herbert's term to cover such developments is the more colorful one of "priestcraft." When one reads the chapter in *Ancient Religion* entitled "An Essay Concerning the First Causes of Religion Amongst the Heathen" (chap. 14), one finds nothing but an account of the corruption introduced by "a race of crafty priests" who distorted the original religion of pure "piety and virtue" already in existence. Herbert had already treated original religion earlier in his book.

The material relevant to this question divides into subjective and objective elements—that is, a more-or-less innate propensity to religiousness, on the one hand, and experiences of the world that evoke and shape that inner sensibility and result in outward manifestations, on the other.

Regarding the former, Herbert asserts that "nature has implanted in man [a propensity] to render a due veneration to all those from whom he has received any benefits [quum iis omnibus a quibus beneficia accepimus, cultum debitum reddere ab ipsa natura homine insitum]" (*RG*, 10/6). But an even more general response to worldly experience has been preprogrammed in human beings, or at least some of them, for

> all pious and good men, as if they were tired and satiated with every thing here, endeavored after something beyond them, though they knew not what it was. From hence first proceeded the notion of an unknown deity. For God inspiring all men with a desire of an eternal and more happy state; he tacitly discovered himself, who is eternal life, and perfectly happy [dum enim author fuit Deus, ut vitae aeternae beatiorisque status desiderium cunctis inderetur, seipsum . . . tacite indicavit]. (*RG*, 8/5)

Thus, the reality of God conforms to the fondest wishes of humankind (an idea that, stripped of its theological presupposition, suggests the Freudian conception of religion as illusion). In fact, Herbert asserts, "belief and hope of a better life" is the inner urge on which "the whole frame of religion turns [tota perfectae religionis machina vertitur]" (*RG*, 270/167).

Herbert's sources did not, however, indicate anything like an actual consensus about monotheism arising from such a propensity; he found, rather, all sorts of nature worship. Here is how he accounted for it: "Now, in regard God cannot be worshipped according to the excellence of his dignity, which the most sagacious reason can never penetrate into; he therefore manifested himself (seipsum patefecit) by the most excellent fabric of the world [cf. Rom. 1]" (*RG*, 8/5). The result was not an apprehension of order bespeaking a supreme intelligence, as the design argument would have it, but an awareness of *transitoriness*. When the ancients contemplated the world, they undertook "an anxious and strict enquiry, whether there was anything here, or any where else, that was eternal; knowing very well that fading and transitory things could produce nothing but what was fading and transitory" (ibid.).

Their search first led them to lift their eyes to the heavenly bodies, and lo, beyond the corruption and transitoriness of this world, they found "a certain eternal and happy state in them only" (*RG*, 9/5). Moreover, the heathen attributed to the stars causality with regard to the world, thinking "their motion, heat, light and influence to be at least the proximate causes of the production of all things which are seen here" (ibid.).[19]

Despite such evidence, Herbert cherished an assumption that behind all this there was some implicit worship of God. Yet his interpretation could easily be separated from that assumption, as the following statement indicates: "Now, although the worship of the supreme God is more ancient in itself, being written in the heart, yet in regard our ancestors received the first indications of him from those splendid incorruptible bodies, the sun and moon, if not the most ancient, yet certainly the most universal worship (such as it was) was paid to the stars; as is evident from many authors" (*RG*, 11/6). But how is this discrepancy between the principle of an immediately known common notion and the apparent fact that the earliest religion was star-worship to be resolved? In face of this difficulty, Herbert is on the verge of discovering history, for he suggests that a process of religious *development* was under way. "At last by degrees, they came to adore the Supreme Deity. ... They could not come to the knowledge of him any other way [quum gradatim ita ad summi Numinis cultum profecti sint ... haut sane aliter Deum congredi potuerunt]" (*RG*, 11/6). Thus, rather than erupting spontaneously out of right reason or consciousness, and rather than being the primeval religion of a lost first age, monotheism, despite its privileged status as the first of Herbert's common notions, was in fact arrived at historically, "by degrees." "Religion being progressive, they began to enquire [religione its ingruente quaeri coeptum est] whether there was any God or Deity that presided over the stars themselves? which opinion soon obtained. ... " (*RG*, 11/6). But Herbert resists the radical implications of his own glimmer of a developmental view: against his own evidence he insists that even "in the first ages," when people were directed by their inner hopes "to the stars,"

19. Herbert notes that the same belief prevails among Indians in his own day: "They worship all those things whose influence they observe to be most prevalent in natural productions: illa enim ea omnia colunt, quorum vires maximas in res naturales experti sunt" (*RG* 10f./6).

they "worshipped God himself in his works. Neither was there any other form of religion [religionis formula] at that time" (*RG*, 11/7).

Two more texts are of interest, for they present ideas about the most elementary possible form of religion Herbert can imagine. Of the two texts, one speculates about how the common man regarded the world while all this high-level philosophical speculation was going on; the other tells how a theory of divine creation and purpose might possibly have arisen. What is notable about these two texts is that in neither of them does Herbert refer to the common notions; either of these conjectures could have as well been proposed by a Lockeian. In the first, about the religious view of the "vulgar," Herbert discovers a people content for the most part to live comfortably in the world, taking no particular care for things "religious,"

> *unless*, observing some internal power or deity, operating in the world, they thought it was in his power to take the blessings they enjoyed from them, or them from the blessings. This latent power or deity [vim latentem sive numen] they readily acknowledged to be the original of all things *whose causes they were ignorant of* . . . [quarum caussas ignorabant, authorem facile faciebant]. (*RG*, 258/160; italics mine)

At length, they supposed it prudent to come to terms with such power, regarding it

> their duty and interest to supplicate this god, to divert evil from them, and bestow his favors on them, and that they ought to pay all respect to his chief ministers [such as the stars]. When they contemplated these things, they either framed a sort of religious worship from those notions they had of God, or some internal dictates, or received it from the priests . . . [ex iis circa Deum notitiis, cultum ejus religiosum, sive ex interno aliquo dictamine constituebant, sive a sacerdotibus accipiebant]. (*RG*, 258/160)

According to Herbert, there were probably a few extraordinary intellects extending their thought to higher levels:

> Let us suppose a man of very extraordinary natural abilities, but hath received no external informations, by traditions, revelations, or otherwise; I conceive he will have the same sentiments concerning this world, when he has made some considerable observations concerning it, as he would have upon the first sight of a musical instrument curiously made, that it was not jumbled together by blind chance; or that which admits of such variety of parts, could be self-productive. (*RG*, 259–60/161)

The design argument. But Herbert's version of it differs from what we will find typically in the next century (when the stress will be on regularity of natural laws, rather than on providence). Herbert gets out of this argument not only the idea of an intelligent maker, but also of purpose. So he imagines a musician playing this instrument, which evokes admiration not only for the artificer, but for the intentionality or purpose manifest in the playing of the instrument.

In both these texts, it is notable that Herbert makes no reference to his theory of common notions. Moreover, both texts anticipate commonplaces of post-Lockeian eighteenth-century thought—namely, that the idea of, and manipulation of, the gods arises from ignorance of causes of things that affect human life, and that the world as a whole seems to manifest an intelligent and purposeful creator. We shall of course encounter these ideas and their critique when we come to Hume.

To summarize, Herbert's foray into comparative religion was motivated by his faith in universal providence and shaped by his theory that the evidence would support his claim that a consensus about certain common elements could be established. As it turned out, the facts he presented did not support his theory. But the effort effectively illustrates the importance of having a theory of *some* sort: the theory gave Herbert an orientation, suggested specific questions to ask of the data, and indicated directions for its organization and interpretation. Moreover, his approach was basically sympathetic rather than condescending, and honest enough to allow conflicting data to surface.

Finding universal elements remains one of the key problems for defining religion and for providing a rationale for comparison at all, beyond merely collecting "interesting" data. Despite his weaknesses, then, Herbert can be credited with a modest contribution to the modern paradigm for studying religion.

Before drawing further conclusions, we need to look more closely at Herbert's departure from traditional assumptions about revelation. We have already observed that even though his agenda is theological, his universalism entails a complete freedom from the necessity of "saving" the biblical framework and its primal history or of incorporating it into the construction of an authentic religion. We have been able to present his whole theory of religion and its origins without recourse to the idea of revelation, and without reference to Adam and his posterity (the only reference to Adam I have found is in another context, where Herbert is contesting the doctrine of transmission of sin from Adam).

We have already stressed that the five common notions, or "catholic truths," serve as a criterion for judgment about rival religious claims. This applies *especially* to claims of divine revelation, with which Herbert is unimpressed:

> Not every religion which proclaims a revelation is good, nor is every doctrine taught under its authority always essential or even valuable. Some doctrines due to revelation may be, some ought to be, abandoned. In this connection the teaching of Common Notions is important; indeed, without them it is impossible to establish *any standard of discrimination in revelation* or even in religion [citra earum opem nullus commode institui possit Revelationis, vel ipsius quidem Religionis delectus]. (*DV*, 289/208)[20]

20. Such a standard is all the more necessary to avoid the evil of implicit faith, for "the

Does Herbert leave any place at all for revelation? Yes—in senses which, by personalizing it, rigorously eliminate it as the basis for exclusive claims and coercive laws. When giving his criteria for testing any claim to revelation, Herbert's standards are so strict as effectively to rule out any appeal to tradition, authority, or sacred texts. Among the conditions of a genuine revelation, the most decisive is immediacy (*DV*, 308/226). The testimony of others is by itself no guarantee of revelation, any more than the report of five common notions would be. In either case, one is capable of making a personal judgment. What Herbert says in the following about the adequacy of the common notions for salvation applies equally to the claim of revelation: "They [the common notions] are ... indeed, sharply disputed, and can be tested [i.e., challenged] adequately by no evidence save that of revelations *made directly to ourselves* [neque ullo satis nisi revelationum nobis ipsis immediate factarum testimonio probari possint]. ... (*RL*, 129; my italics).[21]

With regard to each tradition's claims to revelation Herbert strictly distinguishes them from essential truth derived from personal experience and reason; he relegates them to the categories of history, tradition, the past— all without rational authority. In contrast to Bodin, then, Herbert decisively cuts through the last essential link between the authority of reason and the authority of the past. They are clearly separate, so that the inquirer should distinguish "matters which proceed from right reason [ratio recta] from those which concern faith in past events [fides circa praeterita]; let him ascribe to each its own functions" (*RL*, 121). Right reason does not depend on faith, revelation, or tradition; its catholic truths are inscribed in the mind (descripta in mente) by God as a true and certain norm (norma) (*RL*, 129).

These ideas taken together provide a solid foundation for the historical-critical approach to the Bible to be advanced by the great Spinoza before the end of the century: foremost is Herbert's clear distinction between the source of permanently valid religious truth and the histories and traditions related in Scripture to which religious communities appeal as "revelation." Like Spinoza, Herbert already draws a fundamental distinction that flies directly in the face of seventeenth-century orthodoxies: a distinction between what is in the Bible and "the word of God": "Not everything that is contained in Scripture," he assures us, may be called "the pure and undisputed word of

---

Supreme Judge requires every individual to render an account of his actions in the light, not of another's belief, but of his own" (*DV* 290/209).

21. Despite what many scholars have said, there is no inconsistency between Herbert's skepticism about the revelational basis of the religions and his conviction that he himself received a "revelation" (in content an affirmative response to his prayer about whether he should publish his book; see his own autobiography, *The Life of Edward, First Lord Herbert of Cherbury, Written by Himself*, ed. J. M. Shuttleworth, 120–21). This personal appearance by the deity was experienced as a special "grace" in no way related to the sort of alleged divine communications that authorized the formation of sects.

God" (*RL*, 99).[22] There is a great deal of material there—"no small heap of miracles . . . prophecies, rites, sacraments, ceremonies," etc.—that have no application to us. "God's word" is, rather, that religious message which the whole of the Bible intends. "What [Herbert asks] finally is urged, because of God's mercy to mankind, but love and fear of God, charity towards one's neighbor, repentance and hope for a better life?" (*RL*, 101)—what finally, the alert reader will immediately detect, but the five catholic truths!

Some conclusions may now be drawn. In order to make his case for a universal providence, Herbert had to show that religion in all times and places exhibited certain common manifestations. Although his intent was normative in that respect, it also required that he break away from the limitations of "religion" as understood in the Western Christian tradition. And so, even though he frequently employed the language of that tradition, he consistently altered its meanings by universalizing it. Webb made an insightful comment in noting one way in which Herbert did this: "The belief of the Protestant Reformers that Christianity had been perverted from its original purity and simplicity through the multiplication by an interested priesthood of traditions calculated to exalt their own dignity and increase their influence, was generalized into a theory of the corruption of primitive religion by priests."[23]

But in a way this observation applies more closely to Bodin, in that he construed in very precise terms a "primitive religion" from primeval biblical history, whereas Herbert's picture of pre-priestly religion was much more vague and was construed not through evidence from the Bible but from whatever data about other religions were available to him, for instance, Egyptian religion.

The framework of Herbert's discussion is much more compatible with Cicero than with the Bible, and Cicero's summary of the various theories of primitive religion are echoed in Herbert's work. An interesting parallel is that both Cicero and Herbert were concerned to support divine providence, except that Cicero was combatting the Epicurean thesis that the gods are not concerned with human welfare and destiny (*no* providence) whereas Herbert aimed for an opposite target—the denial of universal providence by the particularistic Calvinist doctrine of double predestination.[24]

---

22. In a rare expression of irony, Herbert echoes the famous statement of Augustine that he would not have believed the Bible without the testimony of the church. After asserting flatly that the liberty of passing judgment on the Bible shall remain with mankind rather than with any church, Herbert remarks: "Quite wondrous matters, certainly, are recorded in the Sacred Scriptures more than in all other histories, wonders however which do not dull the mind, but exercise or sharpen it. But the Church will see about these, which indeed I should never have learned had it kept silent, or believed but for its testimony" (*RL* 99).

23. C. C. J. Webb, *Studies in the History of Natural Theology*, 350.

24. Bedford attempts to make Herbert fit into the camp of Latitudinarian Christians, and

Herbert's enduring legacy is most clear in contemporary approaches that reduce religion to an essential core, such as "manifestations of the sacred," or "faith," as the common element in all religious beliefs and rites. Herbert's unbiased approach (that is, unbiased toward the Western tradition, in the context of his time) incited the search for essential religion at the core of the religions, and for definitions that might be universally applicable. And he had the good sense to understand clearly that religion is not reducible to sets of beliefs (what he says about worship, virtue, and repentance makes that very clear).

Herbert's foray into pre-Christian and non-Christian religion was of course impoverished by his lack of sources, especially contemporary, but Europe was shortly to be inundated by them, and he had already seen the fitness of comparing the most ancient he knew (the religion of Egypt) with that of contemporary "savages" (American Indians) as portrayed in travelers' and missionaries' reports (for example, RG, 21/12–13). Fontenelle would make much of this sort of comparison (see chapter 3), and it was to become an eighteenth-century commonplace. Although Herbert's attempt to construct a universal religion (or piety) did not produce a universalist "church," his sympathetic approach to the sources, together with *some* hypothesis about the data, are essential elements of modern study of religion.

A few comments are in order about the distance between Herbert and Bodin. Their similarities have been noted: both worked out of a post-Christian but still religious perspective; for both, the context of conflict raised the same basic question about how to discern the truth: "right reason" is the basis for "true" (Bodin/Toralba) or universal (Herbert) religion. But there are important differences, some already noted. First, although Herbert's view of nature is not yet that of either of his contemporaries Bacon and Descartes, in terms of consonance with (or even knowledge of) the beginning revolution in astronomy, nevertheless Herbert's cosmos is nothing like Bodin's. The entire magical element of angels and demons is gone. Nature is not animated by them, and human causes alone account for corruptions of religion.

Second, Herbert demotes revelation to almost total insignificance: with reference to religious groups, it is simply lumped with "history," "tradition," and "miracle" as something at best probable, and to be rigorously tested

---

attributes to him "reunionist purposes" (*The Defence of Truth*, 136, 141, 174, etc.). The evidence weighs against Bedford's undocumented claim that Herbert has "no mind whatever to demolish the whole structure of Christian belief," but wanted merely to "pare down to the minimal and assured fundamentals" (141). "Christian revelation" may not be spurious in Herbert's eyes, but neither is it necessary. There is a world of difference between Herbert and Locke, who tend to be lumped together by Bedford. Herbert's "universal" or "catholic" church is not a reunited Christian body but the ideal church of the Common Notions, embracing all humanity (see, e.g., DV 303/222: "The only catholic and uniform church is the doctrine of common notions which comprehends all places and all men," etc.).

against reason and immediate experience. Herbert does not yet work with the notion that miracles and revelation are by definition violations of natural law (he has no notion of natural law in that sense), but he does express an idea that will be important for Hume: the weakness of any claim that depends for its credibility upon mere historical testimony.

Related to the demise of revelation is the lack of authority accorded to antiquity. Unlike Bodin, Herbert nowhere equates "the best" with "the oldest" religion. For Herbert, the best (optimum) is that which most closely aligns with the common notions (DV, 291/209). He looks for ancient evidences not in the Old Testament but in sources for "gentile" religion.

For him, accordingly, the quest for the origin of religion, for the best possible account of its first beginnings, no longer functions to demonstrate a preestablished normative form or tradition (such as in the Hebrew Scriptures). Rather, its new rationale is to test his expectation that specifiable epistemological or anthropological assumptions will in fact be borne out in religion's most elementary forms.

Third, Herbert's global perspective envisages a universal history of religions detached from its biblical framework. The development of religion (both its progress and its distortions) swallows up the traditional framework of salvation history. We have seen Herbert offering conjectures about religion's inner sources as well as the kinds of external circumstances that might have given rise to elementary religion, all without reference to the Bible.

Fourth, we see in Herbert a direction and orientation that was increasingly to differentiate the British from the French way of approaching religion: almost totally absent from Herbert's consideration are questions of religion and society. Bodin and Herbert, of course, shared an urgent concern for peace (see RL, 105). But unlike Bodin, whose political orientation kept him mindful of the social functions and necessity of religion, Herbert left entirely aside the question of religion as a social bond—an essential component of the French discussion—thus anticipating England's individualization of the problem of religion and its more secular social philosophy. The British investigation of religion, following in Herbert's wake, would focus on epistemology, while the French would continue to probe religion's irreducible social dimensions.

Güttler has seen Herbert, "first and foremost of the deists," as standing at the head of an intellectual movement which in England reached its end with Hume.[25] As we shall see, Hume's view of Herbert and his tradition was almost entirely critical, and can be understood by recalling our earlier observation that Herbert's basic argument about the common notions is circular: he appeals to universal consent to prove that the ideas are in some sense innate and, in return, appeals to their innateness as an argument that they must be found everywhere. When we look at the beginning of Hume's Natural

25. C. Güttler, Eduard, Lord Herbert von Cherbury, 236.

History of Religion, we shall see the durability of this dilemma, for these very issues frame Hume's whole discussion. Hume, however, rejects both sides of Herbert's thesis: the lack of universality of religion (indicated by the evidence as Hume construes it) weighs against religion being instinctive; and its lack of anthropological grounding in human nature accounts for its incredible and irrational variety (a variety that Herbert recognized but had trouble accounting for).

In yet another way, there is a crucial relationship between Hume and Herbert, consisting in Hume's rejection of the design argument, with its analogy between the cosmos and a human production.

On the positive side, we see Hume pursuing the historical studies that issued from Herbert's concern to draw conclusions based on data from all the religions of the world (augmented considerably by the work of authors like Fontenelle). Hume's *Natural History* takes data such as the star worship and religious rites connected with the powers of nature, both noted by Herbert, but instead of arguing that they entail an implicit monotheism, as Herbert does, Hume demonstrates that polytheism preceded monotheism.

Finally, in explaining religion Herbert resorted even less than Bodin to biblical revelation. His account of its origins appealed to inner anthropological resources, which were theologically legitimated only insofar as needed to testify to a universal providence. To this he added conjecture about how religion might arise in the encounter with nature. His remarks about the historical development of religion are largely negative, since he explains it predominantly as a corrupting process instigated by "priests," producing mostly "dirt and rubbish." But he also had an inkling of an important constructive principle, that religious consciousness is progressive.

Chapter 3

Demythologizing Religious History: Bernard Fontenelle

A key question from one of the writings on religion of Bernard Fontenelle (1657–1757) immediately reveals why he must turn to the study of history in order to satisfy his curiosity about religion.

Near the end of his *Origin of Myths,* in which he has offered a theory of myth and pointed the direction its study must take, he writes: "It is not a science [une science] to fill one's head with all the extravagances of the Phoenicians and Greeks, but it is one to know what led [de savoir ce qui a conduit] the Phoenicians and Greeks to these extravagances."[1]

An irrepressible explainer, Fontenelle thinks he can account for the rise and fall of religious (broadly speaking, to include mythic) belief without appeal to supernatural causes. But once supernatural causes have been renounced (Judaism and Christianity exempted, of which more later), the student of religion is forced to search out psychological and historical causes.

This in fact is what Fontenelle offers us in the two writings he devoted to religion, *De l'origine des fables* (1724)[2] and *Histoire des Oracles* (1686). One is mainly conjectural theory based on his assessment of human nature in light of classical mythology and contemporary travel literature; the other is a critical-historical examination of the career of ancient oracles at the time of the rise of Christianity. Different in focus, the two essays complement each other by presenting what their author believes is a sound scientific approach to the study of religion. Although its dating is uncertain, I am convinced by Carré that Fontenelle had at least the main conceptions of the *Origin* well in mind at the time that he produced the *History.*[3] Accordingly, I shall try to show the compatability of the two works at several junctures along the way.

1. *De l'origine des fables* (hereafter *OF*), ed. J.-R. Carré, 40. Partial Eng.transl. in Leonard Marsak, ed., *The Achievement of Bernard le Bovier de Fontenelle,* part 4; this quotation, p. 41. References in the text will be to the French first, then to the translation, if available; e.g., the present quotation: *OF* 40/41.

2. Scholars agree that the work was written long before it was published, perhaps in the 1680s. See J.-R. Carré, *La Philosophie de Fontenelle,* 117–18; Leonard Marsak, *The Achievement of . . . Fontenelle,* lxxxvi; Alain Niderst, *Fontenelle à la recherche de lui-même,* 220–21.

3. Carré, 117–18.

With this author, the aery realms of deistic natural theology lie behind;
the religious content of myths and oracles are not of particular interest to
him. Rather, Fontenelle relentlessly, wittily, insightfully seeks only to explain
why it is that people believe what they do when and where they do.

In his own age, Fontenelle was acknowledged from several quarters as a
pioneer. The Encyclopedists ranked him with Locke as one of the fathers of
the Enlightenment. He was read by and clearly influenced both Hume and
Comte; his influence was felt both by the classical British anthropologists
and the positivist French sociologists of the nineteenth century.

It is not surprising that Fontenelle wished to approach the study of culture
from a scientific perspective. He served for forty-three years of his long life
(he died a month short of a hundred) as secretary of the Paris Academy of
Sciences. All scholars, regardless of their assessment of his importance, agree
that he was a superb popularizer of new scientific views. His *Conversations
on the Plurality of Worlds* (1686) not only made his reputation as a writer but
"no doubt did more than any other single writing to diffuse these [Coper-
nician] ideas among the educated classes generally."[4] In the same year, he
published the *History of Oracles*, followed shortly by his *Digression on the
Ancients and Moderns* (1688).

He had been a member of the Académie française since 1691, and was also
a member of similar intellectual societies elsewhere—the Royal Society of
London, the Arcadian Academy at Rome, the academies of Berlin and Nancy.
As secretary, he was obliged to publish annually a complete report of the
papers given before the Academy of Sciences and to compose the eulogies
of its deceased members. As a result, he became "the extremely well-in-
formed, technically competent, authoritative voice for the progress of the
'New Philosophy.' "[5]

If not the most profound, Fontenelle is the most witty and readable author
represented in this book. Although he produced mostly pamphlets, and never
a system, some of his views were, as Lévy-Bruhl says, "strangely strong,
bold and deep," and he was "among the first who had a distinct notion of
scientific progress and of the intellectual development of mankind under
fixed laws."[6] The writings to be examined will show the meaning of these
observations. But we shall be especially interested to show how Fontenelle's
naturalistic, evolutionary, and historical approach advanced the discussion
of religion and prepared the ground for the century ahead, especially through
his discussion of origins in the framework of the development of mind,
together with his critical-historical approach to ancient sources.

Let us begin with the *Origin of Myths*. It was published later (1724) than
the *History of Oracles*, but, as already noted, it might have been written

4. Arthor O. Lovejoy, *The Great Chain of Being*, 130.
5. Edward J. Kearns, *Ideas in Seventeenth-Century France*, 162.
6. Lucien Lévy-Bruhl, *History of Modern Philosophy in France*, 138.

earlier, or at least had its main ideas well formed. Even if chronologically later, it is logically prior to the *History*, offering generalizations whose application can be observed in the study of oracles.

The *Origin* is a brief essay, comprising only thirty pages in its critical edition. It has no chapter divisions, and its organization is not altogether satisfactory. It recognizes a distinction between myth and religion but does not spell out the relationship. Its intent is to explain the workings of the human mind "in one of its strangest creations"—myths (*OF*, 11/34). How are we to account for their bizarre and astonishing contents? Could they possibly have been intended to be taken as true? If not, why would such falsehoods be preserved and bequeathed to subsequent generations? How possibly could such things have gripped people's minds and imaginations for so long?

Fontenelle's answers may be grouped under four headings: the generation (or origin) of myths, their evolution, their literary features, and their proper interpretation. Fontenelle's ideas are unequally developed—some not at all—but they contain seminal ideas for subsequent study.

On the very first page, Fontenelle stresses the fact that the myths are the "ancient histories" of primitive peoples; that they have no other history than these ("il n'y a point d'autres histoires anciennes que les fables"; *OF*, 11/34). Accordingly, one might expect Fontenelle to stress the social aspect of myth, or the ways in which myths reflect ancient social order. But in fact, as Fontenelle unfolds his theory, he presents us more with ancient physics, or *natural* history, than what we would call social or cultural history (that will be Vico's specialty). Clearly, in his view, the myths reveal the state of the ancient mind and its cosmological beliefs but not much about their societies.

The origin of myths in the most general sense is to be accounted for by the almost unimaginable ignorance of the first men. "Men see marvels," Fontenelle writes, "in proportion to their ignorance and lack of experience" (*OF*, 12/34); moreover, the propensity of the ignorant to relate the unknown in marvelous ways is a universal human trait, not determined either by nationality or climate. Noting the similarity between Chinese and Greek accounts of natural occurrences, Fontenelle concludes that the same level of ignorance has produced almost the same effects with all peoples ("la même ignorance a produit à peu près les mêmes effects chez tous les peuples"; *OF*, 32).

Fontenelle stresses the universality of this principle: *every* people's history begins with myth, because of ignorance: "in all that I have said, I suppose in men only that which is common to all (commun à tous), and which must have its effect in glacial zones as well as torrid" (*OF*, 30/39).

Evidence for this assertion is "an astonishing conformity" between the myths of contemporary American Indians and those of the ancient Greeks. For example, both peoples send their unworthy dead to disagreeable bodies of water; their explanations of rain are similar; likewise, Peruvian and Greek traditions both designate certain remarkable characters as "sons of the sun" (*OF*, 31/39–40).[7] None of these remarkable similarities requires to be explained by diffusion or historical connection. Rather, every people autonomously generates similar myths at similar stages in their development. The Greeks were once as primitive and savage as the Americans. Moreover, such examples show that peoples are "drawn from barbarism by the same means, and that the imaginations of these two so distant people are in agreement" in mythic constructs (*OF*, 31/40).

In this fashion, Fontenelle proposes the beginnings of a universal evolutionary framework that will be refined by Comte and, later, provide the indispensable presupposition for the great debate about totemism late in the nineteenth century—namely, whether, in the evolution of mind or culture, every people passes through the same stages. If so, an accurate understanding of one of these stages would have universal explanatory significance. Totemism would become the locus classicus for discussion of the theory with regard to religion, from Robertson Smith to Freud and Durkheim.

Meanwhile, Fontenelle proceeds with his account of the generation of myth with a predictable next step: the production of these prodigies was, according to him, the earliest form of natural philosophy, or science: "Will what I am going to say be believed? There was philosophy even in those crude centuries, and it greatly assisted the growth of myths. Men whose intelligence is more acute than most are naturally inclined to seek the cause of what they see [naturallement portés à rechercher la cause de ce qu'ils voient]" (*OF*, 15/35).

The notion that mythic constructs were the primitive form of natural philosophy is repeated when Fontenelle discusses the Greek account of the heavenly constellations in terms of transformations of gods and goddesses. "All metamorphoses," he notes, "are the physics [la physique] of the earliest times" (*OF*, 26).

A pattern emerges for such primitive explanations: invariably the ideas generated to explain unknown phenomena were "copied from things better known" (for example, a river would be explained in terms of a god pouring water from a pitcher) (*OF*, 15/35). And the very ease of imagining such a thing made it easy also to believe. This is the basis of Fontenelle's suggestion that ancient myth is the earliest form of science: the mind is working in the same way in both cases, even though the images and metaphors we use reflect a vastly more sophisticated technology. "This philosophy of the first centuries revolved on a principle so natural that even today our philosophy has none

7. The idea that contemporary "savages" retained ancient beliefs and practices that modern societies had left behind was an eighteenth-century commonplace; see Frank E. Manuel, *The Eighteenth Century Confronts the Gods*, 213. For further discussion and criticism, see Margaret T. Hodgen, *Early Anthropology in the Sixteenth and Seventeenth Centuries*, 296, 314, 346, etc.

other; that is to say, that we explain [expliquons] unknown natural things by those which we have before our eyes, and that we carry over to natural science [la physique] those things furnished us by experience [expérience]." (*OF*, 16/35–36) The content of myths, then, and the imagination itself, are limited by the familiar; we always represent the unknown "under the figures of the known" (*OF*, 17/36). Fontenelle seems confident that this is basically the right analytical procedure, since experience supports our belief that "the unknown cannot be entirely different from what is known to us at present" (ibid.).

In their most primitive form, what exactly do the myths *explain?* Abstractly put, they account for phenomena of *power*—power whose source is unknown and which cannot be duplicated by human means. Out of such experience the "gross philosophy" of the first ages gives birth to the gods and goddesses (*OF*, 17/36). Lightning-bolts, winds, and tides cause men to imagine beings "more powerful than themselves, capable of producing these grand effects" (*OF*, 17/36). It goes without saying—due to the principle of familiarity, or analogy, stated above—that such powers will be imagined as humanlike, for what other form figure could they possibly have? (*OF*, 17/36).

The power and impressiveness of nature, then, has much to do with the origins of myth, according to Fontenelle. But that cannot be the only force at work in their production and elaboration. For although the phenomena of nature never change, the myths do; they evolve. New gods and goddesses appear. How are we to explain that? By changes that were taking place in human beings—their outlooks, values, and societies. Fontenelle sees that some sort of social construction of (mythic) reality goes on. As social values change, the gods change. That correlation even allows us to "date" different myths. "Nothing proves the great antiquity of these divinities better or marks more clearly the route the imagination took [le chemin que l'imagination a tenu] in shaping them. The first men knew of no better quality than physical force; wisdom and justice had not even a name in the ancient languages, as they still do not today among the savages of America" (*OF*, 18/37). Attributing wisdom and justice to their gods, then, presupposed a recognition of order in the cosmos—something the first people were not yet capable of recognizing (ibid.).

Fontenelle states this fundamental insight in axiomatic form: "It was quite necessary that the gods reflect [or perhaps smell of—se sentissent] both the times at which they were created and the circumstances which brought them into existence [il fallait bien que ces dieux se sentissent, et du temps où ils avaient été faits, et des occasions qui les avaient fait faire]" (*OF*, 19/37). To the extent that people become better informed and more appreciative of better things, their gods improve. Thus, Cicero was unjust in criticizing the crudeness of Homer's gods: "what he in his time saw as qualities befitting gods were not at all known in the time of Homer" (*OF*, 19/38). Fact is, the gods of Cicero's time are better only because better philosophers created them (*OF*, 20/38).

Fontenelle nicely anticipates the contemporary understanding of how paradigms work as he describes the mythmaking process that follows the initial formation of a cosmology. The "philosophy" of the first ages, embodied in its myths, "finds itself entirely suitable to be allied with the history of facts" (*OF*, 20–21). For example, someone falls into a river and his body is never recovered. Since the regnant "philosophy" teaches that the river is occupied by young maidens who control it, it is natural to assume that they have captured him. Or, a man of unknown origin but extraordinary talent appears: philosophy provides an explanation that such people are sons of gods. So the myths, as they are elaborated over time, are nothing more than a *"mélange* of facts with the philosophy of the times [philosophie du temps], which explains very conveniently the marvelous aspects of the facts. . . . " (*OF*, 21).

Fontenelle here realizes that the very categories available for accounting for phenomena are given beforehand and determine what sorts of data are selected as relevant, what questions can be asked, and how they can be answered. In the *History of Oracles*, Fontenelle will present a relevant test case, showing how a current philosophy (Christian) had been applied to explain some "marvelous" facts (about oracles).

So far, then, Fontenelle has accounted for the initial creation of myths—ignorance in search of explanations—their early emphasis on power as the chief divine attribute; their evolution, geared to gradual cultural changes; and their power to order and explain the world. To this he adds two more "principles," so named because they explain further aspects universally (he supposes) present in myths—namely, the abundance of repetition of themes in the course of their elaboration, and their durability. The first principle is that of analogy: "the right that one has to invent things similar [pareille] to those which are received, or to push them further by means of extending their consequences" (*OF*, 26–27/38); for example, one god falls for a human woman, pretty soon all the gods are doing it. Durability is explained by blind reverence for antiquity, the attitude that says: our fathers believed; are we wiser than they? (*OF*, 27/39). These two principles joined together are indispensable to explain the rich elaboration of myths (they could not have been invented all at once) and their durability, for "the one [principle], on the smallest foundation that the weakness of human nature has allowed for, extends a stupidity to infinity; the other, no matter how short a time a stupidity is established, conserves it forever" (*OF*, 27–28/39).

As an additional mark of the durability of myths, Fontenelle notes how they attach themselves to cultural forms that can sustain them, so that they become transformed into religion or into art: "Among most peoples, myths were turned into religion. But in addition, among the Greeks, they were converted, so to speak, into pleasure [agrément]. Since they furnish only such ideas as conform to the shape of imagination most common among men, poetry and painting would be perfectly accommodated to them, and one knows how dearly the Greeks love the fine arts" (*OF*, 34). Unfortunately, Fontenelle does not explain what he means by the suggestive notion that myths get converted into *religion*. What happens to them to make them so? Mere representations of the supernatural do not make stories religious; religions apparently evolved, but how? Fontenelle does not follow up this train of thought. We can share the pleasure the Greeks took in their ancient myths, he says, even though we do not believe them as they did, because we can easily recapture the spirit that rendered the myths so agreeable to them (*OF*, 35). "Religiousness," then, is not intrinsic to myths but depends on their function in the system.

The myths endure long beyond the time when they have been superseded by more rational forms of explanation; they manage to attach themselves to other forms, such as religion and art. And so they endure still (*OF*, 34–35). These facts reveal an important feature of cultural evolution: in earlier times, myths had a double appeal—intellectual and aesthetic (*OF*, 26). Now, they no longer serve to explain anything; yet their appeal endures because, Fontenelle explains, reason and imagination are two such disparate faculties as to have scarcely anything to do with each other. The fact that things no longer have any rational claim to truth detracts nothing from their appeal to the imagination (*OF*, 35).

Fontenelle here anticipates a problem that will loom ever larger with subsequent authors—the problem of explaining the survival of mythic thinking after its explanatory function has expired. Fontenelle notes the appeal of myths to imagination to account for their survival in art, but that does not explain their survival as a component of religious systems (unless we define religion aesthetically). Other solutions to the problem surface with full clarity when we come to Comte, Durkheim, and Freud.

Certain literary aspects of myths are highlighted throughout the treatise. The most interesting has to do with the question of literal versus symbolic or (in Fontenelle's day) allegorical interpretation of ancient myths.

Fontenelle complains that despite intellectual progress in his own day, a new form of foolishness has been committed by intellects who are too admiring of antiquity; convinced that the ancient fables are replete with esoteric wisdom, "men proceed to imagine that the secrets of physics and morality are hidden behind these myths" (*OF*, 38–39/41). Was it possible, the defenders of allegory are saying, that the ancients could have produced and preserved such things without intending some deeper meaning (*OF*, 39/41)? Not only possible, Fontenelle argues, but a fact: the ancient myths were believed by those who produced them; they were the science and history of the ancients, and they are irredeemably absurd, as far as the explanatory power of their contents is concerned. They reveal something about the state of ancient reason and imagination, but absolutely nothing about the natural world.

That they are revelatory of the human mind is what makes them worth studying, even though we can look for nothing there but "errors of the human spirit" (*OF*, 39/41). This brings us back to the quotation with which we began, and which captures Fontenelle's whole approach to the study of myth: "It is not a science to fill one's head with all the extravagances of the Phoenicians and Greeks, but it *is* one to know what led the Phoenicians and Greeks to these extravagances (*OF*, 40/41; italics mine).

The text just requoted provides an excellent entré to our second work, the *History of Oracles* (1686). In this translation and adaptation of a similar work by the erudite Dutch Protestant Anthony van Dale, Fontenelle presents a skillful specimen of scientific, as opposed to mythic or theological, history. His focus here is an early bit of Christian theological history, developed by the Fathers and repeated in Fontenelle's own day (by, for example, Bossuet),[8] that the pagan oracles were produced by demons, that they ceased abruptly at the coming of Christ, and that it was his divine power that silenced them.

We can immediately see a connection between what Fontenelle is confronted with here and a general hypothesis that he put forward in the *Origin of Myths*, namely, that mythic (or theological) history is elaborated by the joining of a ready-to-hand philosophy, or mythic structure, with new—and especially remarkable—facts. This process, as long as it is not subjected to criticism, serves to perpetuate absurdities and obfuscate historical understanding.

In the case at hand, the operative philosophy was the Christian cosmology, extended so as to hold available demons responsible for pagan oracles and then to portray Christ as the supernatural power that caused their demise.

It takes Fontenelle twenty-five chapters to untangle and revise this story, for he must not only provide an alternative to the allegedly supernatural *causes* of the events in question but correct the received account of the facts themselves. His comment on the situation is worth quoting: "I am not so convinced of our ignorance by the things that are, and of which the reasons are unknown, as by those which are not, and for which we yet find out reasons. . . . [For example], some learned physicians have found out the reason why places under ground are hot in the winter and cool in the summer; greater physicians have since discovered that they are not so" (*HO*, 33–34/

---

8. Kearns (above, n. 5) states that Fontenelle wrote the *Histoire* against Bossuet, whose *Discours sur l'histoire universelle* affirmed the demon theory of oracles (174). Bossuet, however, gives plenty of historical reasoning alongside his general affirmation of demonic influence. See *Discourse on Universal History*, trans. Elborg Forster, 181, 246, 255.

23).[9] The analogy with the case of oracles is exact, providing Fontenelle, in the modest role of "greater physician," a perfect occasion to demonstrate his historical skill and psychological insight.

The treatise presents a thorough and exhaustive critique of supernatural causal explanation, and a complete and naturalistic alternative explanation of all the data. Although the case is made with regard to a particular past series of events, the implication is clearly of general methodological import.

Fontenelle argues that the attribution of oracles to demons was more a case of apologetic strategy on the part of Christian writers than one of strict historical truth. It met the pagans halfway, which was easier than making a frontal assault on pagan miracles themselves (*HO*, 26/19). The example of Origen of Alexandria is offered to make this point:

> Origen was inclined to believe of oracles as we do [i.e., not to believe in them], but the pagans, who used them for a proof of the divinity of their religion, had no reason to consent, that they were but the artifices of their priests: so, in order to gain a little upon the pagans, there was a necessity of yielding to them, what they maintained with so much obstinacy, and to let them see, that though there might be something of supernatural in the oracles, yet there was no reason to say, that a true divinity was concerned in them; and so demons were to be brought upon the stage. (*HO*, 83–84/82–83; cf. *HO*, 26/19)

This, Fontenelle suggests, "is probably the cause why in the first ages of the church, men so generally embraced this opinion [ce Sistème] concerning oracles" (*HO*, 85/83).

Evidence from Eusebius is brought to support this interpretation, and Fontenelle concludes of the early Christians, "They admitted demons indeed in a certain *general system* [sistème general], which served their disputes; but when they came to *particular matters of fact* [point de fait particulier], they spoke little of them, or rather directly denied them" (*HO*, 134/142; italics mine).

With these matters behind him, Fontenelle is now ready for a frontal assault on oracles, an exposé aimed at discrediting their supernatural claims (chaps. 10–18). The most interesting material in this section is found in chapter 11, on the establishment of new oracles, for this gives Fontenelle the opportunity to augment his ideas about origins of religious phenomena.

Regarding new oracles, he starts with a suggestion that must appear insidious to those devoted to the supernatural character of the oracular insti-

---

9. *Histoire des oracles* (1686; hereafter *HO*), ed. Louis Maigron, 33f. Eng. transl.: *The History of Oracles and the Cheats of the Pagan Priests* (1688, reprinted in L. M. Marsak, *The Achievement of . . . Fontenelle*, part 2), 23. References in the text will list French first, then English. Thus the present quotation: *HO* 33/23. Fontenelle's methodological principle of the priority of facts joins him with Locke, whom Paul Hazard credited for investing the fact "with its due status and its sovereign dignity" (*The European Mind*, 239). On Fontenelle's contribution, see ibid., 165.

tution (and one may substitute, as Fontenelle no doubt intended, pilgrimage sites or any such location founded on alleged miracle):

> Without doubt, these new oracles caused even those who were the least capable of thinking to make reflections upon them. Was there not reason to believe that these were of the same nature with the ancient ones [i.e., that *both* might be frauds]? And that to make a due judgment on the first beginnings of those [ancient oracles] of Amphiaraus, Trophonius, Orpheus, and of Apollo himself, they needed no more than to consider those [new establishments] of Ephaesion, Antinous, and Augustus? (*HO*, 93–94/95).

Although the implication of imposture is heavy both here and throughout the treatise, Fontenelle makes it clear, as he had in the *Origin of Myths,* that the first beginnings of oracles, as with myth in general, was not by imposture: "I cannot believe that the first establishment of oracles was a premeditated fraud [une imposture meditée]; rather, the people fell into some superstition which gave them a beginning, and afterwards men of wit made their advantages of them" (*HO*, 103/102).

How are the oracles to be explained, then? One possible explanation of an oracle (and of course the first one, or few, would easily spawn a host of imitations, as the law of familiarity took effect), using Mount Parnassus as an example, might be called Fontenelle's holy smoke theory:

> There was on top of Parnassus a hole, out of which an exhalation came, which was of such a nature that it made goats dance and caper, by fuming into their heads; and perhaps somebody whose head was filled with this exhalation became an enthusiast, fell a talking, without knowing what he said, and by chance spoke truth. Immediately, there was something divine fancied to be in this exhalation, and that it contained the knowledge of futurity [aussi-tost il faut qui'il y ait quelque chose de Divin dans cette exhalaison, elle contient la science de l'avenir]; then, they begin to approach this hole with veneration, and ceremonies are by little and little introduced. (*HO*, 98/98–99)

Some such series of events might institute an oracle; the spread of the report of such marvels would then be easy: "find me but half a dozen persons, whom I can persuade that it is not the sun that makes the day, and I will not despair of prevailing with a whole nation to embrace the same opinion: for however ridiculous any thing seems at first, if you can but maintain it for some time, so that it gains the authority of antiquity, it is then sufficiently proved" (*HO*, 96ff./98).

This section on new oracles also provides Fontenelle with occasion to divide all pagan gods according to two types of explanation, the first of which roughly squares with his general theory of the origin of myth as the first philosophy—that gods were postulated by the more clever folk in search of the causes of things. The second type is explained according to the Euhemerist principle: the gods are apotheoses of heroes. In the present work, Fontenelle represents these two types of gods as either gods who were supposed to be essentially of a divine nature [essentiellement de nature divine], or gods which did not become so, till after they had been of a human nature first. The former sort were declared gods by the learned, or by the legislators [sages, legislateurs] with a multitude of mysteries . . . the second sort . . . were made gods by the natural inclination of the people touched by their bene-factions [par un mouvement naturel des peuples touchez de leurs bien-faits]. (*HO*, 96/97)

Once established, oracular institutions preserved themselves mainly by imposture and fraud. Fontenelle's analysis of the psychology involved throws suggestive light on the original motivation of allegorical interpretation. Noting the complicity that develops between those who engineered oracular deliv-erances and their clients, Fontenelle observes that, no matter how uncertain the message,

> those who received these ambiguous oracles took the pains very willingly to justify them, by adjusting the success and the production together. And often-times, that which had but one sense (in the intention of those who delivered the oracle) was after the event found to have two [ce que n'avoit eu qu'un sens dans l'intention de celeuy qui avoit rendu l'oracle, aprés l'évenement se trouvoit en avoir deux]. For the imposters might be secure that their honor would be preserved with all the care imaginable by those very persons whom they abused. (*HO*, 130–31/139)

Another section of the History offers a detailed account of when and how the oracles actually ceased, coinciding generally with the decline of paganism itself (this thesis offered in chapter 4). Christianity is given its due as a historical force among others.

The first and foremost reason for the demise of oracles was the Roman mastery of Greece—a cause not essentially related to the existence of Chris-tianity at all. Even without the rise of Christianity and the legal suppression of paganism, including oracles, in the fourth century, the oracles would have ceased, for the fate of any cultural invention follows hard after that of its inventors: "Now the maxims and opinions of the victors easily obtain amongst the conquered; and therefore it is no wonder that oracles, being a Greek invention, should follow the fate of Greece; and that as with her they flour-ished in prosperity, so with her they lost their ancient glory" (*HO*, 187/213). Fontenelle recognized that gods do not routinely survive the defeat of their creators; indeed, "a vast number of gods fell into contempt when people took notice that the masters of the world would not vouchsafe to consult 'em" (*HO*, 190/218).[10]

The other two causes for the demise of oracles were the rise of skeptical philosophy and the too-often exposed and too blatant "cheats" of the pagan priests (chaps. 6 and 7). Fontenelle had already at least given a nod to the influence of Christianity itself—simply as a historical movement, not as a

---

10. This observation is reminiscent of the contemporary sociological concept of plausibility structures.

manifestation of divine power. In the introduction he had stated as his thesis that oracles ceased "not because the Son of God imposed silence on 'em, all of a sudden; but because the most enlightened Wits were disabused by the publication of the gospel, which still supposes that those human artifices could not be detected in a little time" (*HO*, Preface, ix–x/n.p.). Later he returned to the same theme, noting that Christianity "was extremely hurtful to oracles, for the Christians made it their business to disabuse mankind, and to discover impostures" (*HO*, 180/205). But he asserts as his last word that even without the appearance of Christianity, the oracles would have gone under from the other natural causes noted (*HO*, 180/205).

Turning now to the question of how Fontenelle's ideas advanced the study of religion, we consider, first, his advance beyond Herbert's rationalism via the idea of a *scientific* project; next, his use of a naturalistic scheme to characterize historical development and account for variation and change; finally, the clear separation of his project from theology and his alternative to all religious theories of religion.

In common, Fontenelle and Herbert of Cherbury shared an interest in making universally valid statements about religion. Herbert lifted out five "common notions" and constructed a sort of generic theology that, he claimed, constituted the normative faith of the true "catholic church" of humankind. Fontenelle, on his part, also claimed for his findings a basis in human nature: in the *Origins*, he stressed that "so far in this history of the origin of myths we have brought in only that which is drawn from the foundations of human nature, and which in fact has been dominant in it [Nous n'avons fait entrer ... que ce qui est pris du fonds de la nature humaine, et en effect c'est ce qui y a dominé. ...]" *OF*, 35).

Each writer, then, claims to have transcended the limitations of particularized accounts in favor of generalizations that are universally valid. But there the similarity ends.

While Herbert is constructing a generic theology, Fontenelle is trying to find common psychohistorical *causes* of religious belief. While for Herbert religion is a philosophy of life to be legitimated, for Fontenelle it has become an element of culture to be explained. Herbert is trying to construct a generally valid theology; Fontenelle, a historical social science. Herbert's innatism inevitably discovers a common stock of pristine and valid religious ideas; Fontenelle's psychology and comparative history identify the common propensities that lead to religious invention. Religious history, for Herbert, is the story of devolution and distortion of original religious truth; for Fontenelle religious history gradually gives way, in the evolution of mind, to rationality and science, as the world is progressively disenchanted and higher religion disabuses people of ancient superstition.

The rationalism of the seventeenth century is giving way to the empiricism of the eighteenth, for as with Locke so with Fontenelle: the mind has a history; it is built up by experience. But what is really radical here is that Fontenelle is ready to incorporate the entire explanation of religion within the purview of a psycho*historical* account of the development of mind in society. Thus the outlines of a developmental paradigm for studying religion are beginning to appear.

The evolutionary paradigm emerges in the attempt to combine two indispensable propositions: on one hand, that there is a human nature, or collection of propensities and capabilities, sufficiently universal to guarantee that all peoples will respond in similar ways to their environment. All peoples, for example, have nothing but myths for their most ancient history. On the other hand, there are both vast *differences* among presently living peoples (e.g., enlightened Frenchmen and American savages) and astonishing *similarities* between peoples living in *different* times (e.g., between American savages and primitive Greeks). There appears, then, to be some kind of process in which all humanity is implicated, and which causes all peoples to pass through similar stages, but not necessarily at the same time. That, in rudimentary form, is what Fontenelle's incipient theory of evolution says. It is an attempt to say, in naturalistic terms, what might be true of the species as a whole in light of its variegated histories.

Fontenelle's portrait of a primitive mentality, tied to a theory of progress, makes him a "seminal thinker" in Frank Manuel's judgment: "[Fontenelle] expressed in embryonic form a conception of primitive mankind and the nature of pagan religion which held sway in European thought until the early nineteenth century and was integrated into positivist French sociology."[11] Perhaps equally significant was Fontenelle's intuition that the progress of thinking, including the gradual changes in religious ideas, was somehow integrally geared to general cultural change—that ideas do not develop in abstraction from their context.

Although he rejected allegorical interpretations of ancient myths, Fontenelle did not explicitly make a connection between changing religious ideas and the rise of allegorism. Allegorism was a means of retaining and preserving an outdated myth—one that could no longer be taken literally, either as explanation or as representing the values of society, but that one wanted to retain because of its aesthetic attraction or out of reverence for its antiquity (especially when it was "our" antiquity). Allegory was a way of making the dated myth say something appropriate to a new time, by reinterpreting it in light of whatever new philosophy now framed the representation of reality.

Fontenelle held that such a procedure, while well and good for entertainment, was completely unacceptable as an interpretation of what an ancient myth intended. Lévy-Bruhl sees Fontenelle's view of mythology as "won-

---

11. Frank Manuel (above, n. 7), 42. Carré (above, n. 2) credits Fontenelle with showing the way toward making the "primitive" an object of science by recognizing that, due to a different mentality, the primitive's worldview made as much sense to him as ours does to us (138–39).

derfully correct" on this score: to understand a myth, we must return to the intellectual state of mind that produced it, and that "humanity everywhere went through as a necessary stage of its evolution."[12] From a similar perspective, the nineteenth-century British anthropologist Andrew Lang—a student of E. B. Tylor—wrote a warm appreciation of Fontenelle, allowing that "a better and briefer system of mythology could not be devised" than that found in the *Origin of Fables*. As Lang noted, Fontenelle understood that "the world-wide similarities of myths are, on the whole, the consequences of a world-wide uniformity of intellectual development."[13] As we shall see, several of Tylor's most basic ideas are already found in embryonic form in Fontenelle.

I have put aside until now certain confessional Christian statements made by Fontenelle, always in passing (and always absent, oddly, from Marsak's translations). The theoretical positions spelled out in the preceding pages stand on their own and require no theological basis, addition, or qualification to make them coherent or complete. Nevertheless, Fontenelle did make certain statements, and although they were probably motivated mainly by expediency, they indicate an alternative to the theoretical direction taken by Herbert of Cherbury with regard to the relation of the study of religion to theology.

Even while claiming universality for his hypotheses about religion, Fontenelle claims exemptions and makes exceptions for the Hebrew-Christian tradition: in the *Origin*, the Adamic-Sethian tradition of true religion is exempted from the account of mythic origins and development (*OF*, 11); illumination by "true religion and philosophy" gives Christians an advantage over the Greeks (*OF*, 29); the "elect" people are exempted from the generalization that all primitive history is myth (*OF*, 33); Christianity is credited with liberating people from myths (*OF*, 34–35, *HO* 180/205); in the *History*, demons are admitted to exist even though the theory that they are responsible for pagan oracles is mercilessly ridiculed (*HO*, 7/5); the *History* is presented not as criticism but as apologetically advantageous to Christianity (*HO*, 4–5/4); Christianity is credited with "disabusing" people of frauds such as oracles (*HO*, 180/205); and "true" and "false" religion are clearly distinguished in favor of Christianity; the "false" are purely human productions (ne sont l'ouvrage que l'esprit humain), while the true is God's work (un ouvrage de Dieu seul; *HO*, 3/3).

Could it be, then, that everything Fontenelle has written is meant to apply only to "false" religion; that the Jewish and Christian traditions are entirely exempt?—that the former are mere human fabrications, while the latter is

12. Lucien Lévy-Bruhl (above, n. 6), 135.

13. Andrew Lang, *Myth, Ritual and Religion*, 2:342. The sentence appears in an appendix entitled "Fontenelle's Forgotten Common Sense."

the sole work of God? Certainly the orthodox of Fontenelle's day were not so easily fooled. They, along with most contemporary scholars, saw Fontenelle's work as highly subversive[14] because his criticism and analysis could easily embrace all religions, including Christianity.

But Fontenelle and Herbert reveal two contrasting strategies for *religious* students of religion, and one still hears their echo in contemporary studies of religion. One is the deistic-theological strategy, the other the "two-realms" strategy. The first incorporates the claims, values, and data from one's own religion (usually Christianity) into a wider, generic, or allegedly universal theological wisdom; the two-realms strategy in extreme form proceeds in reductive and explanatory fashion, as Fontenelle does, but quite arbitrarily denies that the conclusions reached have any bearing on religions based on what one takes for divine revelation. For a contemporary version of the contrast, one could cite Wilfred Cantwell Smith, *Toward a World Theology*, in the deist camp, and Peter Berger, *The Sacred Canopy* (especially the appendix) in the second. The deist paradigm has the advantage of universality, but tends to abstractions and eschews explanation as "reductionism" inappropriate to the subject matter, in effect presupposing faith in transcendence as a condition of understanding. The second is boldly naturalistic and particularistic in its explanation but exempts its own tradition quite arbitrarily, without producing reasons or evidence that there is anything unique or unusual about it.

Fontenelle's "exemptions," like Vico's after him, are of course understandable on grounds of expediency, but logically they seem hardly convincing or even possible. There is no way to exempt any people's history from critical scrutiny or any part of nature from universal natural law: these are essential principles of Fontenelle's own work on religion; without them, his entire claim to *scientific* integrity would be compromised.

Whatever reservations one might have about Fontenelle's attempt to protest his orthodoxy, certain things are clear: an evolutionary framework provided a clear alternative to traditional theology, both of revelation and of the innatist, deist type. Without revelation, and without innate ideas to support it, religion had to be accounted for as a response to experience—as explanation

14. Niderst (above, n. 2) concludes that Fontenelle's assault on allegorical interpretation was aimed at destroying Christianity by putting its myth on the same level as those of other world religions. Moreover, the *Origin* could explain the birth of Christianity as well as any other religion, despite the "exemption" (215). Carré (above, n. 2) sees him as undermining belief in the supernatural and in the authority of the learned doctors of the church, whose views he ridiculed (22; cf. 422). According to Manuel (above, n. 7), Fontenelle's *Histoire* constituted "a dangerous threat to all established religious institutions which attested miracles and exorcised demons" (50). In his historical survey of anthropology, John J. Honigmann judges that "the Enlightenment's contribution to the history of anthropology lies not so much in specific ideas that it developed and passed on, as in the lasting impulse it gave to the naturalistic study of society and culture" (*The Development of Anthropological Ideas*, 103).

and as interpretation. Liberated from traditional theological presuppositions, Fontenelle thus pointed the way toward naturalistic theories of religion.

Perhaps enough already has been said to justify Fontenelle's prominent place in our account. His influence on Vico, Hume, Comte, and the anthropological school will be evident. He has been credited as a worthy predecessor of the anthropological school (by Andrew Lang and others), of positivist French sociology, and, by Carré—perhaps his most authoritative interpreter—as the "founder of comparativism in the materials of the history of myths and religions"[5] —even though several other contemporary thinkers, above all Pierre Bayle, were also exploiting the travel literature and making similar comparisons.[6] Salomon Reinach also credited Fontenelle with presenting "the germ of the whole theory of modern anthropologists, who see in fables . . . products of the civilizations of various peoples at comparable periods of their evolution."[7] Leonard Marsak claims that "the importance of Fontenelle's social science cannot be overemphasized."[8] Perhaps the most glowing tribute of all was given by Albert Salomon in a 1957 essay in honor of the tercentenary of Fontenelle's birth and bicentennial of his death: by Salomon's reckoning, the Enlightenment itself must be dated, at its beginning, by the treatises of Fontenelle and Locke in the 1680s and 1690s.[9]

15. Carré (above, n. 2), 132; cf. 113.

16. Ibid., 113–14.

17. Salomon Reinach, *Orpheus: A General History of Religions*, 13.

18. Leonard Marsak (above, n. 1), xcv. Marsak continues: "Conceiving of knowledge and society as functions of each other, he was able to construct out of his experience with science the principles of a new social science. The first of these principles is that properly defined such a science is indeed possible. The second principle is that we must go to the origins of society for an explanation of its subsequent behavior, just as we go to nature to discern its laws. Third, we must trace the variables of human behavior through time for a knowledge of the rules that govern change" (ibid.).

19. "Fontenelle: In Praise of the Enlightenment," 99. In a similar vein, 1680 is for Paul Hazard the beginning of the critical period that gives birth to the Enlightenment, in his *The European Mind, 1680–1715*.

PART III

A SCIENCE OF RELIGION?

Chapter 4

A "New Science"
of Providence:
Giambattista Vico

The prodigious originality and richness of Vico's thought both demand and defy placement in an account of this kind. In profound ways, he was both ahead of and behind his times, a misfit in his age.[1] By his own account a stranger in his own city (Naples), he was not discovered by northern Europeans until almost a century after his death (1744), when his time came to exercise a profound and lasting influence on European intellectual life.

The "new science" which he announced in 1725, "concerning the common nature of the nations," aspired to put human studies—the historical, social, and literary work engendered by the Renaissance—on a scientific basis no less secure than what had been achieved in the natural sciences; it would demonstrate that Bacon's "great instauration" could be extended to the study of humankind. Vico's project, because of the theory of knowledge that grounded it, was programmatically committed to the discovery of origins and entailed a reconstruction of human history from its beginnings. This reconstruction was made possible by Vico's discovery of a new method of extracting historical knowledge from ancient myths.

Against the scientific wisdom of his day, dominated by Cartesian doctrine, he sought to join history with philosophy; in doing so, he "opened up a new epistemological domain."[2] His new science showed how to join the universal with the particular, the permanent with the historical, the ideal with the empirical, the providential with the natural, in ways that had epoch-making implications for the study of religion.

In religion, the achievement of Vico can be anticipated simply by listing some of his theses, whose meaning and implications we shall explore here: that religion is made by human beings; that its causes can be scientifically described and understood; that religion is a necessary and universal com-

1. Alain Pons, "Vico and French Thought," 170. Cf. Frank E. Manuel, *The Eighteenth Century Confronts the Gods*, 149. See Peter Burke, however, for a necessary qualification of the judgment that Vico is a misfit in his intellectual milieu (*Vico*, esp. 48).

2. Pons, ibid. For the commonalities between Vico and Marx, see Lawrence H. Simon, "Vico and Marx," esp. 317. On Vico's discovery of history as a "form of cognition", see Manuel, 150.

ponent of historical-social existence; that it evolves in an irreducible interaction among human nature, language, ideas, and social institutions. Vico's
demonstration of these proposals displayed an astonishing intellectual range,
embracing consummate and pioneering skills in philosophy, anthropology,
sociology, history, and literary interpretation—to all of which Vico added an
extraordinary imagination.

Many of his ideas were revolutionary; yet they were presented in the
framework (he insisted) of a catholic Christian worldview that presented the
new science, not in opposition to orthodox faith (hence its poor "fit" with
the enlightened thought of northern Europe), but as a demonstration of divine
providence in the whole course of human development. Despite his protest
of orthodox intent (which was accepted at the highest levels—the *New Science*
was dedicated to the pope), Vico presented a thoroughly naturalistic account
of all human institutions, including religion, offering "naturalistic theory in
a religious light."[3] By profession a legal scholar and jurist, Vico sought a
genetically grounded understanding of the common institutions and laws of
the nations and in doing so found religion at the very basis of such institutions.
His theories of religion are consequently social to the core. In the exposition
that follows, I shall try to unravel all this by treating in order, first, the basis
of the new science in Vico's theory of knowledge; second, the orientation to
origins entailed by that theory; third, the method of myth-interpretation that
he claimed was the master key to unlocking those origins. Then we shall be
in a position to look more closely at what he says about religion. Consideration
of the theological dimension of Vico's work will come later, since it is not
an integral element in Vico's science.

First, the new science. It was to be a science of society and of history,
philosophically grounded. It claimed that the Baconian project of creating
new and genuine knowledge, so successful in the realm of nature, could be
extended to society—as Vico says, "to the civil institutions of mankind."[4]
This extension is possible, Vico claims, because the mind is fully equipped
to understand human institutions. Indeed, it can do so better than it can
understand nature. To a greater depth than in the natural sciences, we can
understand and explain human institutions.

How can this be? Vico posits a fundamental epistemological principle that
he did not invent but that he gave entirely new meaning—the principle
abbreviated as *verum* = *factum* (the true = the made), or "maker's knowl-

---

3. Leon Pompa, *Vico*, 60.

4. Giambattista Vico, *Principi di Scienza Nuova* (1744; hereafter *NS*), in *Opere*, ed. F.
Nicolini, 365–905; par. 163. Eng. transl. *The New Science of Giambattista Vico*, revised transl.
by T. G. Bergin and M. H. Fisch (1968). *NS* will be cited by paragraph only, since that is
standard in all editions.

edge" as it is now called.[5] We can know what we ourselves have made or created. Vico states this principle as part of his criticism of Descartes, who had regarded history and other humane studies as beneath the notice of serious science because they could not be quantified. Vico writes:

> The rule and criterion of truth is to have made it. Hence the [Cartesian] clear and distinct idea of the mind not only cannot be the criterion of other truths, but it cannot be the criterion of that of the mind itself; for while the mind apprehends itself, it does not make itself, and because it does not make itself it is ignorant of the form or mode by which it apprehends itself.[6]

He agrees with Descartes that mathematical knowledge is certain: the reason is because it is wholly the creation of the mind. But such is not the case with the mind itself, or with nature, which is simply given (made by God, in Vico's terms). Insofar as we can claim any true "science" (*scienza*, knowledge) of nature (i.e., physics), we are entitled to claim it only with regard to what we can reproduce ourselves. Hence, "the things which are proved . . . are those to which we can perform something similar, and the ideas as to natural things which are thought to have the most perfect clarity and on which there is the completest consensus, are those to the support of which we can bring experiments by which we so far imitate nature."[7] That is: we know what we produce, and/or what we can reproduce. This is the key to justifying human studies as a scientific enterprise. In one of the most celebrated passages in his *New Science*, where he is addressing the problem of how we can know anything about human beginnings, given the paucity of sources, Vico announces that "in the night of thick darkness enveloping the earliest antiquity, so remote from ourselves, there shines the eternal and never failing light of *a truth beyond all question: that the world of civil society has certainly been made by men*, and that its principles are therefore to be found within the modifications of our own human mind" (par. 331). That civil society is man-made should not have been ignored by those who sought to reconstruct knowledge on a scientific basis:

> Whoever reflects on this [truth] cannot but marvel that the philosophers should have bent all their energies to the study of the world of nature, which, since God made it, he alone knows; and that they should have neglected the study of the world of nations, or *civil world, which, since men have made it, men could come to know*. (par. 331; my italics)

Let us first pursue the implications of "maker's knowledge" (we shall return later to what is meant by "modifications of our own human mind").

---

5. For a thorough discussion, see Jaakko Hintikka, "Practical versus Theoretical Reason," 86.

6. M. H. Fisch and T. G. Bergin, *The Autobiography of G. Vico* (hereafter *AGV*), Introduction, 38, quoting from Vico's *Ancient Wisdom of the Italians* (1710).

7. Ibid., 39.

The claim that we know what we create determines that the weight of Vico's investigations will fall on *origins*—those creative "moments" in which human institutions come into being (including language and ideas associated with them). We begin with the cryptic axiom, "Doctrines must take their beginning from that of the matters of which they treat" (par. 314). M. H. Fisch emphasizes this point in his introduction to the *New Science,* paraphrasing it as follows:

> For in *this* science, philosophic or scientific wisdom comprehends, though with the greatest difficulty, that vulgar or creative wisdom which is the origin and presupposition of all science and all philosophy. The new science, like all science, must begin where its subject matter begins. But its subject matter is institution-building wisdom, and that began with the first beginnings of institutions. . . . [8]

The new science discovers, then, not only the beginnings of human institutions in "vulgar wisdom," but its own beginnings as well, for the beginnings of institutions and the beginnings of human thought are inseparable. Uncovering the causes and origins of things will at the same time illumine their essential natures, or "principles," the reasons for their existence and persistence. Thus, "in reasoning of the origins of institutions, religious and secular, in the gentile world, we reach those first beginnings beyond which it is vain curiosity to demand others earlier; and this is the defining character of *principles*. We explain the particular guises of their birth, that is to say their nature,[9] the explanation of which is the distinguishing mark of science" (par. 346).

This statement illuminates Vico's axiom that every theory has to start from the point where the matter of which it treats first began to take shape. That is, a real understanding of civil society can be achieved only by an approach that is genetic, as Berlin observes: "for it is only through its genesis, reconstructed by *fantasia* [imagination], guided by rules which he thinks he has discovered, that anything [of human creation] can be truly understood: not by some intuition of timeless essences, or empirical descriptions or analysis of an object's present state." "This," Berlin observes, "marks a genuine turning-point in the conception of history and society."[10]

---

8. M. H. Fisch, *NS*, Introduction, xlif.

9. Cf. par. 147: "The nature of institutions is nothing but their coming into being [nascimento] at certain times and in certain guises. Whenever the time and guise are thus and so, such and not otherwise are the institutions that come into being." Cf. M. H. Fisch, *NS*, Introduction, xxii ff.

10. Isaiah Berlin, *Against the Current*, 104, n. 2. Alain Pons (above, n. 1) reinforces this judgment: "the eighteenth century, especially its second half, was haunted by the problem of the historical origins of societies, of social institutions, religions, laws, languages, and it strove to untangle these phenomena by means of the interpretation of myths. We know that it is in the *Scienza nuova* that this problem of origins is posited for the first time, no longer out of a pure concern for erudition, but in the framework of a global perspective, historical and philosophical at the same time" (170).

Any science, or scientific knowledge, requires a prior statement of principles that are universal and timeless (such as the principles of mathematics
prior to astronomy). But in order to yield any knowledge about the actual
world, these principles must also allow us to order the particulars of experience into some coherent pattern and to discern their causes. Vico claims
to have discovered universal principles which will enable us to have scientific
knowledge of the historical world. Thus, he self-consciously proceeds in two
stages—first stating theoretical truths, then applying them to the actualities
of the world. Theory and experiment, thinking and testing, follow Bacon's
prescription *"cogitare-videre"* (think and see).[11]

Here, Vico seeks the "eternal" and lawlike element that determines the
course of human affairs, analogous to the natural laws discovered and then
confirmed by the natural scientists. In the human realm, however, the fundamental reality with which we have to deal is irreducibly *historical*. The
inquirer must therefore begin by attempting to establish or posit historical
universals—principles that state what must always and everywhere be the
pattern of human existence in time.

Vico's quest in some ways echoes Herbert's search for common notions,
but in Vico's case they are not merely rational (in a way, they are not rational
at all in the modern sense, as we shall see), but sociohistorical as well. On
the success of meeting this demand for universal principles that will account
for and order the facts, the scientific status of Vico's whole project depends.
He cannot merely resort to the ancient "facts," for they are not self-
explanatory.

In a text that sounds very much like Herbert's approach (in its more
"empirical" moments), Vico inventories the world of nations in search of
commonalities: "Since this world of nations has been made by men, let us
see in what institutions all men agree and always have agreed. For these
institutions will be able to give us the universal and eternal principles (such
as every science must have) on which all nations were founded and still
preserve themselves" (par. 332). This sounds like Herbert's search for consensus, but it has a revolutionary twist: the search is not for ideas, primarily,
but for institutions.[12] Vico now proposes a hypothesis:

> We observe that all nations... though separately founded because remote from
> each other in time and space, keep these three human customs: all have some
> religion, all contract solemn marriages, all bury their dead. ... It must have been
> dictated to all nations that from these three institutions humanity began among
> them all. ... For this reason we have taken these three eternal and universal customs
> as three first principles of this Science (par. 333).

11. Leon Pompa, *Vico*, 128. Further analysis is found there.
12. Vico's usual word for institution is *cosa:* Fisch explains why, *NS* Introduction, xliii–
xliv.

These principles, then, might be called historical or social or *institutional* universals, but they embody, and make possible, at the same time, common ideas or beliefs (three "common notions," as it were): belief in providence, in sexual order or virtue, and in immortality.[13] Vico has discovered and maintains the necessary reciprocity of ideas and their social context; this alone would earn him a place of honor in the development of human studies.[14]

Why *these* institutions? Leon Pompa cites another text to show that Vico has discovered these principles of the nature of human institutions not by empirical investigation but by "a severe analysis of human thoughts about the *human necessities and utilities* of social life, which are the two perennial springs of the natural law of the gentes" (par. 347; my italics).[15]

Necessity is the mother of invention of human society[16] and the spring from which Vico proposes his historical universals, or "ideal eternal history," as he calls it, as a guide for explaining the course of actual history. This ideal or hypothetical history is (Pompa explains) " 'ideal' in the sense that [it] is a statement of what is necessary and not [yet] of what is actual; eternal in the sense that, being validly deduced from a set of axioms, it deals with timeless truths."[17] Fisch supplements this interpretation by noting that these three institutions "are principles in the sense that they are the necessary and sufficient generative conditions of the *gens*, the minimal society that can outlive its members and thus make possible an evolution of culture."[18] Regardless of whether any particular religion is true or not (Vico has set aside the question of "true religion" altogether by exempting the Hebrew-Christian tradition from his analysis), *all religions are necessary*, as are the other two principal institutions, "and therefore they must be most devoutly guarded ... so that the world should not again become a bestial wilderness [which is how it all began, as we shall see]" (par. 333). On the universality of religion, and its necessity, Vico disputes the opinion of writers such as Pierre Bayle (and later, Hume), who "affirms in his treatise on comets that peoples can live in justice without the light of God.... These are travellers' tales, to promote the sale of their books.... For all nations believe in a provident divinity...." (par. 334; cf. pars. 1109–10). Of the three institutions, religion

13. Pompa, *Vico*, 30ff., argues that these principles are necessary presuppositions of Vico's science, and not regarded by him as falsifiable empirical observations.

14. Thus, for example, the obscene conduct of the gods of Greek myth reflects the need of the mythmakers to legitimate their own barbarous state (pars. 220–21). Axiomatically stated: "The order of ideas must follow the order of institutions" (L'ordine dell'idee dee *[sic]* procedere secondo l'ordine delle cose; par. 238).

15. Pompa, *Vico*, 99.

16. Just such clichés or popular maxims are often alluded to by Vico as examples of "common" or vulgar wisdom.

17. Pompa, *Vico*, 109.

18. M. H. Fisch, *NS*, Introduction, xxxv.

has priority, both in time and in importance, for "the world of peoples began everywhere with religion. This will be the first of the three principles of this Science" (par. 176; cf. pars. 8, 198, 250, 447).

Vico thus claims to have discovered a universal design or pattern according to which every nation must run its course. This pattern has a determined sequence through three stages, as was discovered already by the Egyptians:

> This new science... discovers the origins of institutions, religious and secular, among the gentile nations, and thereby establishes a system of the natural law of the gentes, which proceeds with the greatest equality and constancy through the three ages which the Egyptians handed down to us as the three periods through which the world had passed up to their time. These are: (1) the age of the gods, in which the gentiles believed they lived under divine governments and everything was commanded them by auspices and oracles, which are the oldest institutions in profane history, (2) the age of heroes... (3) the age of men.... (par. 31)[19]

All nations, Vico formulates it elsewhere, will be found to pass through the same cycle of rise, development, maturity, decline, and fall (par. 245).

We have said something about Vico's theory of knowledge and its implications for pursuing a science of history, with its concentration on origins. We turn next to the problem of method—how the stated universal principles are to be applied to illuminating the actual history of the *gentes*. The great obstacle faced by Vico and others on this score was that their sources were the despair of historians—ancient fables and myths whose value as historical sources was at best problematical (recall from the preceding chapter that Fontenelle could derive nothing from them beyond an insight into the crude state of the primitive mind).

Everybody could agree with Vico that there must be some way we can understand these fantastic imaginative tales and symbols, so seemingly absurd and impenetrable to moderns, because they are at least the product of human minds like our own. But in what sense like or own? Here is where the phrase "modifications of our mind" (par. 331, quoted above) can now be understood in its proper historical or evolutionary sense. It does not mean that somehow by introspection we can immediately discover principles for interpreting ancient myths, as the allegorists proposed, and as (in revised fashion) idealistic interpreters of Vico have suggested.[20] Rather, we must attend to the historical and social nature of "mind" itself, in both its primitive and modern modi-

---

19. According to Frank Manuel (above, n. 1), these are Varro's categories (151).

20. E.g., Benedetto Croce, *The Philosophy of Giambattista Vico;* Richard Manson, *The Theory of Knowledge of G. Vico*, esp. 29, 33, 37, 63. For discussion, see H. S. Hughes, "Vico and Contemporary Social Theory and Social History," 321ff., and, above all, Leon Pompa's discussion of Vico's theory of knowledge; *Vico*, 154ff. Pompa honors Vico's commitment to explanation (as well as interpretation), and rightly notes that "the whole weight of explanation is thrown upon the historical-social conditions in which men find themselves, which determine a large part of the content of their character, thoughts, attitudes and desires" (161).

fications. Vico believes that the myths make, or made, sense. Remote as they are from our form of apprehending, describing, interpreting, or explaining reality, they were entirely appropriate for the ages in which they appeared. If we are clear first about the great distance which exists between that age and our own, its minds and ours, we can hope to discover the sense and the truth that the ancient mythmakers made. Their mythmaking was neither frivolous nor esoteric, but expressed a common, or vulgar, wisdom. "Vulgar traditions must have had public grounds of truth [publici motivi di vero], by virtue of which they came into being and were preserved by entire peoples over long periods of time" (par. 149; cf. 198). Pompa explains the meaning of this public sense by underscoring Vico's theory that "any given society is unifed by communal modes of thought and attitude which are the products of the history of its own institutional developments."[21] This common (communal) sense of things is an expression of human nature in that time, as historically and socially conditioned; its remembered expression of itself is found in the myths.[22] Put another way, Vico claims that "There must in the nature of human institutions be a mental language common [lingua mentale commune] to all nations, which uniformly grasps the substance of things *feasible in human social life* [cose agibili nell'umana socievole] and expresses it with as many diverse modifications as these same things may have diverse aspects" (par. 161; my italics). The "mental language" common to *modern* times is that of reason, but this was not so in the earliest age of the gods, when men were inarticulate and their thought entirely imaginative, like that of children. The logic of the primitive is univocally and appropriately expressed in his myths and fables. Insofar as he begins to frame universals, they are "imaginative universals" (pars. 209, 381)[23] —in the earliest stage, the gods and heroes of the myths, which Vico also calls "poetic characters."

Vico testifies that he spent a good twenty years struggling with the problem of interpreting the myths. His great breakthrough was the discovery of how to make them yield genuinely historical knowledge. Earlier authors, such as Fontenelle, had already discerned that "all barbarian histories have fabulous beginnings" (par. 202), but he had found only limited value in them for reconstructing history: at most, they were sources for exposing the super-

21. Pompa, *Vico*, 139.

22. Ibid., 138ff., on Homer. Vico saw Homer not as an individual poet but as a personification of traditional tellers of tales (139): his poems, "civil histories of Greek customs," are products of "a human nature which imaginatively created poetical persons to stand for its own social institutions and narrated the history of these institutions in the form of myths and fables involving these persons" (140).

23. Vico's notion of an *imaginative* universal seems to constitute a significant breakthrough, since earlier thinkers (e.g., Bacon, Herbert, Spinoza, Fontenelle) would attribute the universalizing capacity to *reason* alone, imagination being strictly distinguished from reason by its very *incapacity* to form anything beyond the concrete individual image. This opens the way to inquire whether there are mythic or religious universals that are not reducible to rational concepts. Cf. Fisch's observation, n. 27 below.

stition of the ancients, beyond which we had (thank God) progressed by the light of reason. But Vico saw more—a way to discover historical truths, and in fact to reconstruct the earliest institutional and mental history, in and from them. His discovery created the "master key" to the new science, for it provided a way in which his principles could be demonstrated by bridging the gap between universal ideal history and actual history, and between our time and the first times. Vico's formulation of that "master key" is perhaps the next-most quoted passage of the entire *New Science*, because it puts us on the path to understanding fully the "modification of the human mind":

> the first gentile peoples, by a demonstrated necessity of nature, *were poets who spoke in poetic characters*. This discovery, which is the master key of this science, has cost us the persistent research of almost all our literary life, because with our civilized nature we cannot at all imagine and can understand only by great toil the poetic nature of these first men. (par. 34; my italics)[24]

Herein, Vico thought he had overcome the barrier created by "our civilized nature" and had found an interpretive bridge affording access not only to the meaning of the myths but to the very springs of society and its institutions. Once the poetic character of the ancient mind was fully grasped, a window was opened into the meaning of the fables, which in turn shed light on the fundamental nature of human institutions. The divine and semidivine characters of the myths were not arbitrary or absurd inventions, or the product of individual creative minds making poetry for pleasure; rather, they had reference to real history. They were "true fables or myths, and their allegories are found to contain meanings not analogical [to modern philosophical truths] but univocal, not philosophical but historical, of the peoples of ... those times" (par. 34).

Vico offers a fundamental critique of rival methods of interpretation practiced by both literary scholars and political philosophers. First the literary: Bacon, and a whole host of philosophers and interpreters going back to Plato, had ransacked the ancient myths and languages for their esoteric and hidden philosophical wisdom, which, it was supposed, the ancients had deliberately concealed in their tales. This is nonsense, Vico asserts. He regards as "impertinent all the mystic meanings with which the Egyptian heiroglyphs are endowed by the scholars [heiroglyphics regarded then as the most primitive form of language], and the philosophical allegories which they have read into the Greek fables" (par. 128).

These interpreters are guilty of the "conceit of scholars" (boria de' dotti), who rightly rejected the "conceit of the nations" (boria di nazioni) that their myths were literally true, but who wrongly substituted their own anachron-

---

24. Cf. Vico's *Autobiography*, 180. Tullio de Mauro, commenting on *NS*, par. 34, stresses the primacy of linguistics, rhetoric, and philology as of "foremost importance" in comparison with other components of his thought ("G. Vico: From Rhetoric to Linguistic Historicism," 282).

istic readings, by which the myths became manifestations of a high rationality impossible in their time, given the stage of the evolution of mind, language, and institutions.[25]

The ancient poetry is simply not the product of a reason like ours. It therefore reveals, not esoteric wisdom, but the social wisdom of the makers of institutions; not the contemplative eternal truths of reason, but the practical identification and imaginative expression of these "necessities and utilities" which first generated everything human.

This great discovery of the common and sociological nature of poetry and myth, Vico argues, "does away with the opinion of the matchless wisdom of the ancients, so ardently sought after from Plato to Bacon's *De sapientia veterum*. For the wisdom of the ancients was *the vulgar wisdom of the lawgivers who founded the human race*, not the esoteric wisdom of great and rare philosophers" (par. 384; my italics).[26] Fisch marks the philosophical importance of this move by Vico, in the context of a discussion of Vico's debt to Lucretius and Hobbes and his liberation from Descartes: "to posit as the primitive and basic modes of generalization not the universals of science and philosophy but those of poetry ("poetic characters" [or "fantastic universals"], as Vico came to call them)—was to emancipate oneself at last from Descartes and give a new dignity to those philological and historical disciplines which he had despised as resting on inferior cognitive faculties."[27] Vico's "key" demonstrated how his universal principles could be found in actual history, for the first mythmakers were the brutish and necessitous but hugely creative founders of human societies themselves. It was they who hoisted the primeval creature to a level which could rightly be called "human."

The myths, then, did indeed conceal some truths, as the allegorists taught, but they were "civil truths, and must therefore have been the histories of the first peoples" (par. 198).

The other scholars whom Vico criticizes were primarily interested in just such civil matters, but they too fell prey to the "conceit of scholars" and misinterpreted the myths in another way. Criticizing Grotius (who, along with Bacon, was one of Vico's two most admired modern authors), Selden, and Pufendorf, Vico says that they lacked

> a critical method applicable to the founders of the nations. They believed them to be wise in esoteric wisdom and did not see that for the gentiles Providence was the divine teacher of *a common wisdom*, out of which among them [only] after the

25. Vico's distinction, developed in pars. 122–28, reproduces that of Spinoza between "sceptics" and "dogmatists"; *Tractatus Theologico-Politicus*, chap. 15: the "sceptics" are guilty of Vico's conceit of nations and the "dogmatists" of the conceit of scholars, when they come to interpreting the Bible.

26. Cf. pars. 128, 222–23, and my "Religion and Bacon's New Learning," 280–81.

27. M. H. Fisch, *AGV*, Introduction, 43. Fisch observes that Hobbes, too, saw the "commonwealth" as a human creation, "but not [by men] such as we are now, at the conscious, rational, intellectualist level on which we elaborate definitions of the social contract" (45).

lapse of centuries the esoteric wisdom [of the political philosophers] emerged. Thus our three authors failed to distinguish the [primitive, poetic] natural law of the nations, which was coeval with their customs, from the natural law of the philosophers, which the latter grasped by force of reasoning. . . . [28]

In this civil sphere too, then, we must avoid anachronism. These early creatures did not "read the eternal laws of justice in the bosom of Jove," as the philosophers claim, but rather "read in the aspect of the sky the laws dictated to them [as they supposed,] by the thunderbolts" (par. 516). We come to the thunder later.

Vico further characterizes these first humans, who could not yet think in any sense like we do. They were inarticulate. When they first began to speak, and to think, their thought was entirely imaginative, not rational. Men shaped the idea of Jove (the first idea of all), for example, not by reasoning, "for they were not yet capable of that, but by the senses, which, however false in the matter, were true enough in their form—which was the logic conformable to such natures as theirs" (par. 502).[29]

We have been alerted to the fact that Vico has an evolutionary (more exactly, cyclical) pattern as a presupposition for his account of human society. We have seen that he discerns in history certain original universals—institutions that were born with humanity and even define it as such; that these institutions are everywhere and will always have their primordial and constitutive value; that they are religion, marriage, and burial of the dead. These institutions define the human as such; they are the very creations by which man became, and is, human (the very word "human" is derived, Vico notes, from *humare*, to bury: par. 537).

What, more closely seen, is the case with the origin of religion itself ? I have held in my introduction to this study that this is the question that divides theology from the study of religion, and Vico is an excellent test case because he advertises his entire new science as a theodicy of providence but at the same time explains religion, along with all culture, as made by man. How do the two systems of causality interact, if at all? Are we dealing with two separate and incommensurable paradigms, or two realms of *causality* at all? We observe first that Vico does not hedge his scientific principles and his theory of knowledge when he comes to treat religion: like everything else

28. Vico, *Autobiography*, 172; my italics.
29. Anthropologist Edmund Leach affirms Vico's insight: "Protoman's direct experience was limited to the feelings and emotions of his bodily senses; therefore, the only way in which he *could* impose an orderly frame of logic upon the world of observation was by using categories derived from experience of his own body to sort out the attributes of the external world. . . . This thesis is not identical to that formulated by Lévi-Strauss but it is of the same kind. Instead of dismissing mythical thought as non-logical or pre-logical (and therefore naive), it presumes that it rests on logical principles. The purpose of Vico's inquiry, like that of Lévi-Strauss, is to discover what these principles are" ("Vico and Lévi-Strauss on the Origins of Humanity," 314).

in culture, it is made by man. No component or dimension of it is exempted from scientific analysis. Were this not so, religion could not have been posited as the first principle of Vico's science,[30] because it would then fall outside the epistemological realm of "maker's knowledge." On the other hand, one could argue that Vico is merely asserting that only idolatry, or "false" religion, can be so understood, while true religion, the response to special divine revelation, cannot be understood at all, since God "made" it. Vico never, so far as I have found, makes such a distinction explicit, but it is clearly implicit in his exemption of Christion tradition from analysis. So let us follow his account of "gentile religion."

Its natural causal ground lies in the necessities of human social existence which lie at its foundation. We recall that Vico has announced that "by principles of this new critical art [of deciphering myths] we consider at what determinate times and on what *particular occasions of human necessity or utility felt by the first men* of the gentile world, they, with frightful religions which they themselves feigned and believed in, imagined first such and such gods and then such and such others" (par. 7; my italics).

The way Vico imagines it to have happened is given several summary accounts; here is one of them (note how the whole is awkwardly jammed into the postdiluvian biblical framework—a matter to be treated later). After the Flood,

> the races of Ham and Japheth were destined to be scattered through the great forest of this earth in a savage migration of 200 years. Wandering and alone, they were to bring forth their children, with a savage education, destitute of any human custom and deprived of any human speech, and so in a state of wild animals. It was necessary that just so much time should pass before the earth, having at last dried off from the wetness of the universal flood, could send off dry exhalations of the sort wherein lightning could be generated, which stunned and terrified men into abandoning themselves to the false religions of so many Joves that Varro was able to count forty of them. . . . (par. 62)[31]

The thunder and lightning, then, occurred in the normal and carefully described course of nature, though Vico sprinkles his accounts with reminders that "divine providence initiated the process" (par. 178) on "certain occasions . . . which our Science studies and discovers" (par. 13).

Vico describes the psychological and mental state which, following initial terror,[32] gave birth to the gods. Incapable of rational thought, man naturally imagined that all of nature was like himself, and so he personified all its activities that bore on him, such as the lightning and thunder:

---

30. So Leon Pompa, *Vico*, 58, 60.

31. For variant versions of this story, see pars. 9, 13, 301, 377, and its source in Lucretius, *De rerum natura*.

32. Vico thinks his account gives substance and correct meaning to the ancient saying, "Primos in orbe deos fecit timor"; par. 191; cf. par. 503.

Thereupon a few giants, who must have been the most robust, and who were dispersed through the forests on the mountain heights where the strongest beasts have their dens, were frightened and astonished by the great effect whose cause they did not know, and raised their eyes and became aware of the sky. And because in such a case the nature of the human mind leads it to attribute its own nature to the effect, and because in that state their nature was that of men all robust bodily strength, who expressed their very violent passions by shouting and grumbling, they pictured the sky to themselves as a great animated body, which in that aspect they called Jove, the first god of the so-called greater gentes, who meant to tell them something by the hiss of his bolts and the clap of his thunder. (par. 377)[33]

Herein Vico recaptures and particularizes the "poetic" spirit in its premier human moment, generating its first thought (although this moment occurs repeatedly, independent of any one instance or locale):

The most sublime labor of poetry is to give sense and passion to insensate things; and it is characteristic of children to take inanimate things in their hands and talk to them in play as if they were living persons. This philologico-philosophical axiom proves to us that in the world's childhood men were by nature sublime poets. (pars. 186–87)[34]

So the first men attributed their own nature to the universe in every aspect of it whose causes they did not know (pars. 180–81), seeing all the world as "animate substance." The great and terrible Jove, the hurler of lightning bolts, was

an image so popular, disturbing and instructive that its creators themselves believed in it, and feared, revered, and worshiped it in frightful religions . . . whatever these men saw, imagined, or even made or did themselves they believed to be Jove; and to all the universe that came within their scope, and to all its parts, they gave the being of animate substance. This is the civil history of the expression "All things are full of Jove.". . . . (par. 379)

Thus in this first poetic "age of the gods" Vico sees a world whose primal institutions form a sort of pantheistic unity—not rational, Pompa observes, but "structured by the human capacities and modes of thought proper to the people who have created them. . . . The first nature is poetic, creative or divine because it is a nature in which the imagination, playing a dominant role, creates a religious world-view which affects the character of all institutions."[35]

33. Edmund Leach notes the difference between Vico's personification and that described by Max Müller as a childish "disease of language": "Vico also seems to regard the personification of nature as the prototypical characteristic of mythical thought, but his approach is quite different. Vico's hero-giants are in no sense childish and trivial; on the contrary, it is the gigantic creative power of their imaginations which makes them what they are" ("Vico and Lévi-Strauss on the Origins of Humanity," 313).

34. On the comparison of children to the primeval poets, cf. also pars. 375, 408.

35. Pompa, *Vico*, 117; 120, commenting on par. 916.

Vico goes further: the imaginative act of personification entailed as well the people's supposing that the lightning and thunder were a *form of speech*, for their own speech was a not yet articulate system of signs, interjections, and so on. In their terror, they themselves created the first names for the gods—for example, "Pa!"—which contributed to the gods being called fathers (par. 448). Again, "by the Latins Jove was at first, from the roar of the thunder, called *Ious;* by the Greeks, from the whistle of the lightning, *Zeus;* by the Easterners, from the sound of burning fire, he must have been called *Ur. . . .* " (par. 447).[36] Thus, Vico explains, by onomatopoeia "the divine character of Jove took shape—the first human thought in the gentile world" (par. 447). In such "sublimity of invention" were born the gods.

Because they took the thunder and lightning as signs, they then invented the art of divination, or auspices, in order to grasp the will of Jove and to get some grip on the future. Religious *practice* began, then, when they "began to exercise that natural curiosity which is the daughter of ignorance and the mother of knowledge" (par. 377). "The first men," Vico explains,

> who spoke by signs, naturally believed that lightning bolts and thunderclaps were signs made to them by Jove; whence from *nuo*, to make a sign, came *numen*, the divine will, by an idea more than sublime and worthy to express the divine majesty. They believed that Jove commanded by signs, that such signs were real words, and that nature was the language of Jove. The science of this language the gentiles universally believed to be divination, which by the Greeks was called theology, meaning the science of the language of the gods. (par. 379)

Religion, at first based on fear of these gods,[37] in turn became the basis of morality and virtue, embodying itself in the second universal institution, marriage. The savages, terrified by the lightning, took cover and remained in caves (hence Jove's title of *stator*, "stayer or establisher," par. 379).

> With this impulse the virtue of the spirit began likewise to show itself among them, restraining their bestial lust from finding its satisfaction in the sight of heaven [i.e., out in the open], of which they had a mortal terror. So it came about that each of them would drag one woman into his cave and would keep her there in perpetual company for the duration of their lives. Thus the act of human love was performed under cover, in hiding, that is to say, in shame; and they began to feel that sense of shame which Socrates described as the color of virtue. And this, after religion, is the second bond that keeps nations united, even as shamelessness and impiety destroy them. (par. 504)

---

36. Isaiah Berlin is worth quoting, where he comments on another of Vico's etymological excursions (on *lex*): "This is a characteristically fanciful piece of genetic sociological philology; yet in due course this sociolinguistic approach led to rich and important branches of the humanities in the form of historical jurisprudence, social anthropology, comparative religion and the like, particularly in their relations with the genetic and historical aspects of linguistic theory" (*Against the Current*, 102, n.1).

37. See above, n. 32; cf. par. 62.

Originally, then, marriage was "chaste carnal union consummated under the fear of some divinity" (par. 505), and families were created (par. 13). And the religions of fear, in other ways as well, gradually reduced the beast to humanity (see pars. 191, 503). The third human institution was burial of the dead and, with it, belief in immortality:

> Afterward, the god-fearing giants, those settled in the mountains, must have become sensible of the stench from the corpses of their dead rotting on the ground near by, and must have begun to bury them. . . . And they surrounded these sepulchers with so much religion, or divine terror, that burial grounds were called by the Latins religious places *par excellence.* Hence emerged the universal belief in the immortality of human souls. (par. 529)

By now we were really "human," for humanity "had its origin in *humare*, 'to bury' (which is the reason we took the practice of burial as the third principle of our Science). . . . " (par. 537).

Vico goes on to derive the institutions of government in the same fashion, all of which, he says, evoke our admiration of providence, which "ordered these institutions of men, concerning which they said truly, though in a false sense, that they were all the work of the gods" (par. 630).

What, now, of providence? Our ability to treat naturalistically Vico's historical explanations of all aspects of culture, including religion, is unremarkable in this sense: that he was only extending to new limits the idea that God does everything through secondary causes—a traditional Catholic doctrine. Following such an assumption, nothing except those events which God brings about directly—all confined within the framework of the Hebrew-Christian dispensations—is beyond naturalistic explanation. Vico's application of this doctrine is, however, quite remarkable considering the extent to which even religion itself is explained—can only be explained—under that same rubric of secondary causes ("we cannot conceive how divine providence could have employed any other counsel to halt them in their bestial wandering" than to employ natural means described by Vico [par. 1097]).

Thus, from the perspective of a strict analysis of Vico's work as scientific, his doctrine of providence, Pompa rightly claims, is simply unnecessary: "The concept of a transcendent providence is not . . . basic to his Science as such, since the claim that there is a transcendent providence is an inference from the conclusions established by the Science. One could reject the inference without in any way casting doubt upon the adequacy of the Science itself."[38] The explication of the critical moments in human history is so natural that "one cannot detect in what it [providence] consists over and above" the human creations that make history.[39] "Nothing is

38. Pompa, *Vico*, 58.
39. Ibid., 60.

added," Pompa concludes, to the Science's explanations by saying that we see providence at work in it. "Such a claim is both gratuitous and empty."[40]

Nevertheless, we require a brief review of the functions of providence in Vico's presentation. Although I am in basic agreement with Pompa's conclusion, there is one important exception to be handled last, namely, the otherwise unexplained existence of an innate religious sense.

Vico called his creation a "rational civil theology of divine providence" (pars. 385, 342), and claimed that the new science would also be "a demonstration, so to speak, of what providence has wrought in history" (par. 342). We have seen how all the sciences are in a sense swallowed up in history: is the new science of history finally swallowed up by providence?

Most noticeably, Vico repeatedly credits providence with elevating the postdiluvian brute to humanity, and sustaining and restraining him therein by essential institutions of man's own making. Humankind must strive to sustain those universal institutions because they make society possible. Vico's rational civil theology offered an orthodox way of explaining what happened to survivors of the Flood who fell outside the biblical framework of salvation history—an increasingly vexing problem for Christian minds as the exploration of the new and old worlds outside of Europe were making their full impact.[41] In this light, Vico's account, right down to the thunderclaps, could be read as a new theodicy (parallel to Herbert's much weaker attempt) showing how God had not neglected any part of humanity despite his special attention to some.

Providence provided everything necessary, seeing to it even that religions would appear, since social "necessity and utility" required their creation. Here is one example that supports Pompa's conclusion: Vico's explanation by way of social necessity tends to make gratuitous any further explanation of why religion exists.

For the sake of engendering a genuine humanity outside the orbit of saving history, providence allows even false religions to appear. But there is a kind of education of the human race under way, for beneath the fantastic forms of the first religions, one true and fundamental religious idea was being formed: "Thus, through the thick clouds of those first tempests, intermittently lit by those flashes, they made out this great truth: that divine providence watches over the welfare of all mankind" (par. 385). But here, too, an objection may be raised: Vico is guilty of the same "conceit of scholars" of which he accuses the other mythologists, for primal religion as he describes it offers scant evidence of such an abstract and rational belief. While such

40. Ibid.
41. Margaret Hodgen, *Early Anthropology in the Sixteenth and Seventeenth Centuries.* The whole book is relevant, but see esp. 230.

evidence may be *consistent* with belief in providence, it does not *require* such an inference.[42]

One of the most interesting applications of the idea of providence in the *New Science* is Vico's profound awareness of the ironies of history—that history takes its course beyond, and sometimes contrary to, the intentions of the people who make it. The fullest exposition of this idea is the much discussed paragraph 1108, which reads in part:

> It is true that men have themselves made this world of nations (and we took this as the first incontestable principle of our Science, since we despaired of finding it from the philosophers and philologists), but this world without doubt has issued from a mind often diverse, at times quite contrary, and always superior to the particular ends that men had proposed to themselves; which narrow ends, made means to serve wider ends, it has always employed to preserve the human race upon this earth. (par. 1108)

Vico goes on to cite examples throughout history, beginning with the first: "Men mean to gratify their bestial lust and abandon their offspring, and they inaugurate the chastity of marriage from which the families arise" (ibid.). This paragraph makes no mention of providence, but the next claims that "the evidence clearly confirms ... that providence directs human institutions" (par. 1109); for "without human discernment or counsel, and often against the designs of men, providence has ordered this great city of the human race. . . . " (par. 342).

Pompa, Simon, and others have noted, however, that even the ironic turns of history can be explained in terms of the common, or social, wisdom of the peoples, operating over and above the narrow intentions of self-centered individuals.[43] Vico himself had observed that early humans by nature attributed everything to the gods, even while they were doing these things themselves (par. 629; cf. 379). Just the same observation could now be made about Vico himself, for his science has quite adequately explained how the vulgar wisdom recognized human necessities for social existence and operated so as to constrain and deflect selfish individual intentions, urging them into structures of survival and progress.

Even if, however, there is an element or design in history that remains unexplained, and if this is appealed to as evidence of providence, then providence explains *everything*—both that which is explained naturalistically (like the beginning of religion via thunder), and that which is not. But an explanation that explains everything explains nothing.

A more profitable way of understanding the function of providence, then, is to see it as providing for Vico not explanation by way of causality, but

---

42. Here I am applying Hume's trenchant comment on the logic of the design argument, to be discussed in the next chapter.

43. Lawrence H. Simon, "Vico and Marx," 319; Pompa, *Vico*, 63.

meaning. No particular historical event or process need be explained other than by naturalistic means, but when one is finished with that, the question remains: what is the meaning and significance of the whole story? Vico, a religious man, could hardly neglect such a question, and his entire answer to it falls under his rubric of "providence." Hume, who was not a religious man, would shortly write a *Natural History of Religion* stripped entirely of any reference to divine influence. Comparing the above account to that of Hume in our next chapter, we can identify as the really significant difference between the two authors not the fact that Hume is more "scientific" in his explanation, but that in his account the history of religions is *stripped of any positive meaning*. That the need for meaning is, however, a constitutive source of religion, and therefore a legitimate concern for the study of religion, is evidenced in the chapter following Hume, as we see Comte, premier advocate of science, reintroducing the idea of "providence" without God, in order to refurbish the meanings of faith, hope, and love in the human saga by way of a religion of humanity as the Great Being.

Heirs of Vico who were to be more in tune with his providential thought as a whole, especially German thinkers, would retain a providential dimension; sociologists such as Weber would understand and focus particularly on the meaning-giving function of religion, even if not themselves religious thinkers.

Another aspect of Vico's theological outlook already mentioned is that "providence" is the rubric under which all human history outside the realm of special grace and revelation is to be understood. In Vico's view, two histories run parallel—salvation history as related in the Bible, and "gentile" history, with which alone the new science is concerned. The two histories are distinguished and follow separate paths from the epoch which began after the Flood. Then, with the rise of the Christian era, Vico sees the possibility of an eventual rejoining of the two histories, for the story of gentile religions can be viewed as *preparatio evangelii*:

> Divine providence has so conducted human institutions that, starting from the poetic theology which regulated them by certain sensible signs believed to be divine counsels sent to man by the gods, and [much later] by means of the natural theology which demonstrates providence by eternal reasons which do not fall under the senses, the nations were disposed to receive revealed theology in virtue of a supernatural [Christian] faith, superior not only to the senses but to human reason itself. (par. 366)

Throughout, then, Vico has observed a sharp distinction between what can be understood and explained scientifically, and the religion of Israel and Christianity, about which men can "know" anything only because it has been "revealed to them" (par. 948).

This distinction is justified for Vico not by rational argument but by faith alone. An ironic possibility of Vico's prodigious effort, however, is that the history of Israel's religion and its continuation in Christianity are easily absorbed by the new science. Indeed, commentators have observed that Vico's discovery of the true Homer as a personified representation of the common wisdom of an entire era can, with few adjustments, be applied equally to Moses.[44]

Thus, overall, we see two possibilities: the providential framework which Vico intended to produce and the ironic naturalistic possibilities which his genius opened up through its penetration of the historical causes of human institutions. In this light, I can agree only partly with Mazlish's assessment:

> What was new in Vico was his insistence that the workings of providence must be explained in reference to *secondary* causes and exemplified in terms of the *empirical* data. This was a revolutionary turning around of the question: a Copernican revolution in theodicy, wherein providence does not explain the whirling of events, but the events explain the workings of providence.[45]

The thoroughness and success with which he achieved his secondary-causal explanations is certainly astonishing, if not philosophically altogether novel. And we have already seen anticipations of Vico's "revolution" in Herbert's formally similar empirical demonstration of providence. What is really revolutionary about Vico, I think, is the tendency of his system to explain providence *away*, without remainder, except as a category of meaning.

There is, however, one final "remnant," one element of providence in Vico's scheme for which he does not explicitly offer any naturalistic explanation—the idea that there is an innate sense of divinity. This, I think, is the most durable remnant of traditional theology not only in Vico but in the study of religion until today and demands close attention. Hume will provide it.

By Vico, the notion is hardly stressed (unlike Herbert, who places great weight on it), but it is explicit in several passages and constitutes the most resistant element to the solvent of naturalistic explanation that informs the rest of Vico's account.

In his *Autobiography*, for example (1725), Vico describes how he discovered "a natural theology of all nations by which each people naturally created by itself its own gods through a certain natural instinct that man has for divinity [per un certo istinto naturale che ha l'uomo della divinità]."[46] In the *New Science* I find three pertinent references. One is to the providential intent that religions be instituted to domesticate man's barbarity: their willingness to submit to religion "can only be grounded in the innate concept [concetto innato] which men have of that divine providence" (par. 27). Another text relates that God brought feral humanity to true humanity "by awakening in them a confused idea of divinity, which they in their ignorance attributed to

44. E.g., James C. Morrison, "Vico and Spinoza," 55.
45. Bruce Mazlish, *The Riddle of History*, 46.
46. Vico, *Autobiography*, 167; *Opere*, ed. Nicolini, 62.

that to which it did not belong" (par. 178). Finally, the longing for something "superior" to save them is evidence of "the light that God has shed on all men" (par. 339). Vico's irrepressible urge to invoke natural evidences here crops up in the observation that "libertines grown old, feeling their natural forces fail, turn naturally to religion"!

Thus, despite at least hints that even this innate sense of divinity might be translated into natural causes (religion springing from fear, curiosity, from the universal tendency to personify everything, from the implicit wisdom that recognized social necessities),[47] it could be argued that Vico here designates a causal ground, or sine qua non, in the world of religion that has no other explanation but the fundamental nature of humanity itself, made by God for Himself.

Some conclusions follow. Surely one of Vico's greatest contributions to the study of religion was his showing the possibility of a science of religion embraced by a universal historical-cultural science of humanity. This achievement is heightened by Vico's insight into the difference between such a science and a science of physical nature. As he saw it, the difference was grounded in the distinction between the "maker's knowledge" which we may have of culture, enabling us to explain and understand it fully, and the external and surface knowledge of things natural and revealed which, since we did not make them, we cannot explain. This distinction allowed Vico to deal with the complexity of the human world in a much more profound way than any author treated so far. As Isaiah Berlin observed, Vico penetrated beyond the "blissful simplicity of Descartes or Spinoza, Hume or Russell (or even Kant)." In fact, "not until the days of Dilthey and Max Weber did the full novelty of the implications for the philosophy of mind and epistemology of Vico's theses about the imaginative resurrection of the past begin to dawn upon some of those who, in their turn, resurrected him."[48]

But the reference to Dilthey and Weber alerts us to an essential dimension of Vico's outlook on religion: his claim not merely to interpret it but to explain it. He would not have understood how one might claim to interpret religion independently of explanation. The hermeneutical tradition, so dominant in religious studies in our time (and not pursued in this book), takes its legitimating text from Dilthey, who asserted that we explain nature but interpret culture. This splits asunder precisely what Vico intended to join together. For Vico, the scientific integrity of the new enterprise depended on the claim that human sciences could explain the causes and discover the origins of human ideas and institutions in a way that could not be done with

---

47. Fear: pars. 178, 191, 503; curiosity: par. 189; social necessity: pars. 7, 347, 1109.
48. Isaiah Berlin, "A Note on Vico's Concept of Knowledge," 377.

nature, which, because it was made by God, could *not* be explained.[49] In an important sense, then, Dilthey gives us Vico in reverse, and Dilthey's tradition tended to reduce Vico's enterprise to an individualistic psychological hermeneutic that sought to reexperience the creative moments of past cultural productions, but without explanation.[50]

Here I agree with H. P. Rickman's assessment:

> we cannot rest content with the understanding of individual expressions. We want explanations, and in the human sphere, as well as in the physical, this means the discovery of general laws that govern the connections between events. Indeed, we cannot claim even to have properly understood an individual expression until we know why it came about, that is, how it follows from others in accordance with some established generalization.[51]

The continuation of the scientific study of culture in Vico's fuller sense will thus be followed, in the remainder of this book, through the works of authors who attempted to extend the *explanatory* side of Vico's work. Hence, we turn to Hume, Comte, Tylor, and so on to continue our study of how the enterprise of "explaining religion" proceeded.

One example, by way of anticipation: in our last chapter, on Freud, we see the explanatory element of Vico's thought being extended. Freud, like Vico, believed that religion was a man-made cultural universal which entailed the scientific opportunity to trace it to its moment of birth, its origins in the psyche and in history. Like Vico, Freud believed that the language of myth was a profound source of truth about human life, even where direct evidence was wanting, if a proper hermeneutic could be developed to understand it. They shared the idea that the advance of the individual's mind from childhood to maturity could provide clues to the development of the species. With Vico, Freud believed that "the nature of everything born or made betrays the crudeness of its origin" (par. 361). For both, the very language of religion bears the memory traces of its origins. Vico even populated his primitive world with the ferocious Cyclopean fathers that Freud would borrow from the British anthropologist J. J. Atkinson (a classicist too) to form his oedipal

49. Berlin gives the two most relevant passages from Vico's *De antiquissima italorum sapientia* (1710): "We cannot demonstrate physics from its causes [a caussis], because the elements which compose nature are outside us." Again: "The useful historians are not those who give general descriptions of facts and explain them by reference to general conditions, but those who go into the greatest detail and reveal the peculiar causes [caussarum peculiares] of each event" (*Against the Current*, 111, 118).

50. Wilhelm Dilthey, "The Rise of Hermeneutics." Dilthey defines *Verstehen*, the key to his whole hermeneutical program, as "that process by which we intuit, behind the sign given to our senses, that psychic reality of which it is the expression" (232). Hans H. Penner and Edward A. Yonan discuss and criticize Dilthey's approach in "Is a Science of Religion Possible?" 123–25.

51. H. P. Rickman, "Vico and Dilthey's Methodology," 453.

theory of totemism.[52] Freud extended Vico's scientific endeavors by trying to formulate universal laws by which the unconscious operates in the context of universal primal institutions.

Another essential aspect of Vico's science is its sociological dimension, to be extended (among our authors) by Comte and Durkheim. The subject matter of Vico's science was not primarily individuals and their ideas but the groups and institutions that determined them. Vico claimed that religion constitutes society (or perhaps that religion and society are mutually constitutive) and was sensitive to the social functions of religion, above all its "binding" (from *religare*) moral force (cf. par. 503). Not only did it constrain man's brutish, selfish instinct and enforce sociability, but it had the bonding power to instill love and loyalty and to promote virtue in social groups.[53]

The present state of social sciences has led some commentators to conclude that Vico was too optimistic about the ability of his science to generate essential social knowledge,[54] but he himself was modest enough to understand that the ironic outcomes of historical activity were best left to providence (or fate, or chance). Comte is perhaps more to blame for promising too much from sociology. He diminished the profundity of Vico's ironic understanding of history, believing that scientific humanity had now become its *own* providence. By making that move, Comte rejected Vico's realism. But Durkheim's recognition that certain social necessities generate both religion and community made for a fruitful extension of Vico's evolutionary sociological insight.

My introduction noted that the question of the origins of religion is generally neglected as a serious problem or is simply set aside on various grounds. As we have seen, Vico would respond to this by demanding how we can know the *nature* of such cultural things as religion, and understand their persistence and necessity, without reconstructing at least hypothetically the circumstances of their beginnings (natura = nascimento). The implications of humanity's evolutionary course, as it is being painstakingly unearthed by paleontologists, have if anything heightened the interest of this question.

Like some contemporary scholars, Vico did indeed bracket one part of the religious phenomena, that is, placed it outside the realm of his science of causes. What he bracketed was the entire Hebrew-Christian tradition. True

52. Vico, pars. 523, 524, 582. See J. J. Atkinson, *Primal Law*, chap. 1, developing his theory directly from that of Charles Darwin.

53. Cf. par. 14, which concludes that "all the virtues have their roots in piety and religion, by which alone the virtues are made effective in action. . . . " Cf. par. 516. On Vico's anticipation of Durkheim, see David Bidney, "Vico's New Science of Myth," 270.

54. J. L. Mackie, "Comment" [on J. Hintikka, "Practical versus Theoretical Reason," *q.v.*], 107: "the fact that social institutions are to some extent human products does not make them peculiarly knowable, just because they are not the products of intelligent manufacture or design, but arise from the interaction of many diverse and conflicting intentions. Hobbes and Vico were mistakenly optimistic. . . . "

religion, he claimed, was not man-made in the sense that gentile religion was, and therefore only God could (re-)think the reasons and recreate the causes of its existence. Contemporary scholars who deny that the problem of origins or explanation is a proper pursuit go much further: they would have us vastly extend Vico's brackets so that they cover causal consideration for all religion. The presupposition for this move is the same as his but universalized—namely, the belief that the cause of *all* religion is transcendent and therefore unknowable *in principle*. This orientation to religion is congenial to the hermeneutical tradition referred to above, and to liberal confessional theologies, but inappropriate when used to block inquiry aimed at explaining religious phenomena.

Any approach to religion has to satisfy Vico's claim that the nature of any cultural product cannot be understood or known ahistorically—that is, without reconstructing its origins and causes. Merely to review the ancient myths of origin (as in a purely descriptive account of religious traditions) repeats what Vico called the "conceit of nations," who took the accounts of their beginnings literally. On the other hand, interpreting all religions as apprehensions of "the sacred," or of "transcendence," repeats the anachronistic "conceit of scholars" even more than does Vico's own thesis that primitive religions manifest belief in providence.

Both approaches ignore the importance of Vico's thesis of the "modifications of the mind" through its evolution. The very fact that the mind has evolved and changed and that its modifications are determined by social as well as historical context, are essential conditions for understanding other minds.

The two stages of Vico's methodology are worth noting. With greatest difficulty, he tells us, Vico learned to leave his own categories of thought behind and recreate the "poetic" apprehension of the world in the thought of the mythmakers fully within the actual historico-social context which determined what they could think. That achieved, Vico then tried to explain this aboriginal experience in *his own* scientific terms, bringing to bear his understanding of history, philosophy, and literary, and psychological processes. The *continuity* of human nature—the fact that this proto-human is somehow "one of us"[55] —made the first step possible—that of reconstructing the creative meaning of primitive poetry, symbol, and myth; but the *modifications* of mind—the development undergone by human nature, society, and mind—had evolved a scientific rationality that required and made possible a modern explanation of the operative causes of primitive experience and knowledge-making. Vico's final aim was to explain the primitive "theory" by his own

55. Cf. John Bowker's discussion of the significance of this idea, as expressed by Joseph Conrad in *Lord Jim* when he tries to explain Jim's final act. "We ought to know," one of the characters says, "he is one of us." *The Sense of God*, 1; cf. 6–7. For Vico, the primitive is a childlike version of "us."

theory—which is what scientific explanation or reduction is concerned with.[56] As Vico said, we explain the human creations by way of "the particular ways in which they come into being; that is to say, their nature, *the explanation of which is the distinguishing mark of science*" (spiegano . . . ch'è la nota propissima della scienza; par. 346, my italics). He would not recognize as science anything less.

One final matter: in what sense, if any, may we regard Vico in the light of our thesis that the study of religion issues from *criticism* of religion? The immediate impression is not promising. Vico did not share the openly critical assaults on religion of the northern Enlightenment, which helps to account for the fact that he was so readily ignored in eighteenth-century Europe. His outlook better fitted the restoration and romantic mood of the nineteenth century, which "discovered" him.[57] He did not present his science as an alternative to a religious worldview, concluding rather that "this science carries inseparably with it the study of piety" (par. 1112, the last). His daring extension of the idea that God works through secondary causes left him enough room to construct his version of a "natural history of religion" as a swollen parenthesis to, rather than in opposition to, traditional salvation history. In some sense, then, Vico seems to contradict our thesis. He can be read from a theological perspective as the maker of a magnificent theodicy that would embrace the extra-Christian world of religions within a general account of providence fulfilled in revelation. And yet, his is the profoundest effort to explain religion encountered so far.

The critical element is in some ways hidden, but it is there. His criticism of the interpreters of ancient texts was not applied by him to the Bible; but it could have been, and to an extent already had been: Spinoza had already identified and devastated what Vico referred to as the "conceits" of the nations and of the scholars in his (Spinoza's) criticism of literalistic and allegoristic biblical interpreters. Vico surely had read and absorbed these ideas.

While the biblical framework was not attacked frontally, the outcome of Vico's work is a splendid example of how new wine bursts old wineskins. His attempt to shoehorn his natural history of all cultures and religions into the narrow spaces of the biblical chronology—filling in what the Bible must have left out regarding what happened to the *gentes* after the Flood—was probably sincere rather than a device merely to avoid the Inquisition. But it leans on Spinoza's great insight that all ancient expressions of religion, including that of the Bible, are and of necessity must be exactly suited to the times in which they were produced, for their authors without exemption

56. See Hans H. Penner and Edward A. Yonan (above, n. 50), and better, Wayne Proudfoot, "Religion and Reduction."

57. See Max Fisch, introduction to Vico's *Autobiography*, 61ff., and esp. 75–76; Alain Pons, "Vico and French Thought," 172.

share all the public and common assumptions—the "vulgar wisdom"—of the people to whom they addressed the words of the gods.

Thus, Vico's providential-biblical history and its foreshortened chronology were expendable and could be discarded as gratuitous without detracting anything from the enduring explanatory structure of his science; his entire reconstruction of the origins of religion could be adopted with no exceptions, for he had already addressed and answered the basic question: if revelation is not given, whence religion?

As already stated, what would be lost if Vico's providential interpretation were discarded would not be knowledge but meaning. That would have to be derived in some other way, perhaps from the historical and evolutionary saga of the promising primate emerging as a social and linguistic being, beset by the necessities of nature but equipped for survival through intelligent sociability, with promethean creativity and lots of luck making himself human.[58]

58. Cf. Peter J. Wilson, *Man, the Promising Primate.*

Chapter 5

Religion within the Limits of "The Science of Man": David Hume

avid Hume (1711–76) stands in this account as the pivotal figure, being our clearest exemplar of the self-conscious turn from a theological to a scientific paradigm for the study of religion. With him a line of criticism definitively ends and construction of alternative theory begins.[1] The view taken here is based on his naturalistic assumptions and on the thorough, explicit, and consistent manner in which he carried them through, both in criticism and alternative theory. He believed it was possible to explain religion within the purview of the "science of man." In pursuit of his program, he produced a critique of each of the theological bases on which the phenomena of religion had been understood, explained, and legitimated up to his own time, and then offered naturalistic explanations of his own which opened the way for more systematic scientific investigations.

1. Typically, Hume is either ignored or misinterpreted by historians of the study of religion. On the scientific side, he is not mentioned by the authors of the article on "Religion" in the *International Encyclopedia of the Social Sciences* (Clifford Geertz, Robert N. Bellah, and James E. Dittes in *IESS* 13:398–421). From the philosophical side, he is cursorily mentioned twice by Michel Despland, *La Religion en Occident*, but gets no substantive attention. Jan de Vries completely misses the point of Hume's *Dialogues* (*The Study of Religion*, 34). Wilfred C. Smith thinks that Herbert of Cherbury represents the Enlightenment view (*The Meaning and End of Religion*, 40), leaving no place for Hume, who demolished such views (cf. Peter Gay's judgment, below, n. 2). E. E. Evans-Pritchard (*Theories of Primitive Religion*), Eric J. Sharpe (*Comparative Religion*), and Jacques Waardenburg (*Classical Approaches to the Study of Religion*) all begin later than Hume. J. C. A. Gaskin frequently marvels at the extent to which Hume is still misinterpreted, despite the enormous amount of analysis devoted to his thought (*Hume's Philosophy of Religion*, e.g., 4–5, 183 and n. 19). While I agree with practically everything in Gaskin's book, I prefer to label Hume as founder of the scientific study of religion rather than of the sociology (146) or the philosophy (173–74 and n. 21) of religion. I note the lack of sociological dimension to Hume's analysis below. In philosophy of religion, Hegel has equal claim (see Despland, 488ff.)—but here one is involved in disagreement about the definition of "philosophy" (empiricist vs. idealistic) as well as different standpoints taken with regard to religion. Hume's "externality" to a religious viewpoint, noted by Gaskin, would disqualify him as a "philosopher of religion" in some circles; if Despland is typical of that enterprise, philosophy of religion is closer to natural theology than to what Hume is about.

In the sphere of logical analysis, and on the plane of ideas, Hume may be seen as completing the stream of critical thought which we have followed from the sixteenth century. He exemplifies best what Peter Gay calls "the historic mission of the Enlightenment"—namely, "to overthrow natural religion."[2] This is not to say that the entire modern critique of religion ends with Hume. Sociological, economic, and psychoanalytic probing would continue. But such later critiques would presuppose the validity of Hume's conclusions. And Hume's own hypotheses would have a direct and documentable impact on later students of religion in Britain, France, and Germany,[3] even though his problems, his perspective, and his data were limited and left considerable gaps to be filled by others (to be noted at the end of the chapter).

In Hume's day, the three theological-apologetic supports of religion served at the same time as the pillars on which any religious account of religious origins would be based. They were (1) specific revelation (i.e., the revelation to the Hebrews related in the Bible); (2) "revelation in nature," also with biblical support, on which the theistic hypothesis was based by way of the so-called design argument; and (3) a religious anthropology, rooted in the (also biblical) idea of the image of God but taking the form of "common notions," "innate ideas," or a *sensus divinitatis*.[4]

Hume's criticism of these three fundamental religious hypotheses is found in the following writings, whose arguments we shall review here with reference to Hume's other writings: (1) "Of Miracles" (Section X of *An Enquiry Concerning Human Understanding*, the 1748 revision of the *Treatise on Human Nature*), containing by implication his critique of prophecy and revelation;[5] (2) the *Dialogues Concerning Natural Religion* (published posthumously in 1779; the first version written in the 1750s), and "Of a Particular Providence and of a Future State" (*Enquiry*, XI), against the argument from design, the bulwark of natural theology in Hume's day; and finally, (3) *The Natural History of Religion* (1757), an examination of the claim that religion is instinctive or innate, and an alternative account of its origin.[6]

2. Peter Gay, *The Enlightenment*, 1:319.

3. We shall note direct links to Tylor, de Brosses, and Comte at appropriate places in the text. An ironic link to the German romantics, especially Hamann, is discussed by Frank Manuel (*The Eighteenth Century Confronts the Gods*, 285–86) and by Isaiah Berlin ("Hume and the Sources of German Anti-Rationalism").

4. The last term was popularized by John Calvin; see my "Zwingli, Calvin and the Origin of Religion."

5. Gaskin (above, n. 1) notes that "it is the only piece in which he systematically attacks the reasonableness of belief in revealed religion" (125).

6. Editions used: *Enquiries Concerning Human Understanding and Concerning the Principles of Morals*, ed. L. A. Selby-Bigge. 3d ed. by P. H. Nidditch. Oxford: Clarendon, 1975. *Dialogues Concerning Natural Religion*, ed. Norman Kemp Smith. Indianapolis: Bobbs-Merrill, 1947. *Natural History of Religion*, ed. H. E. Root. Stanford: Stanford University, 1957. References in the text will refer to section of work and page of edition used.

The aim of Hume's criticism was to clear away the metaphysical and theological rubble in the path of the "science of man." The difference between the situation as he perceived it, and that of Herbert's time a century earlier, is instructive. For Herbert, a universalist rational theology would serve as the antidote to the quarrels between the champions of rival "revelations." Hume discovered that theology had turned this very rationality into a new dogma that religion has its basis in reason. "The religious philosophers [he commented], not satisfied with the tradition . . . indulge a rash curiosity, in trying how far they can establish religion upon the principles of reason; and they thereby excite, instead of satisfying, the doubts, which naturally arise from a diligent and scrutinous enquiry."[7]

Hume's work was to have slight impact on the theologians. In 1802, William Paley produced a best seller, *Natural Theology; or, Evidences of the Existence and Attributes of the Deity, collected from the Appearance of Nature*, which blandly set forth arguments that had been demolished by Hume.[8] The yoking of reason and religion continued among British theologians, and they continued to bask in the late seventeenth-century atmosphere—as Gay describes it—"when manners were beginning to be polished, toleration became fashionable, and pulpits filled with Latitudinarians, Arminians, and rational Catholics."[9]

Hume's "science of man" was the framework which he shared with his Scottish contemporaries, and whose scope he set forth in the introduction to his *Treatise of Human Nature* (1735-37):

'Tis evident, that all the sciences have a relation, greater or less, *to human nature;* and that however wide any of them may seem to run from it, they still return back by one passage or another. Even Mathematics, Natural Philosophy [i.e., natural science], and Natural Religion are in some measure *dependent on the science of man;* since they lie under the cognizance of men, and are judged of by their powers and faculties.[10]

For Hume, all arguments on religion are finally grounded in his analysis of human nature, and even his philosophical arguments presuppose that basis, as recent studies have shown.[11] Hume thus sees the science of man as the hub, if not the new "queen," of the sciences, because every realm and

7. *Enquiry* XI, 135: cf. X, 130. Gay (above, n. 2) quotes Anthony Collins's acerbic judgment on the work of the philosophers: "No one doubted the existence of God until Dr. [Samuel] Clarke tried to prove it" (326). Clarke was a dedicated Newtonian and advocate of the design argument.

8. Paley begins by discussing the implications of finding a watch while crossing a heath.

9. Peter Gay (above, n. 2), 325.

10. *A Treatise of Human Nature*, ed. L. A. Selby-Bigge. Introduction, xix.

11. James Collins, *The Emergence of Philosophy of Religion*, 27-28. Cf. Keith E. Yandel, "Hume on Religious Belief," 112; Marvin Fox, "Religion and Human Nature in the Philosophy of David Hume."

direction of inquiry depends for its integrity on an accurate understanding of the powers and capacities of the mind and the nature of human propensities.

The science of man makes man himself the object of study by extending the experimental method to human motivation and behavior. "The philosophical rationale for this extension [Capaldi writes] is a belief that the cosmos is uniform and that Newtonian science is the model for comprehending it. Specifically: Hume believes that even the categories of the human understanding can be explained, not explained away, by that model."[12]

This seems true especially of the early Hume. A striking example occurs in the last paragraph of his short treatise on the passions where he tries to show that "in the production and conduct of the passions, there is a certain regular mechanism, which is susceptible of as accurate a disquisition, as the laws of motion, optics, hydrostatics, or any part of natural philosophy."[13]

It is not the case, however, that Hume was committed to a mechanical model of human beings, as though, for example, a system of morality could be reduced to mathematical principles, a la Spinoza. His science of man easily accommodates the contemporary argument that resists reduction of all natural phenomena to, say, physics. Each branch of science must, rather, respect the nature of the entities it studies, suggesting a hierarchical rather than a reductionist model of the sciences.[14] Thus, in the *Dialogues*, one of the most significant arguments is a criticism of the Newtonian mechanical analogy urged by proponents of the design argument. In place of this model, which requires a cause external to the system, Hume suggests an organic model precisely in the interest of the more basic principle noted above, that the world, whatever models or analogies we use to explain it, contains *within* itself such principles of explanation as it is worthwhile to pursue (that is, possible to investigate and test on the basis of experience—something not possible on the "design" model).

Despite Hume's lack of concern to compress the world into a single metaphor, nevertheless it is, for him, a single system. Isaiah Berlin observes that the German philosopher Hamann and his friends found Hume congenial because he seemed "to have finally undermined . . . any form of dualism, the doctrine of two worlds, whether of a Cartesian, Lebnizian or Kantian kind; there was only one world, that of direct confrontation with reality, and . . . the recognition of its unity and of the platonic fallacy which underlay all attempts to determine frontiers that divided reality from everyday experience, was of supreme importance to them."[15] For Hume, the reality we confront

12. Nicholas Capaldi, "Hume's Theory of the Passions," 176.

13. "A Dissertation on the Passions," in *Essays Moral, Political and Literary*, ed. T. H. Green and T. H. Grose, 2:166.

14. On the contemporary discussion among natural scientists, see Marjorie Grene, "Reducibility: Another Side Issue?" esp. 20–23.

15. Isaiah Berlin, *Against the Current*, 186.

justifies, by experience, our belief in its regularity; his conviction of the unity and regularity of the world is behind his attack on revelation and the design argument, as well as on the postulation of innate endowments that may exempt human religiousness from the realm of psychological inquiry.

We turn now to the texts, beginning with "Of Miracles."

miracles

Hume tells us that his critique of miracles is at the same time, "without any variation," a critique of prophecy[16] —of claims that specific historical events are "revelations" coming from beyond the natural world. These, in his day, were widely regarded as the prime evidentiary basis for the divine origin of religion (or at any rate, of Christianity).

The essay is in two parts: first, a purely logical argument which Hume makes directly from the definition of a miracle; and second, supporting arguments derived from a criticism of specific cases of miracle-claims.

In structure, the first part is remarkably similar to Anselm of Canterbury's celebrated argument for the existence of God in the *Proslogion,* and it is just as neat and swift: if you understand the definition, you can already grasp a decisive proof embedded within it, and if you *agree* with the definition, you cannot refute the argument. For Hume, the very definition of a miracle contains the seed of its own destruction: "A miracle is a violation of the laws of nature;[17] and as a firm and unalterable experience has established these laws, the proof against a miracle, from the very nature of the fact, is as entire as any argument from experience can possibly be imagined" (114). Miracle, by definition, contradicts our uniform experience, out of which we have inferred that nature operates in a regular, lawful way. "Nothing is esteemed a miracle, if it ever happen in the common course of nature" (115). Thus, the very definition of miracle is testimony to "a uniform experience against every miraculous event, otherwise the event would not merit that appellation" (115). Uniform experience in all places and times amounts to a proof against miracle than which Hume cannot conceive a greater *contrary* proof.

Meanwhile, the entire burden of proof in favor of a miracle rests on testimony of others—testimony, again, that by definition must contradict our entire experience. "The plain consequence is (and it is a general maxim worthy of our attention), 'That no testimony is sufficient to establish a miracle, unless the testimony be of such a kind, that its falsehood would be more miraculous, than the fact, which it endeavors to establish. . . .' " (115– 16). So we are faced with a choice between two possible "miracles": (*a*) that a violation of our uniform experience has actually occurred as reported; or (*b*) that the testimony of the witness(es) is false. Hume says: "I weigh the

16. "Of Miracles" (*Enquiry Concerning Human Understanding* X), 130. Subsequent references are given parenthetically in the text.

17. Cf. 115, n.1: "a transgression of a law of nature by a particular volition of the Deity, or by the interposition of some invisible agent."

one miracle against the other; and according to the superiority, which I discover, I pronounce my decision, and always reject the greater miracle" (116).

The irony here is a little heavy, since Hume does not regard it as the least bit miraculous that testimonies to miracles are deceptive. In his view, they always are. More exactly, "there never was a miraculous event established on so full an evidence" (116) as even to consider a judgment in favor of such an event as the lesser of two miracles.

We need not dwell on Part II, Hume's examination of miracle-stories through history, but merely come to its inevitable conclusion: that religion is so totally founded on belief (what he calls "faith") rather than on evidence, that religious faith *itself* has to be a miracle, for, as the treatise wickedly concludes, "whoever is moved by *Faith* to assent to it [Christianity], is conscious of a continued miracle in his own person, which subverts all the principles of his understanding, and gives him a determination to believe what is most contrary to custom and experience" (131).

There are frequent intimations of the relevance of all this to the justification and critique of divine revelation, since revelation is regarded as only one type of miracle as well as being the "point" of most miracles. With regard to new religions, for example, Hume notes that the prophecies and miracles on which they are founded are regularly ignored by the learned, with the result that the miracle becomes too widely believed to be discredited by criticism. Again, he says that not only can human testimony not prove a miracle, but it cannot "make it a just foundation for any . . . system of religion" (127). The reason is that whatever knowledge of God we might rationally infer from experience is based on "the experience which we have of his productions, in the usual course of nature" (129). As with Spinoza, any evidence of a violation of that regularity would threaten, rather than support, belief in God. Besides, given the long history of demonstrated fabrications, it is always more probable that a miracle-story is based on error or deception than that a miracle actually occurred. Finally, since rival religions claim rival miracles, they tend to cancel one another out: with revelation and miracle, "whatever is different is contrary" (121).

In this treatise, then, the unity of the world means that the world is best construed as a single system of causes and effects, operating in a regular fashion, and even the religionists' definition of a miracle bears witness to that reliable criterion of probability.

We now consider the *Dialogues Concerning Natural Religion*. In the essay on miracles, in the *Natural History* as well as in the *Dialogues*, Hume renders sometimes elaborate lip service to the design argument. Much debate has gone on about this, but the evidence weighs decisively against any claim that Hume takes it seriously from an intellectual standpoint, despite its aesthetic appeal. The best evidence is that he demolishes it in the *Dialogues* (and more briefly in "Of a Particular Providence").[18] To say that he believes it anyway is to ignore his devastating critique as well as the frequent irony in his references to it, for example, when he notes that the design argument favorably "strikes everywhere the most careless, the most stupid thinker."[19] His main mouthpiece, Philo,[20] summarizes the very most that can be got out of the argument from design when he says that our best effort "resolves itself into one, simple, though somewhat ambiguous, at least undefined proposition, *that the cause or causes of order in the universe probably bear some remote analogy to human intelligence*" (XII, 227). Not only is this vague, but religiously and ethically empty, for "it affords no inference that affects human life, or can be the source of any action or forbearance" (ibid.).

The logic of the design argument rests on two structural assumptions, only the first of which Hume accepts: (1) that causes can be inferred from effects; and (2) that a persuasive analogy can be drawn between *natural* productions (like watches, buildings, or footprints) and their human causes, or makers, and the *supernatural* production of the world by a cause we call God. Briefly, here are Hume's criticisms of each of these assumptions as they operate in the argument from design.

In the matter of arguing from effect to cause, Hume applies Occam's razor—the principle of parsimony—which dictates that entities must not be posited beyond necessity. This argument is made succinctly in the *Enquiry:* in reasoning from effect to cause, we are not "allowed to ascribe to the cause any qualities, but what are exactly sufficient to produce the effect."[21] Nor, Hume adds, can we then double back, as it were, and "from the [alleged] cause, infer other effects from it, beyond those by which alone it is known to us."[22] This applies to the claim that we can argue a case for providence and a future state when we have no direct experience whatsoever upon which to base such an inference.

As the concluding statement of Philo quoted above shows, Hume's critique leaves the argument with nothing resembling the all-wise, mighty, benevolent

---

18. Forrest Wood states the case accurately and bluntly: the aim of the *Dialogues* is "to destroy the arguments for the existence of God...." ("Hume's Philosophy of Religion as Reflected in the Dialogues," 189).

19. *Dialogues* XII, 214. Subsequent references will be given parenthetically in the text.

20. Gaskin (above, n. 1) has most recently and thoroughly answered the critics of N. K. Smith, who argued convincingly that, for the most part, Philo is the spokesman for Hume. Any careful reader can discern that Philo never says anything that Hume does not agree with, nor are any of Philo's arguments refuted. Smith's argument is found in his introduction to the *Dialogues* (ed. cit. above, n. 6); Gaskin's defense on pp. 160ff. of his book. Further support can be found in the interesting account of the close relation between Hume's *Dialogues* and Cicero's *De natura deorum* by J. V. Price, who notes especially how clearly Hume's Philo is an adaptation of Cicero's Cotta ("Scepticism in Cicero and Hume").

21. *Enquiry Concerning Human Understanding* XI, 136.

22. Ibid.

single creator of Christianity. Indeed, when it comes to inferences, Hume suggests that we have more compelling and direct evidence that the cause or causes of the universe are immanent, rather than residing outside the world, since the experienced world resembles an organism more than a machine. "Nor is it less intelligible, or less conformable to experience to say, that the world arose by vegetation from a seed shed by another world, than to say that it arose from a divine reason or contrivance. . . . " (VII, 178).

Not only the immanence, but the materiality of ultimate world-making causes, is suggested. If we examine the world of our experience, it seems more likely that matter produces mind than the opposite: "Judging by our limited and imperfect experience, generation has some privileges above reason: For we see every day the latter arise from the former, never the former from the latter" (VII, 179–80).

This quotation touches the very nerve of the design analogy, which seeks to convince us that the material world originated from the creative action of a nonmaterial mind. We have no experience of such an event occurring in nature. The human mind does not make watches without hands. Moreover, in the biological generation which we witness constantly, mind is evidently generated from matter, not the other way around.

As if that were not enough, Hume questions more generally whether the world can be construed as related to its maker as a machine or a building is related to its earthly artisan because the world appears so machinelike as to resemble "productions of human contrivance." Is the inference warranted, "by all the rules of analogy, that the causes also resemble; and that the author of nature is somewhat similar to the mind of man" (II, 143)?

Philo/Hume exposes two gaps in our experience which are fatal to such an argument: first, we have never witnessed a world being made, and have no idea what the situation was before it came to be. Its production is unique, a one-of-a-kind event (or process). We simply "have no *data* to establish any system of cosmogony" (VII, 177). Second, the anthropomorphism of the first cause has no warrant: quite gratuitously, we "make ourselves the model of the whole universe" (III, 156), arbitrarily liken world-making to an architect's house-building, and leave unanswered the question of where the architect came from (IV, 160–61).

The design argument, then, does not do what it is supposed to do; much less can it serve as a basis for an aboriginal explanation of religion. This, of course, is not the focus of the discussion in the dialogue, but the type of thinker Hume was contesting liked to think of original or "natural" man as though he were a philosopher inferring one God from the world which he contemplates (recall Herbert's extraordinary primitive who constructs a design argument de novo). On the question of origins, then, Hume's attack indicates one of the avenues to be closed off: according to Hume, man's experience of nature indeed has something to do with the origin of religion,

nature has to do w/ relig bc of unpredictability?

but it is the anxiety-ridden experiencing of nature's unpredictable and un-manageable power, rather than its designedness, that proves critical (and primal religion is polytheistic before it becomes monotheistic).

natural relg

For Hume's development of that argument, we turn to his *Natural History*. We begin where Hume does, in order to be clear about precisely what problem he is addressing. In the works already considered, Hume has cleared the way for assessing the third and most durable basis for a universal and religious explanation of religion—the claim that there is an innate, instinctive religious sense.[23]

Hume's analysis embraces indifferently the questions of historical origin and of cause. In fact, both his evidence and his argument are more pertinent to the latter than to the former, since he takes no special pains to locate the *very oldest* form of religion. Indeed, he does not believe that any account of beginnings is possible.[24] The question he raises is about the origin of religion "in human nature," and an answer to that question has equal bearing on the current situation and on any aboriginal beginning-point. Relevant data, for Hume, include both ancient written sources and contemporary observation without much discrimination between the two. The constancy of human nature—not yet placed in serious question by evolutionary science—assures him that both sorts of evidence are relevant.

In the *Natural History*, Hume applies to religion his general epistemological conclusions regarding the origin of ideas, already worked out in the *Enquiry:* all ideas originate in experience and therefore are historical rather than innate. Yet, religion presents an especially interesting problem, because its virtual universality suggests that it springs from an instinct of some sort rather than being a historically acquired characteristic.

I shall follow the precise steps in Hume's own introduction, since it is so lucid in stating the problem and economical in coming to immediate focus on the critical issue. Concerning religion, he says, "there are two questions in particular, which challenge our attention, to wit, that concerning its foundation in reason, and that concerning its origin in human nature" (Intro., 21). The former, a philosophical and logical question, has already been dis-

23. Outside explicitly confessional theological positions, this is the most durable resting-place for those who regard religion as an irreducible and elemental dimension of human life. I noted this in my preceding chapter on Vico. Hume would have agreed with Marvin Harris's criticism of innatism (in this case, Lévi-Strauss's), as the "practice of explaining sociocultural phenemona by means of conveniently posited instincts" (*The Rise of Anthropological Theory*, 492).

24. Richard Popkin shows that Hume not only rejected biblical history, because of its miraculous character, but the notion that any historical beginning could be known. He notes that in the *Natural History*, "there is not even lip service to the view that Jewish history precedes other histories . . . Hume's history starts nowhere and goes nowhere" ("Hume: Philosophical versus Prophetic Historian," 92).

posed of in the *Dialogues*. Gaskin's formula is on target: the *Dialogues* concern the *reasons* for belief; the *Natural History* concerns the *causes*.[25]

To begin properly, Hume continues, we must select from all that we know about religion the relevant data, which are as follows: "The belief of invisible, intelligent power has been very generally diffused over the human race, in all places and in all ages; but it has neither perhaps been so universal as to admit of no exception, nor has it been, in any degree, uniform in the ideas, which it has suggested" (Intro., 21). This is a carefully worded summary of the state of knowledge: belief in intelligent power and two interesting and problematic aspects of this belief—that it does not appear to be quite universal, and that it is certainly not uniform in the ideas it produces. Hume denies that a poll of the human race would yield any item of unanimous belief (much less the five common notions which Herbert of Cherbury cherished).

That evidence is already sufficient, Hume thinks, to offer a preliminary hypothesis: that the "sentiment of religion" "springs not from an original instinct or primary impression of nature, such as gives rise to self-love, affection between the sexes, love of progeny, gratitude, resentment; since every instinct of this kind has been found absolutely universal in all nations and ages, and has always a precise determinate object, which it inflexibly pursues" (Intro., 21). Genuine instincts and impressions of nature, then, are defined by exactly the two qualities that religion is found to lack. Religion must therefore belong (on the epistemological-psychological map) in the realm of those items which, unlike the instincts, passions, impressions, and sensations, are not innate, but historically acquired. Hume has expressed himself clearly on the issue of "innateness" in the *Enquiry*. There he lists the same instincts as above—self-love, resentment of injuries, and the passion between the sexes—as examples of innate impressions. He also includes sense-impressions among those things that we may take as "innate," if we redefine innate to mean "what is original or copied from no precedent impression."[26] Unlike such impressions, either outward or inward, which are so "strong and vivid" that it is not "easy to fall into any error or mistake with regard to them," ideas—especially abstract ones—are "faint and obscure," and they are easily confused.[27]

"All our ideas . . . are copies of our impressions,"[28] and depend on them for their existence. They have no other source. Thus, even abstract ideas such as the idea of God come only from "the materials afforded us by the senses and experience," which provide a "precedent feeling or sentiment."[29]

25. Gaskin (above, n. 1), 4.
26. *Enquiry Concerning Human Understanding* II, 22, n. 1.
27. Ibid., 21.
28. Ibid., 19
29. Ibid.

What, then, does this tell us about the "first principles" of religion? Hume answers (we return to the *Natural History*), "The first religious principles must be secondary; such as may easily be perverted by various accidents and causes, and whose operation too, in some cases, may, by an extraordinary concurrence of circumstances, be altogether prevented" (Intro., 21). Now Hume can put the original problem of the treatise more precisely: "What those principles are, which give rise to the original belief, and what those accidents and causes are, which direct its operation, is the subject of our present inquiry" (ibid.).

After briefly disposing of the opinion that there is an original monotheism, Hume presents his version of a conjectured primeval person. What does that person encounter? The answer is *power*, or rather, *powers*. They originate outside of him, and he can neither control nor explain them. And so he worries: "the first ideas of religion arose not from a contemplation of the works of nature, but from a concern with regard to the events of life, and from the incessant hopes and fears, which actuate the human mind" (II, 27). In this "moment," the person is moved by "ordinary affections of human life" as they focus on the future, for example, "the anxious concern for happiness, the dread of future misery, the terror of death, the thirst for revenge, the appetite for food and other necessaries. Agitated by hopes and fears of this nature, especially the latter, men scrutinize, with a trembling curiosity, the course of future causes, and examine the various and contrary events of human life" (II, 28).

Man's uniqueness is that he worries about the future. He feels anxiety about "future causes" that will determine his fate. "These *unknown causes*, then, become the constant object of our hope and fear; and while the passions are kept in perpetual alarm by an anxious expectation of the events, the imagination is equally employed in forming ideas of those powers, on which we have so entire a dependence (III, 29)."[30] Now we are on the very brink of religion. But there is one more step to be explained: how a specifically "religious" *interpretation* is derived from this situation. How it is that, "in this disordered scene, with eyes still more disordered and astonished, they see the first obscure traces of divinity" (II, 28)? For Hume, all passions fix on specific objects; in this case, the focus is on powers that help or harm, but their nature is utterly unknown and uncontrolled. Now personification comes into play: that "universal tendency" among humankind "to conceive all beings like themselves, and to transfer to every object, those qualities, with which they are familiarly acquainted, and of which they are intimately conscious. We find human faces in the moon, armies in the clouds; and by a natural propensity, if not corrected by experience and reflection, ascribe malice or good-will to everything, that hurts or pleases us" (III, 29).

After giving many examples of this "propensity" to personify, including

---

30. On fear and hope, see further "Dissertation on the Passions" (in above, n. 13), 2:139.

the habit of Christians to attribute base motives and temperament to the
Deity, Hume concludes the point as follows:

> No wonder, then, that mankind, being placed in such an absolute ignorance of
> causes, and being at the same time so anxious concerning their future fortune,
> should immediately acknowledge a dependence on invisible powers, possessed of
> sentiment and intelligence. The *unknown causes* which continually employ their
> thought . . . are all apprehended to be of the same kind or species. Nor is it long
> before we ascribe to them thought and reason and passion, and sometimes even
> the limbs and figures of men, in order to bring them nearer to a resemblance with
> ourselves. (III, 30)

Religion arises, then, in two stages: first, the predictable determination of
the passions to fix on definite objects; second, the propensity of the mind to
model all unknown powers after those human volitions of which it is immediately conscious. And "hence the origin of religion: and hence the origin
of idolatry or polytheism" (VIII, 47).

Note that, for Hume, the passions of fear and hope are not yet religious.
Religion is not immediate in the same sense that fear, hope, and anxiety
about the future are immediate. Religious sentiments are not inevitable.
Rather, religion originates *from a particular interpretation* of certain impressions. In that sense, it is in the realm of idea rather than irreducible instinct
or impression. What we call "religious experience," then, involves not one
but two moments: instinctive response, then inference. What Hume questions
is not that people have certain immediate and powerful sensations, feelings,
and apprehensions, but that such feelings are religious, and therefore that
the correct inferences to be drawn from these impressions are necessarily
religious.[31]

One strength of Hume's analysis is that it can account for both the virtual
universality and the astonishing variety of religions. Totally undiscriminating,
religion lacks any regulative principle with regard to its contents, except for
that seemingly universal habit of personification. This was a venerable and
durable idea, but Hume will soon be challenged by those who see that personification is not universal; that power can be construed nonanthropo-
morphically (later we examine Durkheim drawing on the impersonal notion
of "mana" and constructing a sociological theory).

Some further comments are in order here. First, Hume approaches the
problem of the causality of religion by imagining how a primitive *individual*
person, with nothing but his own "nature" and senses to inform him, might

---

31. Freud makes exactly this point in *Future of an Illusion*, 6:32: "Critics persist in describing
as 'deeply religious' anyone who admits to a sense of man's insignificance or impotence in the
face of the universe, although what constitutes the essence of the religious attitude is not this
feeling but *only the next step after it*, the reaction to it which seeks a remedy for it" (my italics).
See Proudfoot's analysis in *Religious Experience*.

no social dimension [margin annotation]

possibly have become "religious." He considers no *social* dimension at all, and his will be a characteristic starting-point of the nineteenth-century British anthropological tradition, in contrast to that of the French, stemming from St. Simon, Comte, et al.

Second, Hume presupposes that human nature is the same everywhere and at all times. Because of this assumption, he draws his evidence without discriminating among times and regards his own conclusions as relevant for contemporary popular religion. This does not mean, however, that the "natural" of the title means to eliminate all chronological considerations.[32] Hume firmly establishes the chronological priority of polymorphous deities, recognizing that monotheism is the product of a more complex cultural state. His initial argument for the priority of polytheism is a chronological "fact": that "1,700 years ago all mankind were polytheists" (I, 23). So, despite the fact that Hume is more concerned to establish logical and psychological than chronological sequence, one should not posit a gap between his logical and historical thinking, as some commentators have done. His procedure is perfectly amenable to chronological arrangement and correction by historical data. In the absence of data, he, like his contemporaries (and like all historians) offers conjecture. As Dugald Stewart, a later contemporary of Hume's, observed regarding historical reconstruction of the course of ancient societies, "we are under a necessity of supplying the place of fact by conjecture ... from the principles of their nature, and the circumstances of their external condition."[33]

Such conjecture can be tested and continually corrected by fresh evidence. For example, Hume's hypothesis that concern for future outcomes will be found to characterize primitive religion is supported by prehistoric cave paintings of animals bristling with spears and arrows—artifacts of magico-religious practices aimed at successful results in the hunt.[34] Primitive evidence of fertility cults and burial practices likewise supports the future orientation of at least some of the most ancient archeological testimony we possess with regard to early religion.

Despite what looks so far like total rejection of the theological tradition, a curious if ambiguous remnant of that tradition persists in the *Natural History*. Hume did not share the optimistic view of human nature and destiny

---

32. E. C. Mossner exaggerates the opposition between chronological and "scientific organization of data," in an otherwise informative essay, "The Enlightenment of David Hume," 28.

33. Quoted by Anand C. Chitnis, *The Scottish Enlightenment: A Social History*, 97.

34. Jack Finegan, *The Archeology of World Religions*, 30–37. On the necessity of hypotheses, W. E. LeGros Clark writes, "... hypotheses are not to be disparaged because they are hypotheses; on the contrary, they are quite necessary preliminaries in the pursuit of any scientific enquiry, for only by the construction of hypotheses is the opportunity given of putting them to the test by further observation and discovery" (*The Antecedents of Man*, 3).

expressed by those of his Enlightenment contemporaries[35] who celebrated man's inexorable progress toward rationality. It is man's Humean bondage to be controlled by his passions and haunted by terrors. So deep are these fears that man feels compelled to propitiate his gods no matter how terrible the means or how awful the consequences. In pursuit of this need, humans typically ignore the principles of morality (which should, in Hume's view, regulate religion) in favor of direct action to propitiate their gods. Because of this persistent weakness, humankind has been and remains an easy mark for "priestcraft," even though such "artifices of man" do not account for the origin of religion: "Thus it may be allowed, that the artifices of men aggravate our natural infirmities and follies of this kind, but never originally beget them. Their root strikes deeper into the mind, and springs from the essential and universal properties of human nature" (XIV, 73).

But what can these "essential and universal properties" possibly be? Could it be that Hume still retains the content, if not the formulation, of the orthodox notion that an original image of God has been ruined by sin? Such an idea has indeed occurred to Hume:

> The universal propensity to believe in invisible, intelligent power, if not an original instinct, being at least a general attendant of human nature, *may be* considered as a kind of mark or stamp, which the divine workman has set upon his work; and nothing surely can more dignify mankind, than to be thus selected from all other parts of the creation, and to bear the image or impression [N.B.: a technical term for what is innate!] of the universal Creator. But consult this image, as it appears in the popular religions of the world. How is the deity disfigured in our representations of him! How much is he degraded, even below the character, which we should naturally, in common life, ascribe to a man of sense and virtue! (XV, 75; my italics).[36]

Thus, despite the fact that there "may be" such a thing as an "impression" on human nature that generates religiousness, when you "examine the religious principles that have, in fact, prevailed in the world, you will scarcely be persuaded, that they are any thing but sick men's dreams" (XV, 75). An orthodox theologian might read this with assent, lament "the Fall," and argue that Hume has quite accurately shown the necessity for a divine revelation, and faith. But such a "miracle," as we have seen, was not likely in the case of David Hume.

---

35. Frank Manuel (above, n. 3), 178. Peter Gay specifies as follows: "Locke, Montesquieu, Hume, Diderot had no theory of progress; Rousseau's thought stressed the fact of man's retrogression and the hope for man's regeneration; Voltaire saw human history as a long string of miseries broken by four happy ages. Only Kant, with his speculative world history, Turgot with his five stages, and Condorcet with his ten epochs, may be said to have held a theory of progress, and these three thinkers stood not at the center but at the bright end of the spectrum of enlightenment thought" (quoted by Marvin Harris [above, n. 23], 40).

36. Richard Popkin has noted how closely Hume here approximates orthodox Calvinism; see "Hume and Jurieu: Possible Origins of Hume's Theory of Belief."

If Hume had perceived nothing else, his clarity about one thing would guarantee his place in the scientific tradition that studies religion: he saw that "first and foremost we are talking not about theologies but about ways of coping with life."[37] That simple generalization is stated as an established rule in a recent essay by Leonard Glick reviewing the anthropological study of religion since Malinowski. Although made without reference to Hume, Glick's statement echoes the approach of Hume's *Natural History* more than that of many of his more rationalistic successors. Hume realized that highly articulated worldviews, philosophies, and theologies arrived on the cultural scene long after the first religious interpretations of the human situation, and that those more "primitive" interpretations were still, in his own enlightened age, far more widespread than philosophy, and more typical of actual lived religion.

In the works examined, we have also seen how Hume placed the study of religion within the purview of the science of man. By so doing, he earned at least a forerunner's place in the research tradition that leads directly to modern anthropology. Thomas Huxley recognized the natural continuity between the two. Describing the scope of anthropology, he observed that "the natural history of religion, and the origin and growth of the religions entertained by the different kinds of the human race, are within its proper and legitimate province."[38]

E. B. Tylor, one of the founders of modern anthropology, specifically acknowledged Hume's importance. In his major work (*Primitive Culture*, 1871), Tylor noted that even after a century Hume's *Natural History* was still "perhaps more than any other work the source of modern opinions as to the development of religion." Accordingly, Tylor not only quoted Hume's text directly but adopted his anthropomorphic principle to explain the rise of animism, Tylor's label for man's original and "minimal" religion.[39] This theory, more intellectualistic than Hume's, informed the dominant evolutionary theory of religion for a whole generation of early anthropologists.

The most important presupposition for science, from Hume's perspective, was that the world is a unified system, amenable to analysis and explanation from a single set of rules and categories. There are no privileged areas, no esoteric mysteries—only a vast unknown, open to investigation. Thus, amidst the darts which Philo in the *Dialogues* flings against the design argument, perhaps none is more important than his pregnant question: why should we suppose that the world has a *transcendent* cause on the model of the machine and its maker? Why may the causes not be contained *within* nature itself ?

37. Leonard Glick, "The Anthropology of Religion: Malinowski and Beyond," 229.

38. Quoted by Sharpe (above, n. 1), 47.

39. E. B. Tylor, *Primitive Culture*, 1:477. He quotes from the *Natural History*, 3:29, as an accurate description of "the personifying stage of thought." For a more recent positive assessment of Hume by an anthropologist, see Wilson D. Wallis, "David Hume's Contribution to Social Science."

That would satisfy our need to recognize that nature is orderly, and it would have direct support from our experience. As George Nathan says: "If the cosmos is seen as a vast machine, it is necessary to account for order by reference to a transcendent cause; but if nature is viewed as an organism, the principle of order may be understood as immanent in nature."[40] By reviving this ancient theory,[41] Hume helped to set the stage for an evolutionary (in Darwin's sense) as over against a hierarchical version of human reality and its unfolding—a change which Hannah Arendt saw as "the turning point in the intellectual history of the modern age, . . . when the image of the organic life development—where the evolution of a lower being . . . can cause the appearance of a higher being . . . appeared in place of the image of the watchmaker who must be superior to all watches whose cause he is."[42]

Hume made this directly relevant to explaining religion when he proposed that spirit is more likely generated from matter than the reverse: here he saw the ultimately biological basis for culture and ideas, including the idea that the gods are creations of the human imagination rather than the other way around. In place of religion from the top down, religion of revelation, Hume suggested a more or less ascending pattern of biological and cultural development.

Furthermore, although Hume did not originate his anthropomorphic principle (it goes back to the Ionian philosopher Xenophanes),[43] he installed it in the context of a coherent epistemological analysis, and his principle provided a useful point of reference for many successors who shared his assumptions, up to the present day.[44]

40. Quoted by Roger Johnson in Roger Johnson et al., *Critical Issues in Religion*, 29.

41. Hume credits "ancient mythologists": *NHR* 4:35.

42. Hannah Arendt, *The Human Condition*, 285. Cf. Margaret T. Hodgen, *Early Anthropology in the Sixteenth and Seventeenth Centuries*, 451: "Overnight, as it were, and in the almost uncanny silence of unquestioning agreement, the hierarchical concept of nature, which once was taken to be an orderly arrangement of forms in space, became a progressive sequence in time." This change spawned, among other things, the genre of "natural histories" in zoology.

43. J. M. Robinson, *Introduction to Early Greek Philosophy*, 52, quotes Xenophanes: "The Ethiopians make their gods snub-nosed and black; the Thracians make theirs gray-eyed and red-haired. . . . And if oxen and horses and lions had hands, and could draw with their hands and do what man can do, horses would draw the gods in the shape of horses, and oxen in the shape of oxen, each giving the gods bodies similar to their own."

44. Without making a systematic search, I have found the anthropomorphic principle in Charles de Brosses, Comte, Feuerbach, Tylor, J. F. M'Lennan, Max Müller, T. Huxley, Fustel de Coulanges, Freud, and the contemporary anthropologists Weston LaBarre (*The Ghost Dance*, 168–69), and Robin Horton, who distinguishes the modern from the nonliterate way of explaining things as follows (in John Saliba's paraphrase): "Western man uses things or objects as models, non-literate man prefers people. The reason for this preference is due to the fact that in non-literate societies the activities of people present the most markedly ordered and regulated area of their experience, whereas their control of nature is not sufficiently developed to be ordered and predictable" (John Saliba, '*Homo Religiosus*,' 97–98). Cf. Horton's discussion in "African Thought and Western Science," esp. pp. 146–47).

Hume's science was in principle open to correction and criticism, since he set no limit to what might be learned from further evidence and experience. His agenda could be summarized in three major problem areas: (1) what is the nature of the human, including psychological makeup, the capacities of the mind, and, ultimately, what distinguishes us from other animals?[45] (2) What experience or experiences are sufficient to account for the rise of religion? (Hume sketched some of these, but focused narrowly on the hypothetical individual—a sort of ideal type—confronting an uncertain future amidst the overwhelming powers that beset him.) (3) How are we to account for the formation, development, and variety of specific forms of belief, not to mention practice, about which Hume said nothing with reference to primitive humankind?

Because of the small selection of authors treated in this book, all of them could in some way be credited with being "pivotal." But I have reserved that distinction for Hume because he turned a real corner. The paradigm for the study of religion is built up over time. It includes essential intellectual moves such as objectification of religion as a problem (Bodin); the application of reason both to construct a universal understanding of religion (deism, suggesting the problem of definition of religion as such) *and* as a critical tool; and some temporal framework for constructing an overall theory (for instance, evolution). But Hume's thoroughgoing naturalism, his clear vision of religion as part of a science of humankind, and his development of alternatives to all the contemporary theological explanations of religion together warrant the paradigmatic role he is accorded here. He in effect closes an era of criticism and opens the paths of future research.

To prepare for what follows, we may note some gaps in Hume's project. The first is *evidence*—in a way the least serious, because he was aware of the lack, and it was easy to add to, revise, and enlarge his theories as new evidence was taken into account. Most of Hume's evidence came from his knowledge of the classics, as the documentation of the *Natural History* shows. His current anthropological evidence came from the observations of amateurs (in his day, every anthropologist was an "amateur"). Herbert of Cherbury had pointed out a century earlier that reports of peoples without any religion came from observers who did not even know the native languages of their subjects.

An excellent example of how amenable to revision by evidence Hume's treatise was, is the work of a contemporary and friend of his, Charles de Brosses, a French historian and major cultural figure. Following Fontenelle's lead, he caused a great scandal in 1760 by challenging the learned allegorists, both ancient and modern, who had treated ancient mythologies as profound symbolism, proposing instead that the earliest religion of mankind was just

45. "We do not have, even today, an agreed on definition of humankind. . . . " (Donald C. Johanson and Maitland A. Edey, *Lucy: The Beginnings of Humankind*, 100).

what it appeared to be from archeological evidence—the direct worship of plants and animals (de Brosses coined the term *fetishism* for this form of religion). De Brosses supported this theory by making a detailed comparison between contemporary primitive peoples of West Africa and the ancient Egyptians who, he argued, shared a devotion to plants and animals.[46] Frank Manuel discovered that de Brosses literally translated about twenty pages of Hume's *Natural History*[47] in order to provide a general explanatory framework for his thesis. In the present connection, de Brosses's text makes for interesting comparison with Hume's, because he frequently substitutes evidence for Hume's conjecture, and is self-conscious about doing so.[48]

De Brosses was credited by Tylor with being "the most original thinker of the last century,"[49] and gets honorable mention in some textbooks for his advance of the study of religion.[50] For our purposes he is significant on two further counts: first, because Auguste Comte would appropriate the theory of fetishism to characterize the first religious and mental state of humankind (of which more in the next chapter). Second, we find among nineteenth-century British anthropologists that the main evolutionary rival to Tylor's animistic thesis was an updated version of fetishism, represented by R. R. Marett.[51]

A second gap in Hume's work, and a surprising one in light of the strong social orientation of other representatives of the Scottish Enlightenment,[52] is the absence of any social component in Hume's reconstruction of the origin of religion. The social dimension of religion was of great interest to Hume for its functions and impact, but not for the idea that the *causes* of religion might be social. He did not try to envisage his aboriginal person as a social being, nor did he entertain the notion (already divined by Vico) that the

46. Charles de Brosses, *Du culte des dieux fétiches, ou Parallele de l'ancienne religion de l'Egypte avec la religion actuelle de Nigritie*, 1760.

47. Frank Manuel (above, n. 3), 188.

48. Among many examples, on p. 206 de Brosses (above, n. 46) substitutes "known" for Hume's "natural" in the sentence, "It seems certain that according to the known progress of human thought. . . . " Again, when Hume observes that affliction more quickly turns men to religion than does prosperity, de Brosses confirms: "This is a fact which experience with savages verifies. We know that they address themselves much more often to their fetishes to turn them away from doing them harm than to give thanks for benefits received" (221).

49. *Primitive Culture*, 2:144.

50. E.g., Jan de Vries, *The Study of Religion*, 32; E. E. Evans-Pritchard, *Theories of Primitive Religion*, 20; Frank Manuel (above, n. 3), 201.

51. R. R. Marett, *The Threshold of Religion*, 2d ed. 1914, 19–23. The less anthropomorphic character of this theory seemed superior to Tylor's animism for, as Marett asserts, "religious awe is towards powers, and . . . these are not necessarily spirits or ghosts, though they tend to become so" (22).

52. Contemporaries of Hume, e.g., John Millar, were engaged in accounting for the progress of humankind from savagery to civilization on more sociological and material grounds, but they did not yet think in terms of integrating religion into their accounts. Cf. A. C. Chitnis (above, n. 33), esp. chap. 5, "The Study of Social Man."

origin of religion must be inseparable from the beginnings of social institutions such as marriage or burial of the dead.

The most obvious reason for this omission is that Hume's point of departure was the "powers and faculties" of human nature, having always and only the individual in view. Further, he was formulating his theory of religious origins with critical reference to theological claims, and these led him in the direction of epistemology rather than toward proposing social origins for religion.

As a result, Hume not only did not connect human sociability with the origins of religion, he also did not share the view of others (including Vico) that religion is a component of the very establishment and maintenance of a social order. His (Protestant-shaped?) individualism, along with his generally critical outlook, appears to have made it quite easy for him to follow Bayle in imagining a society without any religion at all. Of considerable theoretical interest is that this same individualism made it easy for him to contest any claim of an intrinsic connection between religion and *morality*—a connection that is quite unavoidable if religion is derived from social sources, as we shall see in the next two chapters.[53]

Thus, it is no accident that Hume's anthropormorphic theory (as represented by British anthropologists) became the target of direct criticism by Emile Durkheim, who recognized the inadequacy of that theory to explain the rise of religious symbols which, he argued, are not simply enlarged projections of individual human volitions and powers, but representations of society's power.[54]

A third gap in Hume's analysis of religion was its lack of any theory of social dynamics or any developmental theory or framework that might encompass the whole story of humankind and place religion within it.[55] Hume's criticisms of theology, providence, and myth left a vacuum (so it appears in retrospect), to be filled only with the formulation of evolutionary theories by nineteenth-century thinkers. Emphasizing the paradigmatic importance of evolution, Eric Sharpe has located the beginnings of scientific study of religion exactly in the decades following the appearance of Charles Darwin's *Origin of Species* (1859). Sharpe writes: "Comparative religion (at first a synonym for the science of religion) did not exist in 1859; by 1869 it did."[56] Sharpe's approach exaggerates the importance of biology and Darwin, however, since British and Continental studies had been already for a century thoroughly informed by pre-Darwinian ideas of social evolution or progress. Moreover, as Sharpe knows, the so-called evolutionary anthropologists were not really Darwinians insofar as their theories of religion were concerned.

53. On Hume's decisive separation of morality from religion, see K. R. Merrill and D. G. Wester, "Hume on the Relation of Religion to Morality." We see the intrinsic moral implications of a sociological theory with Comte and Durkheim, below.
54. *The Elementary Forms of the Religious Life*, 198–203.
55. Cf. Manuel (above, n. 3), 178.
56. Eric J. Sharpe (above, n. 1), 28.

Fourth, and finally, because he had no interest in the *content* of religions, Hume had virtually nothing to say about interpretation of religious myths and symbols. Because he aimed to explain rather than to interpret, he did not try to bring the contents of religious myths into his realm of meaningful data. But he would certainly have agreed with Vico that interpretation depends on its explanatory presuppositions. As we have seen, Vico had been able to challenge the interpretations of ancient myth offered by the allegorists by reconstructing their context, which he regarded as their causal matrix, without understanding of which no historical interpretation could be valid. As the lived context in which myth is created, historical, psychological, and sociological materials provided indispensable data for explanation, and the only proper basis for interpretation as well.

PART IV

THE PROGRESS OF
REASON AND THE
SURVIVAL OF RELIGION

Chapter 6

Inventing Sociology:
Auguste Comte

Isadore Auguste Marie François Comte (1798–1857), the inventor of sociology, had a bad press in his own day; what little he has in ours is not much better. A man of prodigious intellectual ambition, he was engaged in a struggle with madness through about the last thirty years of his life—and many of his contemporaries thought he lost. His later writings—soporific, pretentious, verbose—are almost unreadable, much like those of his British counterpart, Herbert Spencer.[1] Spencer, in fact, expressed a widespread opinion about Comte when he observed that his work, "considered apart from the question of its truth . . . was a vast achievement."[2] This chapter will contest that assessment. Comte advanced the study of society and of religion's role in it to a new level, not merely with vastness, but with insight.

Comte's writing falls into two distinguishable phases, which we might call scientific and messianic (Comte himself characterized them as "Aristotelian" and "Pauline"). In the first, initiated in a series of programmatic essays in the 1820s and culminating in the *Cours de philosophie positive* (1830–42), he presented his new science of sociology, together with no less than a plan for the intellectual, moral, and political reconstruction of Europe—a program that a Francis Bacon *redivivus* and transplanted to postrevolutionary France might have conceived. In his second phase, embodied in the *System of Positive Polity* (1851–54), he undertook to serve as midwife and high priest of a new religion of humanity that could save mankind (more specifically, its avant garde, white Europe) from a threatening anarchy of spirit and body politic.[3]

Scholars have tended to treat seriously only the first, more sober and

---

1. Frank Manuel, *The Prophets of Paris*, 274.
2. Herbert Spencer, "Reasons for Dissenting from the Philosophy of Comte," 118.
3. I have used English translations throughout. Titles of the works cited, along with abbreviations used for documentation, are as follows: essays from the 1820s cited here are all in Ronald Fletcher, ed., *The Crisis of Industrial Civilisation*, including *Plan of the Scientific Operations Necessary for Reorganizing Society* (PSO; 1822); *Philosophical Considerations on the Sciences and Savants* (S&S; 1825); *Considerations on the Spiritual Power* (SP; 1826). *The Positive Philosophy* (CPP; completed 1842) is cited from the abridged translation of Harriet Martineau (1855). *The System of Positive Polity: Treatise on Sociology, Instituting the Religion of Humanity* (SPP): vol.

scientific phase of the work. But despite the problematic tone of the later writing, Comte's vision is all of a piece. The later writing, while not quite predictable from the earlier, is consistent with it. Comte throughout his career was grasped—obsessed, perhaps—by a paradoxical vision of his own particular moment in history. The paradox consists in his conviction of inexorable progress *and* profound crisis. On the positive side, he saw humankind poised for a final intellectual breakthrough as the outlook and method of positive science was about to take on its last and greatest challenge: understanding and reforming society. This science of society (which he names "social physics," then "sociology") would make possible a transformation of social life itself, for its point was not merely to understand society but to change it. On the negative side, however—and an equal cause of almost feverish excitement—was his sense of a crisis that was deeply intellectual, moral, spiritual, social, and political, and threatened to engulf Europe in anarchy.

This feeling of crisis was especially common, as one of Comte's best interpreters, Lucien Lévy-Bruhl, observes: people coming up in the early nineteenth century "never fail to put the same question to themselves: 'What social institutions should be established after the revolution?' and by this all understand not only the political form of government, but the very principles of social order. . . ."[4]

Comte was burdened not only with the question but, even more, with the answer: for he believed that his new science was the key to social reconstruction. Already in the early writings, then, there is an almost messianic, or perhaps utopian, strain: scientific interest is subordinated to social interest.[5] And the social crisis is from the beginning seen as a moral, or "spiritual," crisis. The old religion has gone the way of the old social and economic system; a new age demands something to replace it. In Comte's own words, from one of the early essays: "Manifestly, society, regarded from a moral point of view, is in a condition of real and profound Anarchy. . . . This anarchy results, in the last resort, from the absence of any preponderating system capable of uniting all minds in a communion of ideas" (*S&S*, 199).

Comte's consideration of religion is involved with both sides of this paradoxical vision of the historical situation. If, on one hand, we have progressed intellectually to the brink of a completely scientific age, something has to be said about the natural and deserved demise of theology; but if we are in a crisis that involves the "absence of any preponderating system capable of uniting all minds in a communion of ideas," something has to be found to *replace* theology, which traditionally fulfilled that very function. As Comte

---

1 (1851), trans. J. H. Bridges (1875); vol. 2 (1852), trans. Frederic Harrison (1875); vol. 4 (1854), trans. Richard Congreve (1877).

4. Lucien Lévy-Bruhl, *The Philosophy of Auguste Comte*, 2.

5. Ibid.

says in the same place, the solution involves "completing positive philosophy so as to make it capable of definitely replacing theology" (*S&S*, 200). This means that we must pay attention not only to his more "scientific" and historical analysis, which preponderates in the early writings, and which explains the progress of intellect from a primitive (theological) to a mature (scientific) state, but also to his attempt to construct a new religion on the basis of his insight that society requires it.

By treating both aspects of Comte's thought, we shall discover *two* theories of religion and be able to show a further advance in the study of religion, going beyond Hume and the British tradition. With Comte, we shall pick up the strands of Vico and of French thought issuing from Rousseau and Montesquieu, and from Comte's sometime mentor Saint-Simon, leading toward Durkheim, who acknowledged Comte as his master.

Like Hume, Comte explained religion. But, unlike Hume, explaining it did not mean explaining it away; on the contrary, Comte's profounder understanding of the social role of religion rendered it indispensable to his scheme for a new social order. Comte's attempt to *construct* a religion may be evidence of a certain madness; but more interesting for us is that the very attempt depends on his presumption that he fully understands the origins of religion—how it came into being. He knows how to explain it fully. (Here is Vico's "maker's knowledge" with a vengeance!) In this context of religion-construction, Comte raises the study of religion to a new level through his insight that it can be defined as an ideological complex that performs certain functions indispensable to society. This insight—that every society, including that of the future, must have at least the *functional equivalent* of religion—is one that only Vico, of our earlier authors, came close to understanding. Comte used the insight to overcome the paradox about religion (stemming from the originally paradoxical vision of the historical situation)—namely, that religion was *both* intellectually obsolete *and* socially necessary. Moreover, his evolutionary understanding of the subject matter of the new science (the science of man, sociology) led him to see religion as something which, along with all ideas and social forms, really evolves.

Thus, with the two ideas of evolution and functional equivalency, Comte solved the paradox of religion and carried the discussion of it beyond everybody: beyond the Christians, like Vico, who simply exempted Christianity from analysis (a move that would, if taken seriously, require the most severe intellectual compartmentalization); beyond the deists who, like Herbert, worked with an abstract, unevolved, steady-state definition of religion whose basic *content* allegedly perdured intact through every age (a view possible only by anachronistic interpretation of primitive cultures, and by reducing religion to ideas completely abstracted from cultural context); beyond the Humean criticism, which although intellectually devastating neglected to ask what religion might be accomplishing (beyond providing discredited interpretations of experience) to explain its stubborn vitality.

In what follows, I shall look first at Comte's general idea of science, with special attention to how it goes beyond Hume.[6] Its essential aim is to discover the laws that govern all of reality—and laws (Comte was convinced) *do* govern every level of reality. What distinguishes science from common sense is that science searches out these laws, including those that govern the actions of human beings. Comte insists that our formulations of these laws are relative, not absolute, because they are subject to testing and revision on the basis of observation. Every law, then, seems to be subject to revision, except, of course, the fundamental supposition that everything is subject to law.

Like Hume, Comte sees astronomy as the great scientific breakthrough and as a paradigm for how science ought to proceed. But he also sees, more clearly than the early Hume, that astronomy is the simplest science, and that social science—the final science—is vastly more complex,[7] appropriately "saved" for last at the top of the hierarchy of emerging sciences.

Astronomy was the first achievement to show the immense leap from common sense to science. While popular wisdom "is limited to empirical generalisations, a science such as . . . astronomy discovers the law which governs the whole of an immense order of phenomena."[8] Gradually, Comte observes, scientific progress has been broadening that mode of discovery, through physics, chemistry, biology, and physiology to Comte's own climactic invention of the final science, "sociology."[9] The scientific spirit and method can at last become universal. Knowledge can be consolidated through "a uniform manner of reasoning that is applicable to all the subject matters that the human spirit can occupy itself with."[10]

Because science is controlled through observation, not imagination, Comte recognizes that there will be a qualitative difference between the kinds of observations, and kinds of laws, formulated for different realms of reality. He is not a reductionist in the sense that all reality will be reduced, say, to the laws of physics.[11] The laws that Comte will formulate for social science are peculiarly fitted to that realm of reality, being derived from observation of social facts, which have their own irreducible and historical integrity. When we come to an examination of the basic law applicable to the social realm (the law of the three stages), its independence of natural-science "models" will be very clear.

6. I have found Lévy-Bruhl (above, n. 4), especially part 1, basic for Comte's understanding of science.

7. Ronald Fletcher, introduction to *The Crisis of Industrial Civilization: The Early Essays of Auguste Comte*, 30, emphasizes the fact that Comte did not think sociology could be reduced to the simpler sciences.

8. Lévy-Bruhl (above, n. 4), 63.

9. So called in *CPP*, 535.

10. Gertrude Lenzer, ed., *Auguste Comte and Positivism*, Introduction, xlviii.

11. For a discussion and criticism of that view of science, see Marjorie Grene, "Reducibility: Another Side Issue?"

Although there is a hierarchy of sciences, Comte repeatedly contrasts the procedures of science to those of theology and metaphysics. In general, the former depends upon observation and discovery, the latter on imagination and invention (*PSO*, 140, 153; this is not, however, a claim in favor of pure empiricism, as we shall see). More specifically, theological and/or metaphysical social theories are inferior to scientific ones because they are *absolutist*, with two consequences: being such, they fail to see the necessity of correlating social theories with the actual state of civilization, and they fail to take account of the fact that the dynamics of civilization itself are controlled by laws immanent to the historical process. As Comte summarizes it, the criticism of theologico-metaphysical attempts to define and create the best society

> essentially resolves itself into two considerations. As regards method it consists in the preponderance of imagination over observation. As regards general ideas destined to guide the operations, it consists, on one hand, in a purely abstract consideration of social organisation, regarded as independent of the state of civilisation, and, on the other hand, in viewing the progress of civilisation as not being subject to any law [but rather, to the mere will of the theoretician, or of the proposed government]. (*PSO*, 140)

Moreover, theology and metaphysics have been too addicted to identifying the ultimate origins and causes of things. We will catch ourselves, he says, "occasionally yielding to the infantine curiosity which pretends to a power of knowing the origin and the end of all things," when we should rather be concentrating on "study of the laws of phenomena" (*CPP*, 526). From this, we would expect Comte's explanation of religion to show the operation of some law that should not on its face seem to require any inquiry about the origins of religion. However, Comte does in fact take us back to first beginnings—not because he is inconsistent, but because the laws that govern *society* are historical or evolutionary. So even though the search for "the absolute origin and the absolute end of things"[12] has been eliminated, we must have at least a hypothetical account of the beginnings of thought itself.

Comte thus proposes that the peculiar laws appropriate to a science of society require profound study of the entire human past, including origins so far as it is possible to recover them (he would not understand what an ahistorical sociology would think it was doing). Only in this way can we identify those fundamental tendencies in history that have resulted in the complex present, tendencies which must be known in order for us to prepare intelligently for the future. Some people, he complains, "may suppose that this historic investigation [to determine how the progress of civilization is to be regulated] need not be pushed back to the origin of civilised society, but that it will suffice to consider its present condition" (*PSO*, 150).

12. *SPP*, 71. Cf. Bruce Mazlish, *The Riddle of History*, 196, 205; Marvin Harris, *The Rise of Anthropological Theory*, 60; Gertrude Lenzer (above, n. 10), liv.

This will not do at all. We must start at the point where the human condition was "barely superior to that of a society of great apes" (*S&S*, 192). Or, as Vico might have said, we must return to the place where the subject matter has its beginning. This is because "the observation of the present state of civilisation considered by itself, can no more determine the actual tendencies of society than the study of any other isolated epoch can do" (*PSO*, 151). Any "laws" having to do with society will have to embrace its entire past, for relevant and useful laws are—must be—laws of development; they must expose that pattern of social evolution which explains the present. The present crisis, in all its confusion, can be sorted out only with that recognition in mind:

> In the midst of such confusion it is entirely beyond the grasp of the human mind to make a clear and exact analysis, or to frame real and precise statistics of the body politic, unless it be enlightened by the past. . . . We therefore are bound to study, as profoundly and completely as possible, all the states through which civilisation has passed, from its origin to the present time. (*PSO*, 152)

These "states of civilisation" consist of material and mental components in reciprocal relationships, but with ideas given primacy in the dynamics of history. As he says in the *Cours*, "It cannot be necessary to prove to anybody who reads this work that Ideas govern the world, or throw it into chaos; in other words, that all social mechanisms rest upon Opinions" (*CPP*, 36).

But Comte is not an idealist, or any kind of believer in some Absolute Idea that "realizes" itself through historical means. There are ideas, and they are powerful, but their power (aside from the question of their truth) depends upon the state of the civilization that provides their context and legitimation. Intellect and society "are not independent, but, on the contrary, exercise a reciprocal influence indispensable to each of them" (*S&S*, 186). Not that it is impossible for certain ideas to be *thought* apart from appropriate contexts, but that it is impossible for them to have any impact upon society unless they conform to the state of civilization, which includes the economic, political, and technological state of things, as well as the intellectual (e.g., *PSO*, 142; *S&S*, 186).[13]

Social science, then, will be historical; its search for laws will depend on a profound understanding of the course—the progress—of civilization since its beginnings. Moreover, it will require for its operation some hypotheses,

---

13. Mazlish (above, n. 12) disputes the opinions of Manuel and Hayek that Comte and Hegel are in essential agreement in their idealism: "with all this impressive evidence for the view that Comte and Hegel are alike, I shall take the position that their differences are more important than their likenesses. Comte's positivism is quite removed from Hegel's idealism, and traces back logically through Condorcet to a Humean empiricism, whereas Hegel harks back to Kant's idealistic epistemology. From these bases, the two thinkers press on in vastly different ways. . . . Comte and Hegel, rather than being fundamentally in agreement, are better thought of as standing in a rather loose thesis-antithesis relationship; and, to pursue the metaphor all the way, they find their synthesis in Karl Marx" (184–85).

or theories. Comte's criticism of Bacon, for whom he had great respect, is his misplaced faith in pure induction. Such procedure, Comte argues, "is impossible. Unless man connects facts with some explanation, he is naturally incapable not merely of combining and making deductions from them, but even of observing and recollecting them. In a word, it is as impossible to make continuous observations without a theory of some kind, as to construct a positive theory without continuous observations" (S&S, 185).[14] "Science" consists not in collecting and observing data until one thinks up a theory to "explain" it all. On the contrary, facts are constituted as "data" only when they are put to work testing a theory, however primitive or misguided. For Comte, this truth is confirmed by history itself; from the very beginning, fruitful observation of nature—any advance in knowledge at all—has proceeded only on the basis of some theory, even though it was a fictitious one requiring correction and eventual abandonment. Theories come and go, but theories there must be, for observations made without them are of no scientific significance whatever.[15]

The social law for which Comte is best known is evolutionary and consists in three stages through which the human mind has passed en route to its present "positive" condition. The first of these stages is the theological, in which the forces of nature are personified as gods; then the metaphysical, a transitional phase in which the gods are replaced by abstract transcendental entities and causes; and finally the scientific or positive, in which all the dynamics of nature and society are understood as conforming to immanent laws. This scheme merits attention, not only because of the importance Comte himself attributed to it, but because an evolutionary framework provided the first temporal paradigm through which modern sociological and anthropological study of religion really came into its own as a new discipline.[16]

We have already seen Comte's insistence that social life cannot be understood without a full documentation of its past. We have also seen that for him theory must precede the collection of data. More specifically, some lawlike relationship among the various epochs of human history must be hypothesized in order accurately to identify what trends are most powerful now and for the future. Comte credits Condorcet with recognizing this (PSO, 160). The state of affairs that seems to require such an explanation is the undeniable advance of civilization—"progress."

14. Cf. CPP, 27, 525, and what Thomas Kuhn says about paradigms: The Structure of Scientific Revolutions, e.g., 85, 109, 111–18, etc. Comte's anticipation of Kuhn is remarkable.

15. Larry Laudan, "Towards a Reassessment of Comte's 'Methode Positive,' " 41. Cf. Marvin Harris (above, n. 12), who asserts that Comte's understanding of the relationship between theory and fact is "fundamentally correct" (61).

16. Eric J. Sharpe, Comparative Religion, a History, 26–28, hinges his historical survey on evolutionary theory as the watershed for the rise of the conception of comparative religion as a science in the decade 1859–69.

The advance of civilisation, notwithstanding unfavorable political combination, clearly proves that civilisation is *governed by a natural law of progress,* independent of all combinations, and dominating them. If this principle were denied, in order to explain such a fact ... we could only have recourse to direct continuous supernatural guidance, after the fashion of theological politics. (*PSO,* 144; italics mine)

But what warrant do we have for arranging the past into stages, or epochs? History has no seams. Comte's answer to this question comes close to Weber's idea about rationalization, but even closer to Kuhn's notion of paradigm changes. What justifies our periodization, Comte says in effect, are paradigm shifts that we can detect through careful study of the past.[17] Explaining the emergence of polytheism from fetishism (the first two phases of the "theological" era), Comte writes: "The great revolution that carried men on from fetishism to polytheism is due to the same mental causes, though they may not be so conspicuous, that now produce all scientific revolutions,—which always arise out of a discordance between facts and principles" (*CPP,* 558).[18]

Thus, any set of principles that unifies an era and generates knowledge spurs investigation; but investigation and experience in turn gradually expose anomalies, until finally a new set of principles replaces the old one, and the process goes on at a new level.

But why must *any "law" at all* be operating? Comte believes that something must be postulated to replace the notion of providence. Only so can we explain what Fontenelle and Vico had noted, the remarkable parallel developments in various nations that had no contact with each other (e.g., North American Indians and Homeric Greeks; *PSO,* 144–45). Such developments "could only have been produced under the influence of a natural progress of civilisation uniformly applicable to all nations as resulting from the fundamental laws of human organisation, common to all" (*PSO,* 144–45).

How Comte conceives the evolutionary dynamic of this law (or these laws) is not very clear. He seems finally to appeal to the instincts of human nature rather than to some sociological law as suggested by the above quotation. For example, when he talks about the law of progress, he claims that it "necessarily results from the instinctive tendency of the human race to perfect itself. Consequently [he concludes] it is as completely independent of our

---

17. Thomas Kuhn argues that science evolves not by a smooth cumulative process but sporadically as periods of "normal science" punctuated by paradigm shifts, or scientific revolutions, which involve "reconstruction of the field from new fundamentals" (above, n. 14, 85).

18. Comte spells this out as follows: the emerging capacity of abstracting species-similarities led to the abandonment of fetishism, which sees individual things as animated, for polytheism, according to which the gods, now more abstract and general in jurisdiction, preside over classes of things. This in turn has the added result of gradually "disenchanting" nature (*CPP* 558–59).

control as are the individual instincts the combination of which produces this permanent tendency" (*PSO*, 146).

Comte's master theory is that this law of progress realizes itself in the way minds (or mentalities) pass, always and necessarily, in civilizations, in social groups, and in individuals, through three distinguishable stages. How Comte knows this is not entirely clear, but it is a discovery as important for him as was Vico's discovery, for Vico, that the ancients were poets. For Comte, this law expresses the very nature of the human intellect, and he thinks that the course of both individual and historical development supports his contention of its universality and necessity. "From the nature of the human intellect each branch of knowledge in its development is necessarily obliged to pass through three different theoretical states: the Theological or fictitious state; the Metaphysical or abstract state; lastly the Scientific or positive state" (*PSO*, 134).

Moreover, as Condorcet held, "the development of the race—being only the resultant of individual development passing from one generation to another—should, of necessity, present a general likeness to the natural history of the individual" (*PSO*, 175).

Because this is so, the study of the individual, though subordinate to that of society, has its place in sociology, for individual careers recur everywhere and always, while societies are discrete and unrepeatable. Thus, "owing to this analogy [between individual and species] the study of man, considered by himself, supplies certain means of verification and reasoning, as regards study of the race . . . which [means] . . . have the advantage of embracing all epochs" (*PSO*, 175). This notion, when given biological reinforcement and status later on, would be of fundamental importance for Freud's theory of religion.

Regarding this analogy, Comte asserts that "all thoughtful persons can verify for themselves its operation in individual development, from infancy to manhood" (*CPP*, 522).[19] On his own behalf, Comte submits this modest report: "Emancipated from theology before the end of childhood, and trained betimes in positive studies, I passed rapidly through the metaphysical period. At the age of twenty-two my philosophical career was opened by a work on the coordination of history, and two years afterwards my discovery of sociological laws irrevocably fixed its course."[20]

These "proofs" of the theory are validated further by historical observations—especially regarding the variety and conflict of points of view in his

19. Further references include *CPP*, 26–27, 545; *PSO*, 175, where Comte credits Condorcet with the idea.

20. Quoted by Gertrude Lenzer (above, n. 10), 311, from Comte's autobiographical sketch (*SPP*, I, preface, xiii–xiv). E. B. Tylor fully agrees with this idea, in the context of his own quotation of Hume and Comte (*Primitive Culture*, 1: 477–78).

own contemporary society, and the world's variety from place to place. For Comte, variation seemed to offer verification of development:

> This science ... possesses general resources for verification ... based on the fact that in the present condition of the human race ... all degrees of civilisation coexist on different points of the globe, from that of the New Zealand savages to that of the French and English [presumed to be civilized]. Thus the connection established by the succession of epochs can be verified by a comparison of places. (*PSO*, 177)

Overall, the data of history and of individual development seem to confirm the fundamental thesis that the whole past must be studied, and segmented into meaningful epochs, in order to understand the present or to deal with it an effective way, for

> observation of the present state of civilisation, considered by itself, can no more determine the actual tendencies of society, than the study of any other isolated epoch can do. The reason for this is, that the existence of a law cannot be established by a single term. Three terms, at least, are needed in order that the connection ascertained by comparing the two first, and verified by the third, may serve to reveal the following ones. (*PSO*, 151)

Turning now at last to Comte's understanding of religion, we must observe first that, in its fullest statement, Comte's law of the three stages embraces not only epochs in the progress of *mind* (focusing on its explanatory theories about the world), but also follows the evolution of the basic social structures that match up with the idea-system. Thus we have the Theological-military, the Metaphysical-feudal, and the Positive-industrial stages. The three-stage law is thus at once a theory of intellectual and social or institutional development. This is of crucial importance for us, because finally Comte's (implicit) definitions and explanations of religion are of two different sorts, depending on which of the two sides he has in mind in any given discussion, the intellectual or the social. As noted above, religion seems on one side to be obsolete, and on the other, necessary. We need to examine this paradox further.

Comte is constantly aware of the intimate relationship between ideas and society: the three stages are constituted by the basic types of ideas that have served, over whole epochs, to organize and advance knowledge *and* to unify society and legitimate its institutions. The two functions are never far apart in Comte's mind.

For example, when he describes the first or Theological epoch, he considers both aspects as follows: first, the epistemological: "In the first state supernatural ideas serve to bind the small number of isolated observations which then constitute science. In other words, the facts observed are explained, that is to say, conceived *a priori*, by means of invented facts. Such is the necessary state of all knowledge in its infancy. With all its imperfections this forms the only mode of connecting facts possible at that epoch" (*PSO*, 134). For example, merely sensing thunder is not knowledge, but hearing it as the

threatening voice of the gods is knowledge, because it combines theory and
rudimentary observation.

The theological stage *had* to come first in line, because it alone could be
created entirely out of the imagination, prior to any systematic observation.
Thus,

> the earliest advances of the human intellect could not be effected in any other way
> than the theological method, the only one susceptible of spontaneous development.
> It alone possessed the important property of presenting from the outset a provisional
> theory, vague and arbitrary, it is true, but direct and easy, which immediately
> grouped the primary facts and, by cultivating our faculties of observation, prepared
> the advent of a positive philosophy. (*S&S*, 185)

But in addition to enabling the very dawn of knowledge, the theological
idea also served a unifying social function (otherwise it would not deserve to
be designated as that idea which characterizes a whole epoch); and we would
not be wrong to characterize this function as "religious": "no real and coherent society can form and maintain itself except under the influence of
some system of ideas, fitted to surmount the opposition of individualising
tendencies, always so strong at the outset, and to make these concur in
maintaining a settled order. . . . " (*S&S*, 187). We must therefore give proper
credit, he would say, to the theological philosophy, even though its time is
past: "To it we must naturally ascribe the original establishment of all social
organisation" (*S&S*, 187), as well as the beginning of the progress of thinking.

We shall follow both strands of Comte's thinking, because in the end they
will yield two different ways of explaining religion. When we recount his
version of the origin of religion at the dawn of the "theological" age, we find
religion explained rather like Hume explained it. But when we explore the
sociological vein of Comte's thought, we encounter the idea that, although
the traditional theology is no longer plausible, its psychological and social
functions demand to be carried out in some way. This trend is richly elaborated in Comte's account of modern history, his analysis of the present
crisis, and his prescription of a new religion of the Great Being. Here, his
explanation of religion will anticipate Durkheim.

First, then, the origin of religion.

Comte subdivides the theological age into three periods, the first being
that of "fetishism." This first stage arises from the fundamental human need
to reduce the world to some kind of rational order, a need that expresses
itself necessarily, first, in a "fictitious" or theological fashion.

To account more precisely for the appearance of fetishism, primarily as a
form of explanation, Comte draws directly on Hume, although the term
fetishism is a coinage of Hume's French contemporary Charles de Brosses
(see chapter 5). De Brosses incorporated parts of Hume's *Natural History of
Religion* into his own work on primitive fetish gods, as we have already seen.

"Fetishism [Comte writes] . . . allowed free exercise to that tendency of our nature by which man conceives of all external bodies as animated by a life analogous to his own, with differences of mere intensity" (*CPP*, 545). This notion, Comte asserts, is supported "by all the precise information that we can obtain of the earliest social period" (*CPP*, 545). Fetishism is the beginning of theology, arising as man obeys "his propensity to transfer to outward objects the sense of existence which served him for an explanation of his own phenomena, and therefore for an absolute explanation of all out of himself" (*CPP*, 547). More precisely, and of critical importance for differentiating the theological from the positive type of paradigm, fetishism supposes "external bodies, even the most inert, to be animated by passion and will, more or less analogous to the personal impressions of the spectator" (*CPP*, 546). As with Hume, the motivation to do this is to trace the appearance of "unknown effects" to their causes (*CPP*, 547). The universe is conceived of as the product of will(s), not law(s)—that is the essential thing.

In explaining *why* the anthropomorphic response is a "primary tendency of man," Comte anticipates Freud, as he refers again to the individual's life history, wherein each person begins "by supposing himself the centre of all things" (*CPP*, 523). The infantile illusion of omnipotence gives fetishism its "spontaneous origin" (*CPP*, 524), whereby the person imagines himself

> in all respects, the center of the natural system, and consequently endowed with an indefinite control over phenomena. This opinion, it is evident, results directly from the supremacy exercised by the imagination, combined with the natural tendency which disposes men in general to form exaggerated ideas of their own importance and power. Such an illusion constitutes the most prominent characteristic of the infancy of human reason. (*PSO*, 138)

Thus, child and primitive human both imagine that the causal mechanism of the world is like his own, in which "all phenomena are regulated by superhuman will" (*CPP*, 526). Only much later, when he has been *disillusioned*, does man begin to understand that all phenomena are regulated not by wills but by laws. And that is the first principle of the positive philosophy.

Despite the illusory structure and nature of fetishistic thinking, Comte evaluates it entirely differently from Hume, and here surfaces an essential difference between the latter's critical spirit and the constructive passion of Comte: fetishism, for Comte, is the essential and productive first step in man's evolutionary journey. Despite its inability to advance knowledge very far, it did "initiate everything":

> It . . . succeeded in completing one great step in human progress, one quite in accordance with its nature, and the necessary starting point of our whole intellectual advance. . . . The human intellect required this first step to awaken it. It drew from our natural affections [i.e., the propensity to personalize everything] the earliest hypotheses which were capable of connecting and guiding our observations, these having at that time no rational guide whatever. (*SPP*, II, 78)

Not only is fetishism credited with launching the intellectual career of humankind by providing a theory that enabled thinking, but it embodied a principle that has been recovered only in modern times, after a long reign of theisms and metaphysics. These systems bifurcated the world, adding on top of the animated world of fetishistic nature "an invisible world, peopled by superhuman agents, who occasion all phenomena by their action on matter, otherwise inert" (*CPP*, 525; cf. 558). Despite the necessity and plausibility (in its time) of this development, it turns out that "at bottom the fetishist reasoner . . . is less distant from scientific truth than the theological dreamer who in spite of all the evidence, persists in taking matter to be passive" (*SPP*, II, 75). Behold, then, the inner compatibility of the fetishist with our modern scientific selves: against the theologians who represent to us "these immense beings [of nature] as purely passive *under wills external to them*" (*SPP* IV, 188; my italics), we now recognize and admire, like the fetishists of old, the power of order which is *immanent* in nature. In fact, we do so (as a sentimentalizing, older Comte puts it) "in a higher degree than the fetishists, with the involuntary gratitude which corresponds to our appreciation of the universal order, an appreciation especially resting on experience" (*SPP*, IV, 188).

The advance of the theological age was marked by the move first to polytheism and then to monotheism, each reflecting important progress. The latter move represents "an admirable simplification of theological philosophy," which turned the mind increasingly to the study of nature, for it "reduced the action of the chief supernatural power, in each special case, to a certain general direction, the character of which was unavoidably vague. Thus the human mind was authorised, and even strongly impelled, to study the physical laws of each class of phenomena regarded as a mode of action of this power" (*S&S*, 185).

The advance of intellect finally overthrew theology, then metaphysics, bringing about a complete *reversal* of the ancient anthropomorphism. Having discovered that external reality is in fact governed by impersonal and necessary laws, it learned, gradually, to apply these laws to persons and to human society, giving rise to the human sciences. This great reversal is described as follows: "In the early ages men transferred to the external world the expressions proper to human acts; whereas now we apply to the phenomena of life [including human] terms originally appropriated to inert nature, thus showing that the scientific spirit, which looks from without inward, is more and more influencing human language" (*CPP*, 549). The proof of man's intellectual "maturity" is the ability to "apply the study of external nature to his own" (*CPP*, 524).

Thus, in place of the projection of the human will onto the realm of natural causes, Comte sees modern science as the application, or "introjection," of natural-law analysis even into the explanation of human behavior. The impersonal laws of physical nature, rather than the spontaneous impulses of the psyche, become the normative model for all theories of reality. Comte regards this as "the most precious result of our intelligence"—the discovery that an immutable natural order is "the only solid ground which can apply to the whole of our nature, individual or collective" (*SPP*, II, 27).

This is sufficient for us to see how, in Comte's way of thinking, theology has run its course and given way to other modes of explaining the world. Inexorably, the "positive" mode has taken over (after a transitional period of metaphysical thinking, with which we need not concern ourselves here). If we think of religion as necessarily accompanied by theology of some sort, it would seem, taking Comte's thought this far, that religion is as obsolete as theology. But when we turn from considering religion as explanation, via theological theory, to religion as a unitive element of any society, it is a different story.

The importance of this second perspective on religion emerges as we pursue how the law of the three stages functions in his thought. It will be recalled that the purpose of Comte's historical sociology was to clarify the contemporary social situation so that appropriate action could be taken and crisis averted. The three-stage law is invoked exactly for that purpose: "the existing disorder is abundantly accounted for by the existence, all at once, of three incompatible philosophies—the theological, the metaphysical, and the positive. Any one of these might alone secure some sort of social order; but while the three co-exist, it is impossible for us to understand one another upon any essential point whatever" (*CPP*, 36).

A profound study of history shows, however, that as a matter of "incontestable fact" the positive philosophy alone "has been advancing during a course of centuries, throughout which the others have been declining" (*CPP*, 36). Here is one side of the now-familiar paradox: progress. The other side—crisis—is next analyzed in terms of a shorter "three-age" perspective beginning in the Middle Ages. It is from this analysis that religion derives its new lease on life as a social force.

The present crisis must be understood historically as it developed out of (first) the theological-military, or Catholic-feudal age, then the transitional age of critical philosophy (sixteenth to eighteenth centuries, from the Reformation through the Revolution), and the positive-industrial age, now pending the solution of the present crisis.

The first of these three eras (the medieval) was a great constructive period in which ideology and society were in tune with each other because a common faith underwrote social institutions and gave civilization coherence. The third and present age has the same potential, as yet awaiting its fulfillment. What was not understood in the middle period was that it was entirely lacking in such constructive social potential. Its critical and destructive power was necessary to make way for a new age, but the critical philosophy itself was incapable of providing the basis for a new order. Its "purely critical spirit" has fulfilled its necessarily destructive mission, through such new doctrines as the reformation cry for "unlimited liberty of conscience." "Regarded simply as a means of combatting the theological system the dogma in question favours the progress of the human mind. But it ceases to do so and loses all its value when conceived as a basis for the great social reorganisation reserved for our epoch" (*PSO*, 115).

Equally unsuitable as a basis for a new social order, Comte insists, is the political notion of popular sovereignty. For our purposes, however, two other criticisms by Comte are of more importance: the Enlightenment's unduly negative view of the past and its illusion that a new society could be built *without* what Comte calls a "spiritual power."

The first criticism alerts us to the distance between Comte and some of his eighteenth century predecessors. They tended—especially when dealing with religion—to regard past epochs as in all respects retrograde rather than progressive. But if they are correct in this view of the past, "we are landed in a perpetual miracle, and the progressive march of civilisation becomes an effect without a cause" (*PSO*, 165). Comte thinks he has a better and more scientific way of evaluating past eras:

> We should regard institutions and doctrines as having reached, at every period, the greatest perfection compatible with the corresponding civilisation. . . . In a final analysis, then, instead of regarding the past as a tissue of monstrosities, we should, generally speaking, consider society as having been, on the whole, guided with all the wisdom which the situation allowed. (*PSO*, 165)

After all, "the human mind has not continued down to our time in a state of madness" (*PSO*, 184)!

This more generous view of the past includes a willingness to reassess the value of religion. And this leads to Comte's second criticism of the critical philosophers: their denial of the necessity of any "spiritual power" in society: "we see how profoundly vicious is that disposition with which the critical philosophy has imbued nearly all minds, and which disposes men to conceive the new social order as subsisting without any spiritual power" (*SP*, 234, cf. 239). But what exactly is "spiritual power"? Is it the "religious dimension" in the vaguest sense—that is, the presence of some unifying idea, aim, or loyalty? Clearly it is more than that, in Comte's mind. For him, it is the most precious legacy of the Middle Ages, which Comte is bold to defend against the almost universal disapproval of the leading minds of the critical period. The spiritual power of medieval invention was an institutionalized class of leaders—in the feudal age, priests—charged with the care and keeping of all theoretical matters, and—most important—*independent* of the political arm of society. Medieval society, Comte writes, was

> vivified and consolidated by the creation of a spiritual power, distinct and independent of the temporal power . . . which maintained towards the latter the natural attitude of a theoretical towards a practical authority, modified of course by the special character of the ancient system. This great and beautiful conception was

the principal cause of the admirable vigour and consistency which distinguished the Feudo-Catholic system during its flourishing period. (*PSO*, 126)

What medieval priests once did, scientific men are to do now: the *savants* are commissioned (perhaps *ordained* is the right word in this context) to fulfill the role of the medieval *sacerdotium*. Above the parochial concerns of nationality, they are united by easy means of communication and mutual understanding; they possess common ideas, a uniform language, common and permanent aims (*PSO*, 132). Through control of education, they will manage the future government of opinion, be custodians of knowledge and social morality. In fact, their most important aim will be to fuse the greatest number of citizens into "one moral communion" (*SP*, 229). especially by cultivating in people "the social point of view" (*SP*, 237). This is especially needed in an age of rampant individualism and self-centeredness, encouraged by the critical philosophy.

> Minds, no longer united by any real bond, diverge on all essential points, with that license which unregulated individualism must produce. Hence the entire absence of public morality; the universal spread of egotism; the preponderance of considerations purely material; and, as a last inevitable consequence, corruption erected into a system of government, as being the only kind of order applicable to a population become deaf to all appeals made in the name of a general ideal and alive only to the voice of private interest. (*S&S*, 199)

This rampant egoism calls for a strong moral arm in society. But Comte is not just preaching. Behind those sentiments lies a real theory of how society works. His reflection on history seems to have been the source of this theory, which he manages at one point to compress into one remarkable paragraph from *Considerations on the Spiritual Power* (1826). Here he maintains that "the whole" of society must find ways to exert on "the parts" sufficient influence "to make them converge towards the general order from which they always tend naturally to deviate" when left to their own devices. This "influence" may be either "directive" or "repressive," or both, and it may be exerted in one of two ways (corresponding exactly to what was earlier described as the medieval distinction between temporal and spiritual power): through "material" or "moral" means.

"Material" influence is ultimately based on *force* or, "what comes to the same thing" in modern industrial states, *wealth*. "The second [influence, the moral] consists in the regulation of opinion, sentiment and will, in a word of tendencies. Its basis is that moral authority which in the last resort belongs to intellectual superiority and knowledge. In this way the two great inequalities [in wealth and knowledge] on which all society is based concur to maintain social order" (*SP*, 227).

We are moving in the direction of Durkheim and Freud. Indeed, Comte's notion of repression, while far from psychoanalytically grounded, recognizes that civilization causes discontent by the "continuous state of sacrifice" that it requires from individuals: "each person . . . must experience . . . a certain degree of sacrifice without which it [society] could not maintain itself, having regard to the opposition of individual tendencies which is, in some degree, absolutely inevitable" (*SP*, 236). Repression of sexuality is recognized as one of the most important tasks; it requires the existence of a spiritual authority (*SP*, 241).

In sum, Comte has consigned theological thought to the oblivion it deserves in light of the inexorable evolution of mind. But he has also perceived that society requires powerful unifying and repressive structures to make it work. Thus, though traditional religion with its theological legitimations and self-definition is impossible for the learned,[21] some sort of religion seems necessary.

As Raymond Aron summarizes: "Every society necessarily involves consensus, agreement between groups, agreement between individuals, a unifying principle. Religion is this unifying principle."[22]

But an obstacle stands in the way. The new truth system being constituted by modern science lacks an essential element of the older theological system, especially in its earliest phase—emotional appeal. Comte recognized the importance of feeling in his early essays; in his later "messianic" phase, he outdoes himself in his efforts to make his idea of the Great Being emotionally attractive. Let us briefly follow this line of thought, since it contributes to a full understanding of how Comte understands and explains religion.

As a young advocate of the new positive worldview, Comte was aware that some means needed to be found, most appropriately through the office of the fine arts, to appeal to people's passions by presenting them with a "vivid picture" of the new order (*PSO*, 156). This was no problem in earlier ages. "The preponderance of the affective over the intellectual life, always conspicuous, was in its full strength in the earliest stages of the human mind. The empire of the passions over the reason, favorable to theology at all times, is yet more favorable to fetish theology than to any other" (*CPP*, 548).

The link which Comte sees between the passions and religion is not, finally, regarded as a liability, as it was with Hume. The personal nature of fetish religion gave it a powerful and harmony-creating emotional appeal: "All substances being immediately personified, and endowed with passions, powerful in proportion to the energy of the phenomena, the external world

---

21. Comte makes an exception for some people of high culture, however—those emotionally unstable types liable to be plunged "by some passion of hope or fear into the radical fetishism—personifying, and then deifying, even the most inert objects that can interest their roused sensibilities" (*CPP*, 548).

22. Raymond Aron, *Main Currents in Sociological Thought*, 1:108. Cf. *SPP*, 16–17, where religion in its "true sense" is described as "a complete unity, whereby all the motives of conduct within us are reduced to a common object, whilst our conduct as a whole submits with freedom to the Necessity imposed by a power without."

presented to the observer a spectacle of such perfect harmony... which yielded him a satisfaction to which we cannot even give a name...." (*CPP*, 548).

Yet, inexorably, the rationalizing intellect undermined the plausibility of the old system and robbed it of further value; for "it is the intellect which in the end determines the character of religion for the individual, and still more for the race" (*SPP*, II, 24). But the affective needs which fetish religion fulfilled are still there—and these must be fulfilled in some way.

This sets the stage for how the older Comte defines and proposes to meet the social crisis of his time. Our source here is the late work *System of Positive Polity* (1852ff.), part of whose subtitle is *Instituting the Religion of Humanity*. Here, Comte sees the heart of the crisis as the rupture between man's cognitive and affective life (between what he knows and what he loves). The primeval unity of knowledge and affect has been irreparably broken. What man knows about nature is one thing; that to which he can attach his emotions and imagination is quite another. That split, Comte believes, opened up radically with the breakdown of the medieval worldview. By degrees, the modern study of nature rendered useless all theological and metaphysical explanations of things,[23] revealing a world of lawlike regularity which—however admirable—was not *lovable*. "The [new] Order based on reality," Comte observes, "was unable to satisfy the emotions so well as the Order based on fictions" (*SPP*, II, 47).

Comte now is convinced that some "adequate combination" of belief and affection is a sine qua non of social viability and harmony. The older Comte begins at length to sound like his namesake Augustine of Hippo in calling for a reunification of the objects of belief and love. In fact, he finally proposes a new religion through which modern persons may recover the lost capacity not only to believe what they love, but to love what they believe (to use Augustinian language).[24]

Science has radically depersonalized the universe, and rightly so. But who can regard abstract laws with affection and devotion? How can psychic unity be restored? Comte's first statement of a solution sounds almost like a recantation—a proposal to reanthropomorphize the universe. He says: "this final statement of the problem also indicates its natural solution. It is this: to invest with a moral purpose that natural Economy; which at first is to us but a merely physical, and then becomes an intellectual system" (*SPP*, II, 46). But how possibly can the new cosmos, unimaginably vast and governed not by provident will but by inexorable impersonal laws, be reinvested with

---

23. Lucien Lévy-Bruhl (above, n. 4), 31–32 provides a fuller discussion.

24. Cf. *SPP*, 1:46, where the "crucial problem" to be solved by religion is to reconcile belief with affection. "When belief directly conspires with affection, human unity will be fully established.... We ... perceive the extreme difficulty of reconciling the two, a difficulty which forms indeed the crucial problem to be solved by true religion."

moral purpose? The answer is: by attaching our affection to that place where "moral purpose" *really exists:* humanity. Humanity itself, the "Great Being," is a new and worthy object of affection. But how can this make sense? If humanity itself must submit to nature's laws, how can it take the place of *theology's* "great being(s)"? Answer: it does so insofar as it masters nature and thus gains direct control of man's destiny—"submitting itself [to be sure] to the conditions in which it exists, but modifying them by its own wisdom" (*SPP*, II, 51). Belief in humanity, confidence in its future as our *own* "providence," thus "becomes thoroughly in harmony with the affections; for it directs towards this Great Being, whose property is sympathy, all the homage which is due to the beneficent control of the Order of nature" (*SPP*, II, 51).

Humanity is not only learning to control nature to an increasing extent, but it embodies something lovable that nature lacks—the "property of sympathy," which seems to mean: we humans love ourselves, and, through long struggle, have mastered nature for our own benefit. Our knowledge is not only power, but *lovable* power because it is directed toward our benefit (about self-destructive tendencies nothing is said). The same cannot be said for nature: "The Order of nature is certainly so imperfect, that its benefits are only dispensed to us in an indirect way, by means of the loving ministry of that active and intelligent Being, but for whom our existence would be scarcely tolerable" (*SPP*, II, 51). "Sympathy," combined with control, puts humanity in the driver's seat formerly occupied by divine providence. The "only real author of the benefits received" is humanity itself (*SPP*, II, 52). Humanity is in the process of earning its new title as the "Supreme Power" and object of "direct adoration," because it alone possesses "all the forces capable of voluntarily taking part in the amelioration of the race, even without excepting our worthy helpmates amongst the animals" (*SPP*, II, 54). Elaborating this thought, Comte calls up a veritable "cloud of witnesses"—heroes of humanity who in the past have carried it forward step by step: "Thus each step of sound training in positive thought awakens perpetual feelings of veneration and gratitude; which rise often into enthusiastic admiration of the Great Being, who is the Author of all these conquests, be they in thought, or be they in action" (*SPP*, II, 45).[25]

Comte's vast scenario for the new worship thus unfolds in a way reminiscent of Feuerbach's thesis that theology is finally revealed to have been anthropology from its very beginning. With Comte, the first, fetishistic stage saw man interpreting all reality after the model of the human agent. Fictitious as this view was, it bore witness to the secret truth that man is god, to which each stage in religious history contributed further confirmation, if we understand it right. The Christian notion of incarnation added a crucial chapter, for

25. This is a sentiment worthy of the ritual orgy scene in Aldous Huxley's *Brave New World*, 52–57.

a divine mediator pointed . . . indistinctly to a growing tendency in humanity to find its highest providence within itself. The Human Type had furnished fetishism with its general basis. . . . It assumed still further prominence under Polytheism, which left the imagination free to clothe the governing Powers of the world with all the attributes of Human Nature idealized. . . . The original theory of incarnation could not but issue eventually, in the entire disappearance of the fictitious being; as soon as the Real Being had acquired sufficient majesty and power to take the place of its indispensable precursor (*SPP*, II, 94–95).

The religion of the *incarnation* thus inaugurates the final religious age with the truth that humanity is the "bearer" of the divine—not merely capable of receiving it but *engendering* it.

Comte's exposition of the religion of the Great Being becomes unbearably verbose, as with organ tones he abandons any pretense of further historical observation and analysis. But even in his lavish promotion of the new religiosity he provides further material about how, in his view, religion functions. As in the earliest writings, he clearly sees the unitive and integrative functions of religion. But the emphasis has shifted from the stern *moral* focus of the early "spiritual power" to individual feelings. Only religion, he says, "exerts an influence at once over the understanding and the feelings, neither of which separately would suffice to establish a true unity either for individual or collective life" (*SPP*, II, 11).

This also gives religion a social function, that of "*regulating* each personal life, no less than in *combining* different individual lives" (*SPP*, II, 8). Unity in individual life contributes to harmony in collective life (*SPP*, II, 9). Although his analysis is now virtually buried in exhortation, Comte clearly sees religion as *capable of being socially generated* and capable of uniting a society by "causing all our feelings to converge towards universal benevolence" (*SPP*, II, 45). His definitions of religion's functions almost invariably include the dual elements of "*regulating* each individual nature and *rejoining* all individuals [to one another]."[26]

What all this adds up to is quite simply evidence that Comte had come to understand that the unitive or integrative function of religion requires a psychological appeal to the emotions, not merely an intellectual consensus about worldview. He made no converts to his Church of the Great Being, and that perhaps invalidates some of what he said—at least his choice of an object for devotion. His Great Being is admirable, perhaps; but who can generate passion for a collective?

Durkheim would understand this. But some of his interpreters (or, rather, critics) think his idea is the same as Comte's—that people in a conscious way worship society. This is not Durkheim's idea, but the connection between his ideas and Comte's is clear. Comte's prescription provided a clue for

---

26. Bruce Mazlish (above, n. 12), 188–89, n.8, quoting from Comte's *Catechism of Positive Religion* (1852).

Durkheim's description of the latent power that actually does generate religion. Durkheim would adopt Comte's idea of society not as the newly designated *referent* of religious language but as the *causal* matrix out of which collective and symbolic representations of social experience are generated.

Some conclusions remain to be drawn. The first concerns the remarkable facts that Comte has given us, in effect, *two* explanations of religion, and that out of these two we can anticipate the divergent trends to be traced in the following chapters.

But how and why two theories? The root of the answer already appeared at the beginning, when we described the paradoxical sense of his times from which Comte developed his whole program: on the one hand, his conviction of inexorable progress of the mind toward mastery over human destiny; on the other, his trepidation in the face of a social crisis that threatened to ruin everything.

The first theme produced his evolutionary theory explaining religion as a necessary first stage of the advance of the mind in its way of apprehending and knowing the world, from fetishism to positive science. The second yielded a theory of society that explained the necessity of unitive and repressive powers in order for society to exist at all, "religion" or "spiritual power" being the name for whatever fulfilled these functions.

The first of Comte's two theories, as we saw, is the one he adopted from Hume. Here, religion is a spontaneous expression of the infantile illusion that we, with our wills, are the model for the mechanism of the world; accordingly, all phenomena are explained by analogy to human acts. It is an individualistic, anthropomorphic, psycho-intellectual theory of religion, grounded in human nature's inextinguishable (and laudable) need to make sense of experience, but now outdated because of its childlike anthropomorphism.

But even as he absorbed this theory into his own system, Comte took the further step of crediting fetishism and subsequent religious ideas with a positive and necessary social role, as well as an intellectual one. The very existence of a society, he held, depends upon a consensus about its objects of belief, devotion, and value. In that sense, religion or its equivalent is necessary, something that society will inevitably generate in the very process of creating and preserving itself.

That is Comte's second explanation of religion. And it opens (or reopens, if we recall Vico) a whole realm of social thought that the critical philosophy (for example, Hume's) failed to grasp. Moreover, the modern problem of religion, both for intellects and for society, now appears in a much fuller sense than before: what will serve the "religious function" in the present age, in the face of the loss of traditional belief and the anarchy which threatens? Is a return to "old-time religion" the answer?

For Comte, there could be no such return to anthropomorphism of nature

(Comte was too literal-minded to think about symbols yet). There being no gods, Comte turned to the next closest thing to serve as the new moral-personal religious object—the human collectivity, mediator of all benefits, master of nature, controller of destiny, constrainer of anarchic individualism, worthy focal point of our deepest affection and gratitude. The Great Being deserved to become the replacement for the fictitious gods of yore.

Comte's two explanations of religion give us a clear preview of an emerging division between early British anthropology and the sociological approach to be taken in France.

As we shall see, E. B. Tylor recognized his debt both to Hume and to Comte (he quotes directly from both).[27] Tylor's own celebrated theory of *animism* is nothing more than a labeling of the Hume-Comte explanation of religion. Spencer, Frazer, et al. were to follow suit, and Freud would draw heavily on these authors as well. But in France, Emile Durkheim would transform Comte's "second theory"—his prescriptive notions—into a new descriptive theory to explain the social generation and persistence of religion, and to demonstrate its irreducibly social nature. Durkheim would reject outright the Humean-Victorian anthropomorphic thesis and relocate the primordia of religion in the experience of belonging to a group, or society. He would take Comte's normative criticism of fetishism (and Protestantism)—its inadequacy to create social unity[28] —and use it to expose the British theory's inadequacy as a scientific explanation of religion. Durkheim's social theory of religion is, in a way, Comte's Great Being transformed into that all-embracing social reality whose power over individuals is sufficient to explain religion, which through its symbols ultimately represents society and one's solidarity with it. Such is the direction to be traced in the chapters to follow.

My second concluding point has to do with what I regard as Comte's two most important ideas: his evolutionary theory and his notion that society must have religion or its functional equivalent; put another way, that the word *religion* may be used to denote certain social functions that occur in any society.

First, Comte's evolutionary idea makes difficult, if not altogether implausible, notions of religion of the deistic type, with its conviction that there is for all time an essential or generic religious idea or "experience." If the

27. See n. 20 above.

28. Comte faulted the social utility of fetishism (despite giving credit to its intellectual contribution) as being too individualistic and "too special to give rise to any belief really common to many" (*SPP*, 1:76). It lacked the capacity for institutionalization that belongs to Comte's conception of "spiritual power" as it needs to be adapted to modern times; cf. *CPP*, 550: the fetish deities "could afford little assistance to the development of common ideas. . . . The worship . . . was of a kind that required every man to be his own priest, free from intervention between himself and gods that were constantly accessible." This exactly parallels his criticism of Protestantism.

human as such has evolved out of something prehuman, if consciousness itself evolved, along with brain, mind, language, and all cultural forms, then no exemption can be made for religion except on what are properly called theological grounds, namely, on the basis of a postulate that religion is a response to something that does not evolve. The very variety of religion over time and space, however, provides counterevidence as strong as any positive support one can muster for such a supposition.

Evolutionary theory suggests that nothing in culture is absolutely permanent, including religion as some sort of theology, whether deistic or fetishistic. Tylor, for example, would offer what became a classic definition of religion for anthropology: religion is belief in spiritual beings. Defined thus, however, religion becomes something capable of simply evolving *away;* once such beliefs are no longer held, religion is destined to disappear. Meanwhile, it lingers on (and on, and on) as a "survival." But how?

On the other hand, "religion" denotes a set of functions peculiar to humanity, meeting psychological, intellectual, or social needs. In that sense, it can be regarded as what Parsons has called an evolutionary universal;[29] as such, it can look like practically anything so long as it meets those essential needs, performs those necessary functions.

We now see how Comte's two ideas, of evolution and of functional equivalency, create a dilemma that for the first time forces the problem of definition to the surface. Once his ideas are taken seriously, students of religion will have to define what they are talking about when they discuss religion. If they take the first tack—using a substantive definition—then they inevitably encounter times and places without any "religion." The "deistic" types, for example, will be able to deal only with the so-called higher religions; the Tylorians will wearily wonder when those "survivals" are going to go away; the Freudians will explain why they are so tenacious, despite their irrationality, but also argue that they *should* disappear. But if students of religion take the second, functional route, then whatever fulfills those functions may continue to be called "religions," whatever their form. With such an understanding, religion never ceases to exist despite its transformations: "belief in spiritual beings," for example, may disappear, but the functions it served continue to be met through other beliefs, such as belief in the Great Being, and those functions may continue to be studied as "religious."

If we wish to say in some meaningful sense that religion has evolved, we need to take seriously Comte's second idea of religion as functional. The continuity from age to age is found not in certain ideas supposedly constituting essential religion, but rather in certain psychosocial needs and functions of

29. Talcott Parsons, "Evolutionary Universals in Society." Parsons characterizes such a universal as an evolutionary adaptation that "so increases the long-run adaptive capacity of living systems in a given class that only systems that develop the complex can attain certain higher levels of general adaptive capacity" (340–41).

universal application in all times and places. What evolves are all the forms of religion—its beliefs, practices, rituals; but we shall know it is religion by identifying and testing what it does. Still, without some vestige of a substantive definition in play, it is not yet clear how one can make meaningful the assertion that it is *religion* that is evolving. Durkheim's introduction of the "sacred" attempts to solve this problem.

Comte's idea of functional equivalency proved to be one of his most fruitful for the ongoing study of religion. It is curious, therefore, that the idea appears so unobtrusively in his writing, for Comte usually made a habit of announcing all his discoveries (including the law of the three stages) with great fanfare. Quiet though its appearance is, it puts the discussion of religion on a new level. All our subsequent writers will agree that religion *as explanation* can no longer endure in the modern world. It does not provide or enable knowledge about the world as it did in earlier epochs. But religion as *function*, Comte suggests, must endure. Indeed, it must be cultivated, promoted and if necessary reinvented. Comte thus gives a new twist to Voltaire's wisdom about God: if *religion* did not exist, it would be necessary to invent it.

Chapter 7

Evolutionary Anthropology:
Edward Burnett Tylor

A new era in the "science of man" opened up in the 1860s in Britain, as fundamental advances on three scientific fronts converged to set all of human studies in a radically new framework. Those fronts were: geology, led by Sir George Lyell; biology, revolutionized by Charles Darwin; and archeology, advanced by startling discoveries of prehistoric human remains in France and England by Boucher de Perthes and others.[1] Lyell's *Principles of Geology* (1832) extended the time frame of the earth's history far beyond not only the biblical chronology, by way of which theologians placed creation around 4000 B.C.E., but far beyond any recorded or even imagined human history. Darwin's *Origin of Species* (1859) set forth the theory of gradual evolution by natural selection, a scheme that gained plausibility from the long eras of time allowed by the new geology and installed the human species firmly in the evolutionary process of nature. Finally, hard evidence of heretofore only imagined primitive culture—culture so rude that its only artifacts were stone tools—turned up beneath the very ground on which civilized French and Englishmen trod. The question to be asked was both profound and obvious: how did humanity climb from there to here, from Stone Age to civilization?

In 1884, Edward Burnett Tylor (1832–1917) became Reader in Anthropology at Oxford University, the first such position in the academic world.[2] This honor was bestowed in recognition of his leadership, along with John Lubbock and Lewis Henry Morgan, in the creation of a new evolutionary anthropology. But 1865, the year in which Tylor published his *Researches into the Early History of Mankind,* and Lubbock (later Lord Avebury) his *Prehistoric Times,* may be taken as the inaugural year of the evolutionary

---

1. Jacob W. Gruber, "Brixham Cave and the Antiquity of Man"; George W. Stocking, Jr., "Matthew Arnold, E. B. Tylor, and the Uses of Invention." R. R. Marett, describing Tylor's setting, said, "One might speak of the second Renaissance of Europe that began about the year 1858. Immense vistas opened out on all sides, with philology, biology, and archeology alike eager to break the dusty windows of the academies and let in light and air" (*Tylor,* 163–64).

2. Erich J. Sharpe, *Comparative Religion,* 54. Cf. John W. Burrow, *Evolution and Society: A Study of Victorian Social Theory,* 81.

131

phase in the development of anthropology, a period lasting into the first
quarter of the present century.[3]

The importance ascribed to religion in Tylor's magnum opus, *Primitive
Culture* (1871), has earned him a prominent place in the annals of comparative
religion as well as in anthropology.[4] Thoroughly attuned to the new scientific
advances, and championing their relevance both for the understanding of the
species and the advancement of civilization, Tylor also fits comfortably into
the research tradition being studied here: his work reflects the concerns and
advances theories already familiar to us from Hume, Comte, and even the
earlier deism. But Tylor gives religion a central role in a grand and global
saga of the evolutionary struggle for civilization.

In his effort to understand religion, he offered what he intended as a new
universal cultural category—animism; he was able to accommodate masses
of evidence to his developmental framework, and he developed the notion
of "survivals" to explain the persistence of archaic forms.

Our investigation will concentrate on Tylor's two-volume masterwork,
Primitive Culture.[5] Six of its nineteen chapters are devoted to "animism,"
three more to "mythology," and one to "rites and ceremonies." It synthesizes
most of Tylor's earlier work, and, although he lived until 1917, Tylor did
not develop his theories further. In these volumes one finds "the earliest
detailed anthropological study of religion."[6]

Tylor envisioned and outlined what he called a "science of culture" (the
title of his first chapter), a developmental study of mind having as its master
concept the notion of animism. "My task [he explains] has been here not to
discuss Religion in all its bearings, but to portray in outline the great doctrine
of Animism, as found in what I conceive to be its earliest stages among the
lower races of mankind, and to show its transmission along the lines of
religious thought" (*PC*, II, 359). For Tylor, animism constitutes not only
the fundamental common denominator of religious history but of primitive
culture as a whole. Discovery of Stone Age artifacts directly beneath those
of civilization challenged scholars to explain both the continuity of human
history and the stages through which it was passing. Tylor hoped to arrange
the cultural evidence in an ascending causal order:

> On the one hand, the uniformity which so largely pervades civilization may be
> ascribed, in great measure, to the uniform action of uniform causes; while on the
> other hand its various grades may be regarded as stages of development or evolution,

3. Idus Murphree, "The Evolutionary Anthropologists: The Progress of Mankind. The
Concepts of Progress and Culture in the Thought of John Lubbock, Edward B. Tylor, and
Lewis H. Morgan," 273.

4. Sharpe (above, n. 2), 53. Cf. Margaret Hodgen, *Early Anthropology in the Sixteenth and
Seventeenth Centuries*, 382.

5. Edward B. Tylor, *Primitive Culture: Researches into the Development of Mythology, Philosophy, Religion, Language, Art and Customs*, 2 vols. (hereafter *PC*; 1871; 3d ed. used, 1889).

6. Edward Norbeck, "The Study of Religion," 330.

each the outcome of previous history, and about to do its proper part in shaping the history of the future. To the investigation of these two great principles . . . the present volumes are devoted. (*PC*, I, 1)

In what follows, we shall first spell out the general assumptions and hypotheses on which Tylor constructs his "science of culture"; then we shall turn specifically to his treatment of religion.

Culture, the object of Tylor's science, was equated with "civilization": "that complex whole which includes knowledge, belief, art, morals, law, custom, and any other capabilities and habits acquired by man as a member of society" (*PC*, I, 1).[7] More specifically, as the work unfolds, we see that Tylor is writing the history of the mind. Repeatedly, he refers to his project as describing "the course of mental history," the "laws of intellectual movement," the "history of laws of mind," the "history of opinion," "intellectual history," and so on.[8] In this, he is firmly in the tradition of Auguste Comte, and, as we shall see, his whole treatment of religion will be relentlessly focused on its cognitive element—religion as belief, to the neglect of the entire social and functional side that Comte's work had opened up.

But can there be a "science" of culture? Tylor, operating with the Comtean understanding of science as law-based, is aware of the difficulties:

The world at large is scarcely prepared to accept the general study of human life as a branch of natural science, and to carry out, in a large sense, the poet's injunction to "Account for moral as for natural things." To many educated minds there seems something presumptuous and repulsive in the view that the history of mankind is part and parcel of the history of nature, that our thoughts, wills, and actions accord with laws as definite as those which govern the motion of waves, the combination of acids and bases, and the growth of plants and animals. (*PC*, I, 2)[9]

The echo of Comte, and of Hume's treatise on the passions, is reinforced by another Humean notion, as Tylor drives home an argument for a naturalistic account of *every* element of culture, including the religious: "the moment that the story [which is recorded in ancient texts] falls out of our scheme of the world's habitual course, the ever repeated question comes out to meet it—Which is the more likely, that so unusual an event should have really

---

7. Stocking (above, n. 1), sees Tylor's equation of culture with civilization as a serious methodological flaw, because it gives the word an evaluative and humanistic meaning inappropriate for anthropology (783–84).

8. See, for example, *PC*, 1:158, 273, 275, 368, 374, 425, 496, 499. John Skorupski offers an analysis of Tylor as his prime representative of the intellectualist tradition in *Symbol and Theory: A Philosophical Study of Theories of Religion in Social Anthropology;* cf. p. 2 et passim.

9. Laws govern the formation of myth: "a wide collection of evidence, will show plainly enough in such efforts of fancy at once a development from stage to stage, and a production of uniformity of result from uniformity of cause" (*PC*, I, 18). This view echoes Hume's discussion of the passions (see my chap. 5).

happened, or that the record should be misunderstood or false?" (*PC*, I, 280).[10]

Eschewing all supernatural explanations, Tylor insists on the universal applicability of the laws of cause and effect as a "more practicable ground" for ethnography than one can find in philosophy and theology, for,

> as each man knows by the evidence of his own consciousness, definite and natural cause does, to a great extent, determine human action. Then, keeping aside from considerations of extra-natural interference and causeless spontaneity, let us take this admitted existence of natural cause and effect as our standing-ground, and travel on it so far as it will bear us. (*PC*, I, 3)

How far, ultimately, this course will bear us toward the explanation of religion remains an open question, but Tylor makes no "exemptions" of the sort familiar from the writing of Fontenelle and Vico, including the explanation of religion itself.[11] Most especially Tylor contests the orthodox theological views of his day, that contemporary savagery was the result of degeneration from a higher state, and that contemporary civilization was a gift of God—the result of a head start by supernatural intervention.[12] It is specifically against the doctrine of degeneration that Tylor presents his alternative of development, or as he less frequently calls it, evolution.

Like the astronomers and geologists before him, he holds that the laws of nature operate the same—not only everywhere in the universe, but "every-*when*" as well.

> If anyone holds that human thought and action were worked out in primaeval times according to laws essentially other than those of the modern world, it is for him to prove by valid evidence this anomalous state of things, otherwise the doctrine of permanent principle will hold good, as in astronomy or geology. That the tendency of culture has been similar throughout the existence of human society, and that we may fairly judge from its known historic course what its prehistoric course may have been, is a theory clearly entitled to precedence as a fundamental principle of ethnographic research. (*PC*, I, 33)

This principle of eschewing any resort to supernatural causes in the new human sciences coincides with the procedure of the more established sciences: "the claim to ground scientific opinion upon a basis of revelation is in itself objectionable. It would be, I think, inexcusable if students who have seen

10. The "ever repeated question" is, of course, precisely the question that Hume raised about miracles (see chap. 5).

11. Cf. *PC*, I, 427: theological systems are studied as inventions of "human reason, without supernatural aid or revelation; in other words, as being developments of Natural Religion."

12. "At the present time it is not unusual for the origin of civilization to be treated as a matter of dogmatic theology. It has happened to me more than once to be assured from the pulpit that the theories of ethnologists who consider man to have risen from a low original condition are delusive fancies, it being revealed truth that man was originally in a high condition" (*PC*, 1:36; cf. 38).

in astronomy and geology the unhappy results of attempting to base science on religion, should countenance a similar attempt in Ethnology" (*PC*, I, 37).

Tylor's appeal to uniform mechanisms and laws in the whole course of civilization is not simply an arbitrary analogical extension of an abstract law from one realm of nature to another. It is based on evidence—that of archeology. "The master-key to the investigation of man's primaeval condition is held by Pre-historic Archaeology. This key is the evidence of the Stone Age, proving that men of remotely ancient ages were in the savage state" (*PC*, I, 58). The hard evidence of Stone Age culture was being unearthed on the very sites of European civilization. In light of this "general support given to the development theory of culture by Prehistoric Archaeology," the burden of proof now shifted to the degenerationists to find evidence of their alleged high culture at an even earlier geological stratum (*PC*, I, 61). And Tylor will not buy the theory that the Flood can be injected into the record as a compromise solution.[13]

It should be noted that Tylor's developmental theory does not presuppose an optimistic doctrine of human progress of the type familiar from Condorcet, Turgot, or Comte.[14] The argument against the degenerationists was not that of progress versus pessimism; rather, it was framed over the issue: how are we to account for the present existence of civilization and, to a secondary degree, of contemporary savagery? Archbishop Richard Whately, against whom Tylor specifically wrote, had postulated a supernatural explanation. To account for civilization, he argued, "there must have been . . . a Revelation made to the first, or to some subsequent generation of our species. And this miracle (for such it is, as being an impossibility according to the present course of nature) is attested, independently of the authority of the Scripture-accounts, by the fact, that civilized Man exists at the present day."[15] Whately and Tylor shared the conviction of the superiority of civilization to savagery, but they differed radically on how to explain it and what role they accorded savagery in human history. For the theologian, savagery was the degenerate wastage of a lost element of the species. For Tylor, it was surviving evidence

13. On this score, Tylor criticizes Charles de Brosses (whom he admires and cites often), and might also have mentioned Vico: "De Brosses, whose whole intellectual nature turned to the progression-theory, argued that by studying what actually now happens 'we may trace men upward from the savage state to which the flood and dispersion had reduced them' " (*PC*, 1:36). De Brosses is credited with being "a most original" and "powerful" thinker (*PC*, 1:161; 2:144), with reference to his discovery of fetishism. Other citations occur at 2:166, n. 2, 171–72, n. 1, 246.

14. The progress of humankind is clouded with ambiguity. "To have learnt [for example] to give poison secretly and effectually, to have raised a corrupt literature to pestilent perfection, to have organized a successful scheme to arrest free enquiry and proscribe free expression, are works of knowledge and skill whose progress toward their goal has hardly conduced to the general good" (*PC*, 1:28). Cf. 1:29 on the higher level of religious toleration among savages.

15. Whately is quoted by Murphree (above, n. 3), 272. Note that Hume's classical definition of miracle still holds for Whately.

of the childhood of the species for, in his view, present-day "savages" and "barbarians" (the two stages prior to "civilization") were roughly equivalent to peoples whose existence was attested in the evidence of prehistoric archeology and ancient historical texts.

Pressing the point, Tylor argues that "the degradation theory would expect savages to hold beliefs and customs intelligible as broken-down relics of former higher civilization. The development-theory would expect civilized men to keep up beliefs and customs which have their reasonable meaning in less cultured states of society" (*PC*, II, 357). In support of the latter alternative, we are brought to Tylor's notion of "survivals" of earlier cultural elements. A survival can be any belief or custom that does not make sense—explain itself—in the context of the modern world. Calling something a survival already implies an explanation of anomalous cultural elements: they are the relics of another age and another mental condition. Thus, Tylor defines them as "processes, customs, opinions, and so forth, which have been carried on by force of habit into a new state of society different from that in which they had their original home, and they thus remain as proofs and examples of an older condition of culture out of which a newer has been evolved" (*PC*, I, 16). Survivals can be everything from obvious technological relics (like horse-drawn plows) to the more ambiguous matters of politics, morals, and religions. On this score, Tylor is more comprehensive than discriminating: "The principal criteria of classification are absence or presence, high or low development, of the industrial arts, . . . the extent of scientific knowledge, the definiteness of moral principles, the condition of religious belief and ceremony, the degree of social and political organization, and so forth" (*PC*, I, 26–27). In the context of belief, in fact, "survival" is merely another word for "superstition," the new term being introduced "simply to denote the historical fact which the word 'superstition' is now spoiled for expressing" (*PC* I, 72). In this realm, survivals are "opinions belonging properly to lower intellectual levels, which have held their place into the higher by mere force of ancestral tradition. . . . [Some of these are but] time-honored superstition in the garb of modern knowledge" (*PC*, II, 445; cf. I, 17; II, 102–03).

The notion of survivals is vulnerable to the criticism that anything that does not make sense in terms of Tylor's rationalistic criteria can be labeled a survival.[16] On the other hand, one must appreciate the fact that Tylor grants that *same* rationality to his subjects that he claims for himself. He is convinced that everything in culture made sense at *some* time, even if not now, and that it can be appreciated and explained if one has the patience to reconstruct the mental outlook that produced it. That principle of rationality, one of Tylor's

---

16. For a full-dress critique, see Margaret Hodgen, *The Doctrine of Survivals*. Malinowski also rejected the notion of survivals because it "inhibited the study of social facts as living items of a culture; . . . it encouraged, in fact, an antiquarian rather than a sociological attitude toward contemporary society" (reported by John W. Burrow, *Evolution and Society*, 240).

lasting contributions to the study of cultures,[17] is basic to his explanation of the development of religion. Also of importance to him is the fact that the principle is not readily accommodated to degeneration theory (*PC*, II, 102–03).

The following from Tylor sums up the main argument so far: "In carrying out the great task of rational ethnography, the investigation of the causes which have produced the phenomena of culture, and the laws to which they are subordinate, it is desirable to work out as systematically as possible a scheme of evolution of this culture along its many lines" (*PC*, I, 20–21). Such a scheme will have explanatory power because the lower phases are "explanatory of the higher" (*PC*, II, 363; cf. 357)—not so much because they *produced* the higher but because they make its meaning clear by reconstructing its past. A summary statement following the description of rites and ceremonies is Tylor's clearest statement of this point:

> Through their varied phases of survival, modification and succession, they have each in its own way brought to view the threads of continuity which connect the faiths of the lower with the faiths of the higher world; they have shown how hardly the civilized man can understand the religious rites even of his own land without knowledge of the meaning, often the widely unlike meaning, which they bore to men of distant ages and countries, representatives of grades of culture far different from his. (*PC*, II, 442)[18]

How Darwinian is Tylor's notion of development? On the whole, not very. It is well established that "social Darwinism" is a misnomer, in the sense that social evolution was well worked out before Darwin. Harris, in fact, asserts that "Darwin's principles were an application of social-science principles to biology," rather than the reverse.[19] The most "Darwinian" statement in the whole work, to my knowledge, is that in which Tylor almost echoes Herbert Spencer's term "survival of the fittest" with reference to cultural forms: "History . . . and ethnography over a wider range combine to show that the institutions which can best hold their own in the world gradually supersede the less fit ones, and that this incessant conflict determines the general resultant course of culture" (*PC*, I, 69). Conflict, crisis, and struggle, however, rarely appear in Tylor's account of development and are never appealed to as explaining any specific cultural innovation. Generally, Tylor prefers a more genteel image of evolution—Lady Civilization toiling in the world, moving sometimes forward, but often deviating, stumbling, suffering delay. But "it is not according to her nature [to stumble], her feet were not

17. E. E. Evans-Pritchard, *Theories of Primitive Religion*, 29: Tylor's belief in "the essential rationality of primitive peoples" still holds good. Primitive systems, Evans-Pritchard adds, are always coherent "and up to a point . . . critical and sceptical, and even experimental, within the system of their beliefs and in its idiom. . . . "

18. Cf. *PC*, 1:19, quoting Comte to this same effect.

19. Marvin Harris, *The Rise of Anthropological Theory*, 122–23.

made to plant uncertain steps behind her, for both in her forward view and in her onward gait she is of truly human type" (*PC*, I, 69). For Tylor, the vista of an orderly development according to laws of the mind (of which more in the next section), the conviction that cultural forms that do not make sense now once did, the ability to identify survivals through comparison of cultures at various levels, and the vast accumulation of evidences from all over the world together promise an accurate general account of human development from the earliest ages. The record is sparse for prehistory. But archeology has given us a beginning, and the fuller evidences from direct history allows for reconstruction. After citing examples of technological progress (firearms, navigational equipment, and so on), Tylor confidently claims that we can

> reconstruct lost history without scruple, trusting to general knowledge of the principles of human thought and action as a guide in putting the facts in their proper order. . . . And thus . . . there will come again and again into view series of facts which may be consistently arranged as having followed one another in a particular order of development, but which will hardly bear being turned round and made to follow in reversed order. (*PC*, I, 15–16)

Nowhere does Tylor set down a rigorously coherent body of "laws," but a basic principle so far unmentioned which is absolutely essential for his project of reconstruction is the idea of the psychic unity of humankind—a term not current for Tylor, but a principle that even his critics allow has stood the test of time—especially in the sense of allowing the essential rationality of the most primitive humans. Impressed by the unity of humankind, Tylor cites an Italian proverb which conveys the sense of today's cliché about the global village: "All the world is one country." The validity of the comparative method for establishing developmental sequences depended on the essential sameness of the human capacity and the human condition:

> To general likeness in human nature on the one hand, and to general likeness in the circumstances of life on the other, this similarity and consistency may no doubt be traced, and they may be studied with especial fitness in comparing races near the same grade of civilization. Little respect need be had in such comparisons for date in history or for place on the map; the ancient Swiss lake-dweller may be set beside the medieval Aztec. . . . (*PC*, I, 6)

Tylor's confidence that he can understand the savage mind because it is essentially rational is the basis for his conviction that he can understand the continuity of human religiousness from the earliest times in which it affords a glimpse of itself. That confidence is further bolstered by the assumption that the preferred form of savage rationality, as we shall see, is empiricism.

The outcome of Tylor's massively documented consideration of mythology and animism will be that religion itself is a survival. This conclusion is supported by the fact that he discerns no form, essence, or rationale of religion that has superseded the common denominator of all religion from time immemorial—*belief in spiritual beings* (that do not exist). His concept of religion lacks entirely the second, functional dimension so important in the work of Comte. As John Burrow notes, he was an "antiquarian before a systematic anthropologist," and "sociologically incurious," showing no knowledge of economics or political theory.[20]

Tylor holds that his "rudimentary definition of religion" is broad enough to cover the abundance of the evidence. Most competing definitions (such as theistic ones) are too narrow, having "the fault of identifying religion rather with particular developments than with the deeper motive which underlies them. It seems best to fall back at once on this essential source, and simply to claim, as a minimum definition of Religion, the belief in Spiritual Beings" (*PC*, I, 424). This belief exposes the very root of religions, for it "characterizes tribes very low in the scale of humanity, and thence ascends, deeply modified in its transmission, but from first to last preserving an unbroken continuity, into the midst of high modern culture" (*PC*, I, 426). To those who might object that he has offered a "bare and meagre" definition, "it will be found practically sufficient; for where the root is, the branches [i.e., practice] will generally be produced" (*PC*, I, 426).

Animism generally embraces two "dogmas": (1) that individual creatures have souls that are capable of continued existence after death, and (2) that the world is populated with "other spirits, upward to the rank of powerful deities" (*PC*, I, 426).[21] Animism is thus a quasi universal, in the sense that it identifies the *definiens* of all religion, or at least most of what we know from the available evidence. Tylor does not try to give it any metaphysical status; obviously, it is not, for him, the product of divine revelation. Nor does Tylor affirm any innate idea or sense of religion such as earlier deists had postulated as the root of religion. Rather, it is a universal empirically arrived at, and empirically limited as well:

> It cannot be positively asserted that *every* existing tribe recognizes the belief in spiritual beings. . . . It would be . . . unwarranted to set down every tribe mentioned in history, or known to us by the discovery of antiquarian relics, as *necessarily* having possessed the defined minimum of religion. Greater still would be the unwisdom of declaring such a rudimentary belief *natural or instinctive* in *all* human tribes of *all* times; for no evidence justifies the opinion that man, known to be capable of so vast an intellectual development, cannot have emerged from a non-religious condition, previous to that religious condition in which he happens at present to come with sufficient clearness within our range of knowledge (*PC*, I, 424–25; italics mine).

20. The advantage of Tylor's definition is that it presides over an exceedingly long temporal period; see the next two quotations in the text. For John W. Burrow's criticism, see *Evolution and Society*, 245.

21. Tylor holds that his definition can embrace fetishism, as defined by de Brosses and Comte: *PC* 2:144–45. His sense of the development from there to "idolatry" (polytheism) is roughly the same as Comte's.

Within the limits of the evidence, then, animism serves as an inductively constructed evolutionary universal,[22] a concept that serves both to identify the continuing essence of the religious idea and to serve as a baseline through all the historical varieties of religious belief to the present.

The text just quoted indicates another important element of Tylor's idea: he is quite aware that the *temporal origin* of religion is unknown and forever eludes the grasp of science. Were it possible to locate savages who were without religion, "these might be at least plausibly claimed as representatives of the condition of man before he arrived at the religious stage of culture" (*PC*, I, 425). Within a Darwinian framework of man ascending from higher primates, such a prereligious state is not only plausible but simply to be granted; this in fact is where Tylor by implication leaves the matter: "Nonreligious tribes may not exist in our day, but the fact bears no more decisively on the development of religion, than the impossibility of finding a modern English village without scissors or books or lucifer-matches bears on the fact that there was a time when no such things existed in the land" (*PC*, I, 425). Tylor will not try to go beyond the evidence as he reads it; "it is desirable . . . to take our basis of enquiry in observation rather than from speculation" (*PC*, I, 425).

Since the nineteenth century is notorious for its proliferation of theories of the "origin" of religion, it should be noted that Tylor makes no claim to have identified a first beginning of religious belief or practice. On the other hand, he presents what he clearly thinks is a plausible theory of how belief in spiritual beings might possibly have arisen. His aim, however, is to establish the essential continuity of religious belief (as well as practice) through the whole history for which we have any evidence, and this demonstration aims to refute the degenerationists, with whom the "main issue" of contention is whether animism is a "primary formation" of human culture, from which a rational and plausible development to modernity can be construed, or whether it is a "degradation" of a pristine, "higher" form of religion generally lost but by divine intervention reissued and preserved only in Christianity. Tylor's answer is modestly hedged but firm: "The evidence for the first alternative, though not amounting to complete demonstration, seems reasonably strong, and not met by contrary evidence approaching it in force. The animism of the lower tribes . . . is a system which might quite reasonably exist among mankind, had they never anywhere risen above the savage condition" (*PC*, II, 356–57).

What, then, is Tylor's explanation of animism? We note first that this is an empiricist's theory from a man who is convinced that savages are empi-

---

22. Evolutionary universal is a term I have borrowed from Talcott Parsons, "Evolutionary Universals in Society."

ricists as well, in the sense that all their ideas derive from experience. Nowhere is this more clearly stated than in the following:

> It is in large measure possible to follow them [i.e., the threads which connect modern thought with archaic] as clues leading back to that actual experience of nature and life, which is the ultimate source of human fancy. . . . The office of our thought is to develop, to combine, and to derive, *rather than to create*, and the consistent laws it works by are to be discerned even in the unsubstantial structures of the imagination. Here, as elsewhere in the universe, there is to be recognized a sequence from cause to effect, a sequence intelligible, definite, and where knowledge reaches the needful exactness, even calculable. (*PC*, I, 274; italics mine)

So we should be able to give some account of the rise of animistic belief from experience, and (as we shall see) animism in turn accounts for the appearance of mythology.

Animism itself is a product of thought that begins, not with nature, but with puzzling aspects of the self: "the conception of the human soul is the very 'fons et origo' of the conceptions of spirit and deity in general" (*PC*, II, 247). And what is the origin of the notion of the soul? It is "originally based," Tylor guesses, on "direct evidence of the senses" (*PC*, II, 356). His earliest statement of this idea is found in the *Researches* (1865), where he writes that "a man who thinks he sees in sleep the apparitions of his dead relatives and friends has a reason for believing that their spirits outlive their bodies, and this reason lies in no far-fetched induction, but in what seems to be the *plain evidence of his senses*."[23]

Tylor later adds the problems of distinguishing between a live body and a dead one and explaining what happens in sleep, trance, and death (*PC*, I, 428). He summarizes in *Primitive Culture:* "At the lowest levels of culture of which we have clear knowledge, the notion of ghost-soul animating man while in the body, and appearing in dream and vision out of the body, is found deeply ingrained. . . . Savages . . . appear to hold [this doctrine] on the very evidence of their senses, interpreted on the biological principle which seems to them most reasonable" (*PC*, I, 499–500).[24] For present purposes, it is sufficient to stress how strongly Tylor believes that this doctrine makes, or made, sense as a plausible interpretation, given the savages' lack of philosophical sophistication. To have grasped this point is for him the very condition for serious study of early religion and culture. "Kindly interest" in such phenomena requires that students "look for meaning, however crude and childish, at the root of doctrines often most dark to the believers who accept them most zealously; they will search for the reasonable thought which once gave life to observances now become in seeming or reality the most abject and superstitious folly" (*PC*, I, 421).

---

23. *Researches into the Early History of Mankind and the Development of Civilization* (1865), 8; italics mine. Cf. *PC*, 1:285, 447, 478, 499–500; 2:194.

24. For further description of the primitive doctrine of the soul, *PC*, 1:429.

Thus, the most immediate concerns of conscious, personal existence itself are identified as the generative seed of "religious" thought. And that initial focus on the self in turn explains the nearly universal reign of anthropomorphism in myth and religion: the initial idea of a personal "soul" is extended to explain causality throughout all of nature as well, so that the entire realm of external reality is explained as the operation of personal wills (*PC*, II, 356). Tylor has thus traced to its existential root the anthropomorphic principle articulated by David Hume ("whose 'Natural History of Religion,' " Tylor notes, "is perhaps more than any other work the source of modern opinions as to the development of religion" [*PC*, I, 477]).[25]

In Tylor's view, then, animism is a "perfectly rational and intelligible product of early science" (*PC*, I, 447), the attempt of "ancient savage philosophers" (*PC*, I, 428) to explain psychic realities that they encountered every day. And religion is a development from animism, that "ancient and world-wide philosophy of which belief is the theory and worship the practice" (*PC*, I, 427). Identifying and summarizing its two organizing principles, Tylor notes "First, that spiritual beings are modelled by man on his primary conception of his own human soul, and second, that their purpose is to explain nature on the primitive childlike theory that it is truly and throughout 'Animated Nature' " (*PC*, II, 184).

By grounding myths in animism, and animism in experience, Tylor also claims to have exposed in yet a new way the futility of allegorizing myths in the style of Bacon and others, that is, attempting to run them aground by finding in them a deep and primal wisdom (a familiar theme from Fontenelle and Vico). Whereas the allegorizer "believed himself to be reversing the process of myth-making, he was in fact only carrying it a stage farther in the old direction, and out of the suggestion of one train of thought evolving another connected with it by some more or less remote analogy. Any of us may practise this simple art, each according to his own fancy" (*PC*, I, 277). Contrary to the allegorizers, myths were literally meant by their creators (*PC*, I, 289–90; cf. 297), and their proper interpretation is therefore only obscured by being "plastered with allegory or euhemerized into dull sham history" (*PC*, I, 275).[26]

From these principles the elaboration of myth is explained. Myth is the form taken by interpretations of experience founded on animistic presuppositions. Tylor sees the relationship as causal:

25. Here, Tylor quotes from Hume's *Natural History*, 29–30, and then from Comte's *Positive Philosophy*, 524. The anthropomorphic principle serves to explain the practice of religious sacrifice as well: *PC*, 2:393.

26. The sacerdotal class that emerged later was largely responsible for allegorization of myths whose original sense had either been lost or no longer fit the spiritual condition of later times: *PC*, 2:363.

First and foremost among the causes which transfigure into myths the facts of daily experience, is the belief in the animation of all nature, rising at its highest pitch to personification. This, no occasional or hypothetical action of the mind, is inextricably bound in with that primitive mental state where man recognizes in every detail of his world the operation of personal life and will (*PC*, I, 285).

The mythic process, with the idea of the soul as its *fons et origo*, proceeds to "conceptions of spirit and deity in general," passing from souls "into the characters of good and evil demons, and . . . ascending to the rank of deities" (*PC*, II, 247). All spiritual entities, including vampires, werewolves, and so on, have thus been shown, to Tylor's satisfaction, to "have their origin not in fancy, but in real phenomena interpreted on animistic principles" (*PC*, II, 194).

The above account satisfies Tylor as an alternative to the traditional theological explanation of the appearance of "natural" religion. Tylor quotes Bishop Joseph Butler as a representative of that tradition; we have encountered it in Bodin's Toralba and in Herbert of Cherbury. For Butler, natural religion is "a primeval system which he expressly argues to have not been reasoned out, but taught first by revelation." Tylor simply directs attention to the evidence, concluding that Butler's system "differs in the extreme from the actual religions of the lower races" (*PC*, II, 356, n. 1).

The developmental course of animism can include in its commodious embrace not only modern religion but the great philosophical tradition of the ancient Greeks. The earliest philosophical theory of perception, set forth by Democritus, is in direct continuity with the animism of the "savage philosophers" to which it is indebted (*PC*, I, 498). Even more obvious is the animistic continuity "from the philosophy of the savage thinker to the modern professor of theology. Its definition has remained from the first of an animating, separable, surviving entity, the vehicle of individual personal existence" (*PC*, I, 501).

The fundamental continuity between "savage" and modern religion, then, lies in its anthropology—its dualistic doctrine of the person which retains the notion of the soul (cf. *PC*, I, 23).

It seems arguable that, in Tylor's view, animism itself is wholly a survival—a once rational but now reliquary legacy of savagery. Over the millennia, animism has drastically contracted from its greatest expanse as a comprehensive world philosophy. Science has gradually deanthropomorphized the universe, replacing the idea of personalistic causality, life, and will, with the impersonal notions of natural laws and forces (*PC*, II, 183). Animism has thus come full circle, reduced again to the place from which it began—a doctrine of the personal human soul, and that doctrine itself has of course been greatly modified and refined in religious history.

But now, for a fully scientific account of the person, the soul itself seems expendable. It is being replaced, in the investigations of biology and "mental

science," with a "groundwork of pure experience" (*PC*, I, 501). The last
refuge of the soul "in modern thought is in the metaphysics of religion, and
its especial office there is that of furnishing an intellectual side to the religious
doctrine of the future life" (*PC*, I, 501). Contemporary theology, then,
tenuously and tenaciously preserves the last connecting link between "the
savage fetish-worshipper and the civilized Christian" (*PC*, I, 501–02), as well
as with all the other religions of the modern world. In Tylor's view, the
world is now divided between only two completely opposed doctrines: animism and materialism. This great schism has far deeper significance than
the hostile but "superficial" divisions between the great *religions* of the world
(*PC*, I, 502). Animism seems to have about finished its long career in the
climb toward civilization. The animism of savages made sense because it was
built on "point-blank natural evidence and acts of straightforward practical
purpose" (*PC*, I, 500). But it was produced "in a mental condition of intense
and inveterate ignorance" (*PC*, I, 23) and depended on the savage's inability
to make a clear distinction between imagination and reality, and between
subjective and objective realms of being (*PC*, I, 445).[27] And so today, animism
is a survival found in various degrees of decline: "the old in the midst of the
new, modification of the old to bring it into conformity with the new, abandonment of the old because it is no longer compatible with the new" (*PC*,
I, 500). In great measure it is "only explicable as a developed product of the
older and ruder system" (*PC*, I, 500).

How can we translate the implications of Tylor's thought? Since he identified animism with religion, or at least with its indispensable core, is it the
case that the gradual demise of animism entails the demise of religion itself—
branch with root? A negative argument could be made by noting that Tylor,
by focusing only on the cognitive core of religion, has in fact left the rest
untouched. Even if in his own mind he has gutted the inner justification of
religious belief by showing its gradual replacement by the doctrines of modern
science, he has ignored or bracketed out an exceedingly large terrain, not
only of practice, but of the inner life—for example, the notion that religion
is ultimately rooted in emotion, the passions, or feeling (Hume, Schleiermacher), and that its cognitive function is quite secondary. Or that it is
rooted in ritual action, and that myth is basically the rationalization of ritual/
religious action (W. Robertson Smith),[28] rather than the other way around,
as in Tylor's view. Or, that it has an irreducible ethical dimension (Herbert,
Kant). Or, that it is rooted in the unconscious (Freud). Or that social, rather
than individual experience, is the "fons et origo" of religion (Durkheim).

27. Andrew Lang credited Fontenelle with anticipating Tylor on this point (as already noted
in chap. 3, n. 14).

28. William Robertson Smith, *Lectures on the Religion of the Semites* (1889), 18: "it may be
affirmed that in almost every case the myth was derived from the ritual, and not the ritual from
the myth."

The question of those omissions must remain open for now, but Tylor's conclusion is persuasive—that it has not been a "wanton incredulity or decay of religious temperament," that has led to the retreat of animistic belief, but "the alteration in natural science, assigning new causes for the operations of nature and the events of life. The theory of the immediate action of personal spirits has here [i.e., in the realm of the mind], as so widely elsewhere, given place to the ideas of force and law" (*PC*, II, 183). Furthermore, the refusal of theologians to give up the fight for a theological or revelational scheme to answer questions that belong to natural science has only discredited religion.

On the other hand, Tylor's claim (following on the heels of Comte's) that the evolution and dynamics of mind are amenable to scientific explanation awaited the theoretical breakthrough of Sigmund Freud, with his discovery and mapping of the unconscious. Freud's work can be seen as an extension of Tylor's (and Hume's) thesis that, with regard to the mind (or "soul"—a term Freud did not eschew), "the consistent laws it works by are to be discerned even in the unsubstantial structures of the imagination. Here, as elsewhere in the universe, there is to be recognized a sequence from cause to effect, a sequence intelligible, definite, and where knowledge reaches the needful exactness, even calculable" (*PC*, I, 274). Freud's notion of the soul and of the roots of religion would, of course, be incomparably richer than Tylor's purely cognitive treatment.[29]

Two other notions found in Tylor will surface in new guise in the writings of Freud on religion: that the source of religion is to be found in the "childhood" of the species, and that analogy—from primitive times to ours—is an important principle of scientific discovery.

For Tylor, savagery and all its works belong to the childhood of the human race (see *PC*, I, 284, 478; II, 184). This old idea was given more than metaphorical implication once the developmental model of humanity became normative. In this childhood state, according to Tylor (following Comte), the animistic philosophy was created by analogical extension of the doctrine of the personal soul to a general doctrine of personal causality comprehending the whole natural realm; it provided "explanation of the course and change of nature, as caused by life such as the life of the thinking man who gazes on it" (*PC*, I, 296).[30]

Despite our better knowledge, analogical thinking persists and ought to, for from it "we have gained so much of our apprehension of the world around us. Distrusted as it now is by severer science for its misleading results, analogy is still to us the chief means of discovery and illustration, while in earlier

---

29. Robert Lowie rejected the charge of "intellectualism" frequently leveled at Tylor by those who grounded religion elsewhere than in the mind: "the charge is pointless because Tylor is concerned with tracing the origin of a concept, that is, of a cognitive element of consciousness. Further, he derives it very largely not from ratiocination about observed phenomena but from the immediate sensory testimony of dream life" (*Primitive Religion*, 109).

30. As already noted (above, n. 25), this idea is credited to Comte.

grades of education its influence was all but paramount" (*PC*, I, 297). The importance of analogical models in the process of scientific discovery looms large both in the history of science and in contemporary discussion about the nature of scientific explanation.[31] The Freudian theory of religion would find a fruitful analogy between psychological development and the biological notion that the development of the individual recapitulates that of the species ("ontogeny recapitulates phylogeny"). Freud would also trade heavily on the analogy between religion and neurosis. Discussion of these matters appears in my last chapter.

Further implications of Tylor's thought revolve around its individualism and its mentalism (or dualism, or idealism, depending on one's definition of the issues involved). Tylor's (typically British) individualism has at least two serious flaws: first, his explanation of religion lacks any social component, and second, it renders inexplicable any essential relation between religion (qua animism) and *morality*. So marked are these features that they seem to require a Durkheim to be invented—with critical help from Tylor's Scottish contemporary and critic, W. Robertson Smith.

Idus Murphree, I think, exhibits a tendency to make Tylor's thought more sociological than it really is. He emphasizes that Tylor's definition of culture describes man "as a member of society,"[32] but that obvious fact has absolutely no theoretical importance in Tylor's theory of religion. Religion has its roots in the ruminations of those curious individuals who wondered about the difference between living and dead bodies and the nature of dreams. Rite and cult are of no theoretical interest to Tylor, except as the "practice" that follows straight from animistic "theory" (cf. *PC*, II, 362). Murphree, however, wants to interpret Tylor's definition of culture to mean that culture is "a community product": "he [Tylor] assumed that it could be studied as a collective, societal phenomenon because, for all its complexity, it was a whole with characteristics general and predominant enough to make it the manageable subject of the science of culture."[33] However, Tylor has no Durkheimian notion of "social facts" beyond the conglomerate of individuals, and thus Murphree is right to add: "What *accounted for* that homogeneity Tylor was *not sure*, but that entire populations were *somehow* induced 'to unite in the use of the same language, to follow the same religion and customary law, to settle down to the same general level of art and knowledge' *seemed evident*."[34] This statement of where Tylor ends is not a bad approximation of where Durkheim *begins*—with the question of what it is that conduces to the existence of a social order.

31. On the importance of analogy (or "models") for scientific discovery, cf. Marjorie Grene, "Reducibility: Another Side Issue?" 22–23.

32. Idus Murphree (above, n. 3), 286, on *PC*, I:1.

33. Ibid.

34. Ibid.; italics mine.

For Tylor, religion is belief, and everything else belongs "outside its central scheme." The most sociological statement I have found in the entire work is the notion that heavenly society, as conceived in myth, reflects the earthly:

> The higher deities of Polytheism have their places in the general animistic system of mankind. Among nation after nation it is still clear how, man being the type of deity [= the anthropormorphic principle], human society and government became the model on which divine society and government were shaped. As chiefs and kings are among men, so are the great gods among the lesser spirits. (*PC*, II, 248)

So uncharacteristic is this in the pages of Tylor's work, however, that it strikes the reader almost as an insertion. More important, Tylor does not integrate this observation in any way with his basic theory.[35]

A further consequence of Tylor's individualistic theory of religion is that (like Hume's) it is without ethical dimension and does not suggest in any way *how* religious and ethical systems would become so closely bound together. "The lower animism is not immoral, it is unmoral" (*PC*, II, 360). The reason is that animism is "a philosophy of man and nature," and Tylor insists that "the popular idea [we saw it in Herbert and Vico] that the moral government of the universe is an essential tenet of natural religion simply falls to the ground" (*PC*, II, 360).

The ethical element found in higher religion is an evolutionary development; thus, "doctrines which in the lower culture are philosophical [referring to animism as "savage philosophy"] tend in the higher to become ethical; . . . what among savages is a science of nature, passes among civilized nations into a moral engine" (*PC*, II, 103). Fine. But if we ask *how it is* that religion and morality become connected, and why, we are left high and dry. The only specific discussion of the development of a moral dimension comes in Tylor's argument that, with regard to the afterlife, the doctrine of mere continuance is the earlier, while that of retribution, with its ethical twist, comes later. His argument for this placement on the evolutionary scale is that "the continuance-theory, with its ideas of a ghostly life like this, is directly vouched for by the evidence of the senses in dreams and visions of the dead. . . . On the other hand, the retribution-theory is a dogma which this evidence of apparitions could hardly set on foot, though capable of afterwards supporting it" (*PC*, II, 103). Tylor offers no explanation of the cause of this momentous development in the history of religion.

Further confirmation that he has no interest in explaining how animism might lead to ethical conceptions is his linking of primitive animism with early Greek epistemology rather than with its ethics. I have not found Tylor relegating morality to the rank of a mere "attachment" to religion; it is simply

---

35. Tylor of course understands that the content of myths reflects the evolution of societies; thus, sun-worship is characteristic of agricultural and not hunter-gatherer societies, because "tillers of the soil . . . watch him day by day giving or taking away their wealth and their very life" (*PC*, 2:286).

omitted in texts such as the following: "In the course of history, religion has in various ways attached to itself matters small and great *outside its central scheme*, such as prohibition of special meats, observance of special days, regulation of marriage as to kinship, division of society into castes, ordinance of social law and civil government" (*PC*, II, 361; italics mine). Perhaps, like Hume, Tylor had an idea of the genealogy of morals entirely distinct from that of religion. At any rate, if Tylor's account is correct, it reinforces the views not only of Hume and other Enlightenment critics of religion, but also indirectly of those theologians such as Schleiermacher and Otto, who sought to identify a sui generis essence of religion that was somehow premoral. Against that view would come Durkheim, whose thought (following Comte's) explains the inseparable connection between a sociological explanation of religion and an irreducible ethical substance.

A further implication of Tylor's views for anthropology, and one that has a fundamental bearing on the study of religion, is the question of Tylor's mentalism, to which Marvin Harris, an advocate of cultural materialism, has called particular attention."[36] Although, as mentioned above, Tylor divided the world between "animists" and "materialists" in a way that clearly implied his attachment to the latter view, he is surely not a materialist in his understanding (such as it is) of the causal dynamics of the evolutionary process. Over the millennia, mind determines itself. Belief itself is a "cause" (see, for example *PC*, I, 285). By its very rationality (to savage man), animism simply "explains its own origin" (*PC*, I, 500). The presupposition here is that beliefs that are rational in their context are self-explanatory; causes need not be sought beneath reasons.[37] On the other hand, this theoretical position is mitigated by the fact that Tylor is outspokenly *not* an "idealist" in the epistemological sense. As we have already seen, he is an empiricist: the mind does not create but responds to the experiences of nature and life (cf. *PC*, I, 274, 478). Thus, he is at least open to the idea that the way life is experienced determines the development of religion. For example, accounting for the demise of Manichaean-type dualism, Tylor says: "That the adoration of a Good Deity should have more and more superseded the propitiation of an Evil Deity, is the sign of one of the great movements in the education of mankind, a result of happier experience of life, and of larger and more gladsome views of the system of the universe" (*PC*, II, 330). But since Tylor makes no specific causal connections between the developments of material culture and the evolution of mind—between which Harris sees an intrinsic link, and without which historical laws have not been stated nor causes explained—Harris's characterization of Tylor is quite correct.

36. Marvin Harris (above, n. 19), 202ff.
37. Larry Laudan vigorously defends this view against the so-called arationality assumption advanced by some sociologists of knowledge: *Progress and its Problems: Toward a Theory of Scientific Growth*, chap. 7.

Tylor's mentalism, however, should not be identified with his simply holding that there is (or was) a *reason* for everything. What makes Tylor "mentalistic" is, rather, the claim that those reasons are not merely rationalizations but the actual *causes* of actions and events. As Harris says, "the basic point of *Primitive Culture* seems to be that the human mind has the ability to perfect itself by thinking more clearly," and the so-called laws of evolution are mere sequences of the unfolding of reason's power.[38]

The foundation of nineteenth-century anthropology, and of the beginnings of comparative religion, was the comparative method inlaid upon an evolutionary framework. The doctrine of development was the fundamental premise of the naturalistic explanation and interpretation of cultures, and it stood in essential polemical counterpoint to the degenerationist doctrine of orthodox and deistic theology.

Harris reminds us of the daring of the evolutionists: their choice of the new doctrine meant turning away "from the much more convincing and satisfying rationales of divine revelation and divine commandments. The enduring significance of the late nineteenth-century use of the comparative method was that it completed the demonstration, begun in the previous century, that Western man's institutions from Christianity to motherhood had a natural and not a divine origin."[39]

While scholars have rightly criticized "the license of the [Victorian] times for imaginative reconstructions of origins," it trivializes their work to characterize the enterprise as a "game."[40] The stunning discoveries of the new geology, biology, and archeology, after all, presented phenomena that could not be accommodated to received theological tradition—which was no less "imaginative," though far more weighted with the cumulative authority of Christendom. Some comprehensive paradigm for ordering the new data had to be offered, and evolution—the notion that human institutions are "as distinctly stratified as the earth" (Tylor)[41] —provided that framework.

Evolutionary thinking is not a major concern in contemporary anthropology, oriented as it is toward fieldwork and the synchronic, structural-functional study of particular cultures rather than to grand theory. But it is by no means rejected as a presupposition, and some argue vigorously that it is

---

38. Marvin Harris (above, n. 19), 202ff.

39. Ibid., 210.

40. John J. Honigmann, *The Development of Anthropological Ideas*, 149, referring to "the 18th-century game of delving speculatively into the mind of early man."

41. Tylor, "On a Method of Investigating the Development of Institutions; Applied to Laws of Marriage and Descent," 269. Institutions, Tylor goes on, "succeed each other in series substantially uniform over the globe, independent of what seem the comparatively superficial differences of race and language, but shaped by similar human nature acting through successively changed conditions in savage, barbaric and civilised life."

indispensable if anything is to be explained.[42] Indeed, in the modest form stated by Tylor, it is difficult to contest, and so closely approximated to history itself as to seem almost trivial:

> On the whole, it appears that wherever there are found elaborate arts, abstruse knowledge, complex institutions, these are results of graduate development from an earlier, simpler, and ruder state of life. No stage of civilization comes into existence spontaneously, but grows or is developed out of the stage before it. This is the great principle which every scholar must lay firm hold of.[43]

In two ways, however, Tylor's theory of evolution (and perhaps any significant theory) differed from straight history. First, it was inherently comparative because it was intended as a species history (or history of the "race," in his terminology) and was therefore intent on construing the entire saga of culture as a single history. Its sequences, rather than those of direct and immediate succession within a single culture, were developed by identifying "strata" of culture through cross-cultural comparison without necessary reference to contiguous times or places. The second feature of evolutionary as contrasted to historical reconstruction was that it at least implicitly claimed to offer some sort of *explanation* of the sequences, just as in biology, Darwin's real contribution lay in explaining the process through his theory of natural selection.

With Tylor, both elements are evident. Obviously *Primitive Culture* aims at a comprehensive species history and is, accordingly, massively comparative. Its explanatory component consists of Tylor's belief that the mind operates and develops in a regular manner, according to natural laws. Both elements are evident in Tylor's statement of the first principle in the study of myth:

> legend, when classified on a sufficient scale, displays a regularity of development which the notion of motiveless fancy quite fails to account for, and which must be attributed to laws of formation whereby every story, old and new, has arisen from its definite origin and sufficient cause. So uniform indeed is such development, that it becomes possible to treat myth as an organic product of mankind at large, in which individual, national, and even racial distinctions stand subordinate to universal qualities of the human mind. (*PC*, I, 415–16)

The "regularity" to which Tylor refers is that of the epistemological process already reviewed, and summarized in such references as "the operation of outward events on the inward mind," or to the mind "acting on appropriate facts in a manner suited to the intellectual state of the people producing it," and so on. (*PC*, II, 446–47). Because of the regular operation of "mental

---

42. Leslie A. White, *The Evolution of Culture*, is a classic and clear exposition of an evolutionary anthropology. As Harris (above, n. 19; 641) notes, White quoted with approval Tylor's conviction that evolution must be grasped as a first principle (White, 125).

43. Tylor, *Anthropology* (1881), 20.

law," the course of mythmaking is revealed to be even "more uniform than history" (*PC*, I, 282).

Yet Tylor is ever mindful of evidence and nowhere loses his consistent respect for data. Natural science has presented a model for skepticism and rigor which the ethnologist dare not ignore (*PC*, I, 280). The strongest argument against the degeneration theory is that with regard "to definite evidence . . . it does not seem to have any ethnological basis whatever" (*PC*, I, 36). Even-handed to the last, Tylor also rejected a suggestion of the superevolutionist Spencer for the same reason: in opposition to Spencer's notion that animal worship evolved from human nicknames, Tylor comments: "All this might indeed possibly happen, and when it did happen it might set an example. . . . Yet, while granting that such a theory affords a rational interpretation of the obscure facts of totemism, we must treat it as a theory not vouched for by sufficient evidence, and within our knowledge liable to mislead, if pushed to extremes" (*PC*, II, 236–37).

Tylor's refined and critical historical sense is further seen in his assessment of myths as historical sources. While the content of legend and myth is hopeless as a source of knowledge, so that, "far from their elucidating history, they need history to elucidate them," they are an invaluable source in another way:

> unconsciously, as it were in spite of themselves, the shapers and transmitters of poetic legend have preserved for us masses of sound historical evidence. They moulded into mythic lives of gods and heroes their own ancestral heirlooms of thought and word, they displayed in the structure of their legends the operations of their own minds, they placed on record the arts and manners, the philosophy and religion of their own times, times of which formal history has often lost the very memory. Myth is the history of its authors not of its subjects; it records the lives, not of superhuman heroes, but of poetic nations. (*PC*, I, 416)[44]

Despite the narrow mentalistic basis of his approach, then, Tylor's critical, cautious placement of the data of religious life into an evolutionary framework still points in a positive direction. Recent works by scholars such as Bellah and Geertz, Rappaport and P. J. Wilson[45] bear witness to the continued fruitfulness of evolutionary investigations bearing on religion.

I shall reserve further criticism of animism for Durkheim. But its interest and importance may not be entirely discounted. Even Harris credits the notion with "immense utility," because of its "power to account for another series of universal experiences of the greatest significance to man: the difference between life and death, health and sickness, wakefulness and sleep,

---

44. This passage is one of the best evidences that Tylor had read Vico, or at least was thoroughly acquainted with his thought (see chap. 4).

45. Robert N. Bellah, "Religious Evolution"; Clifford Geertz, "The Growth of Culture and the Evolution of Mind"; Roy A. Rappaport, "The Sacred in Human Evolution"; Peter J. Wilson, *Man, the Promising Primate.*

trance and ordinary consciousness."[46] The term has passed into the general language of ethnology, as witnessed by Harris's own use of the term, where he refers to religious explanations as "hypotheses of sustained animistic interference."[47]

In an odd sort of way, Tylor's intellectualism is more deistic than Humean, despite Tylor's acknowledged debt to Hume. Tylor's cognitive interests programmatically omit the emotional or affective element of religion. Meanwhile:

> Those to whom religion means above all things religious feeling may say of my argument that I have written soullessly of the soul, and unspiritually of spiritual things. Be it so: I accept the phrase not as needing an apology, but as expressing a plan. Scientific progress is at times most furthered by working along a distinct intellectual line. . . . My task has been here not to discuss Religion in all its bearings, but to portray in outline the great doctrine of animism, as found in what I conceive to be its earlier stages among the lower races of mankind, and to show its transmission along the lines of religious thought. (*PC*, II, 359)

Insofar as he attributes causal power to sheer ratiocination as a source of religion, Tylor duplicates the second (inferential) step in the Humean analysis but does not exploit the affective, experiential moment that calls up that inference. In that sense, Tylor is pre-Humean. It would remain for scholars like Freud—who took up the whole of Hume's analysis via Tylor[48]— to descend into the chaotic arena of feelings in an attempt to subject that realm, too, to the operation of universal natural laws, and to explain religion psychoanalytically.

It has been an ongoing concern of this book to note the extent to which the study of religion emerged out of criticism of religion. With Tylor, we are well past the time when criticism of religion is the springboard for the proposal of alternatives. The triumph of the scientific revolution brought this about. The new anthropology and sociology generated their own agendas, embracing culture as well as nature. Having demonstrated uniformitarianism—the universal extent of the operation of natural laws—in space through astronomy, the principle was now extended to time, becoming the presupposition for the new geology, biology, and—through the "master key" of archeology (*PC*, I, 58)—to culture and history itself. In epistemology, psychology, and sociology the search was on for the laws that govern the progress of knowledge and culture. Tylor was still arguing with theologians, but that argument was not what motivated his theories. Rather, the situation was reversed: theology now found itself in the position of defending its supernatural outlook against the dominant evolutionary view.

---

46. Harris (above, n. 19), 202. Robert H. Lowie (above, n. 29, 108ff.) offers a generally positive assessment of Tylor, including a defense against Durkheim's attack.

47. Ibid., 634.

48. Sigmund Freud, *Totem and Taboo*, 77 (see chap. 9).

Tylor rejected the wish of the theologians to be excused from the universal process of evolution by claiming an exemption for religion, or a particular form of religion, in the name of an entirely autonomous supernatural realm of law and causality. The situation is an index to the plight of theology in modernity. It is as though the old two-realms doctrine, so venerable in Christian tradition in its various guises, had now reversed itself. In the sixteenth and seventeenth centuries, it was used by theologians such as Luther and advocates of science such as Bacon and Galileo to carve a niche in the Christian universe for the works of human reason, whether in politics (Luther) or natural philosophy (Bacon). Now it was reversed: Tylor left behind the remnant of the idea (still found in the "exemptions" of Fontenelle and Vico) in favor of a comprehensive doctrine of truth; now it is theology that is seeking to preserve a last corner of the universe for itself, attempting to exempt the *religious* element in culture from the processes that produce all the rest of it.[49]

Although a sworn enemy of "superstition" (*PC*, II, 445), the gentle Tylor does not try to drive theology from its corner, but suggests that the results of the new ethnography should now be incorporated into a modern theology:

> The ethnographic results may . . . be left as materials for professed theologians, and it will not perhaps be long before evidence so fraught with meaning shall take its legitimate place. . . . The time may soon come when it will be thought as unreasonable for the scientific student of theology not to have a competent acquaintance with the principles of the religions of the lower races. . . . (*PC*, I, 23–24)[50]

The terms of the tension between a science and a theology of religion have changed in the century since Tylor, but the tension remains in the seemingly irreducible conflict between naturalistic and "transcendental" explanations of religion. There is no basis for productive dialogue until theologians take evolution seriously. Tylor would have agreed: theology's perplexed condition, he thought, was due to "the partial and one-sided application of the historical method of enquiry into theological doctrines, and the utter neglect of the ethnographical method which carries back the historical into remoter and more primitive regions of thought" (*PC*, II, 450).

---

49. Hans W. Frei, *The Eclipse of Biblical Narrative: A Study in Eighteenth- and Nineteenth-Century Hermeneutics*, notes the "reversal" that took place in biblical interpretation as a result of this process: "all across the theological spectrum the great reversal had taken place; interpretation was a matter of fitting the biblical story into another world with another story, rather than incorporating that world into the biblical story" (130).

50. The durability of what I have characterized as the "deistic" approach to the study of religion would have surprised Tylor, as would the enduring inattention to preliterate religion in theological education.

PART V

RELIGION EXPLAINED

Chapter 8

Sociogenic Theory:
Emile Durkheim

Emile Durkheim (1858–1917) and Sigmund Freud (1856–1939) were almost exact contemporaries, and, in a way quite different from all our previous authors, they are our contemporaries as well. Their continuing vitality for the study of religion is evident from their pervasive presence in the literature of the field. The basic explanatory structure that grounds scientific study of religion today can be traced directly to them. No one interested in explaining religion can ignore their contributions.

Included on everyone's list of "classics" in the study of religion, Durkheim and Freud are not the sort who are merely honored but unread. Of many contemporary examples of the continued vitality of their thought, let me cite two. The anthropologist Melford Spiro writes:

> Most theorists seem to agree that religious statements are believed to be true because religious actors have had social experiences which, corresponding to these beliefs, provide them with face validity. Thus Durkheim and Freud, agreeing that the cognitive roots of religious belief are to be found in social experience, disagree only about the structural context of the experience.[1]

Spiro goes on to express some preference for Freud's theory (purged of its ethnocentric "father") and notes that anthropological field studies have been able to confirm hypotheses derived from Freud.[2]

A second, more indirect testimony comes from Mary Douglas's *Purity and Danger*. She poses the question of why magic is effective among primitives. "Miracles apart," she answers, "such a power could only work at two levels, that of individual psychology and that of social life." Then, after an analysis of two cases, she comments on the first that "manipulation of the social

---

1. Melford E. Spiro, "Religion: Problems of Definition and Explanation," 102. This summary has the advantage over that of John J. Honigmann (*The Development of Anthropological Ideas*, 151) because it narrows the difference between Durkheim and Freud. Honigmann finds that "they differ profoundly in how to identify the source [of religious sentiments]. Freud, in the manner of Tylor, explains religion psychogenically, whereas Durkheim's explanation is sociogenic. In place of guilt, remorse, and the desire to undo evil, he makes the sense of constraint and feeling of elation experienced by belonging to a group the source of religious feeling."

2. Ibid., 103.

situation is the source of its efficacy," and, on the second, that we see not an absurd "Ali Baba" type of magician at work but, as a model, "the magisterial figure of Freud."[3]

In its present differentiated state, the study of religion can be approached from several angles. Lukes, for example, divides his treatment of Durkheim into three areas: interpretive, functional, and causal.[4] In these final chapters I focus only on the last, that is, on how the existence and persistence of religion is to be explained. A thorough treatment would of course entail attention to interpretive and functional questions, but such questions—of what it means and how it works—are distinguishable from our focus on origins or causes.

These final chapters treat Durkheim and Freud in the historical framework of what has preceded. Both of them were thoroughly read in the work of the British anthropologists, and both were drawn into the then heated discussion of totemism as an elementary, puzzling, but decisive form in the evolution of religious and—as they believed—of social and cultural life itself. My purpose will be to show how the work of Durkheim and Freud brought to a plateau the explanatory tradition studied here, by extending that tradition into two specialized theories of religion that are different, not wholly compatible as they stand, yet both indispensable and posing still, for those working within the paradigm of the human sciences, the challenge of producing a unified theory of religion.

Their theories have been well anticipated in what we have already studied. We found two such theories in Comte, and I have suggested that they indicated two future lines of inquiry. Now we can follow those lines in the writings of Freud and Durkheim. One line, represented especially well by Hume and Tylor (as well as by Comte's first theory), models the rise of religion on the individual person struggling to cope with and explain his experience of the world. This line of thought is grounded in an *anthropology* (a theory of the person); it is individualistic, developmental (childhood to maturity), tends to be intellectualistic (seeing the core of religion as a way of thinking), and identifies personification, or anthropomorphism, as the distinguishing mark of religious thought, which in turn exposes it as a "survival" in that it has been surpassed by scientific thinking.

The second line of tradition is best anticipated by Vico and by Comte's second theory: religion is here grounded in a *sociology* and explained by social "necessities and utilities," to use Vico's phrase. It models the rise of religion on elemental social exigencies, sees individual religion as derived from col-

3. Mary T. Douglas, *Purity and Danger: An Analysis of Concepts of Pollution and Taboo*, 86–89.

4. Steven Lukes, *Emile Durkheim: His Life and Work*, 462–77.

lective experience, and regards religious ideas as inseparable from the social matrix which generates and even necessitates them in all times and places.

Earlier, we gave Comte special recognition for revealing the paradoxical situation of religion in modern culture, by seeing, on one hand, the progressive obsolescence of theological thought as explanation and therefore, in a broader sense, as no longer capable of making sense of the world. On the other hand, Comte also saw the necessity of those constraining and unitive functions which traditionally belonged to religion and without which society could not exist.

Durkheim and Freud presuppose the accuracy of Comte's general analysis of the problem. Both agree that religion is no longer "true" in the literal sense of statements it makes about the world and the gods. But religion has been, and may continue to be, socially necessary. The extent to which both thinkers accepted religion as a given, and the profound degree to which both understood its psychological and social significance, forced them to take it most seriously in their theoretical work.

For Freud and Durkheim, religion was more than a mere "survival," and "explaining religion" did not explain it away. On the contrary, they both explained why religion could *not* merely be *explained* away. From the outset, they shared the view that if Tylor's explanation of religion is definitive, then the stubborn survival of religion in the modern world is inexplicable. Both argued that religion must have generative sources more powerful, constant, and persistent than mere reasoning. Furthermore, both argued that those generative forces or causes operate behind the conscious reasons identified by believers, and are necessary to explain them.

Both of our authors took the Enlightenment critique of religion for granted. Like Marx before them, they might have said that the intellectual critique of religion was complete,[5] but with Comte they might have complained that that critique did not provide sufficient basis for a new theory of religion, one that could account for all its aspects, its persistence and new anticipations of its possible future (or demise).

Durkheim complained that if God, or "spiritual beings," are not given, then the British approach "makes religion a system of hallucinations, since it reduces it to an immense metaphor with no objective value." Religious man, in the animists' view, "lives in a world peopled with beings and things which have only a verbal existence"; all that religion amounts to, if they are right, is "a system of lying fictions, whose *survival is incomprehensible*."[6] Tylor has not understood religion, whose primary aim, Durkheim contends, "is not to give men a representation of the physical world; for if that were its

---

5. Karl Marx, "Contribution to the Critique of Hegel's Philosophy of Right," 41.
6. Emile Durkheim, *The Elementary Forms of the Religious Life* (1912; hereafter *EF*), 100, my italics. This criticism is specifically aimed also at Max Müller, who characterized myth as a "disease of language" (and of thought).

essential task, *we could not understand how it has been able to survive*, for, on this side, it is scarcely more than a fabric of errors" (*EF*, 257; my italics). The primacy of this problem for Durkheim is demonstrated even further in his careful recasting of the question that had occupied thinkers since Hume, in order to purge it of unscientific guesswork. Speculations about "first beginnings" are vain, Durkheim asserts; they are only "subjective and arbitrary constructions which are subject to no sort of control." "What we want to do," he continues, "is to find a means of discerning the *ever-present causes* upon which the most essential forms of religious thought and practice depend" (*EF*, 20; my italics). Durkheim has clearly seen the Comtean paradox—that the progress of mind, while undercutting religion, can subvert the foundations of society as well. Though he does not share his messianic mission to save civilization by inventing a new religion, he builds on Comte's idea that religion performs necessary unitive and constraining functions in society.[7]

Freud, too, is aware of the inadequacy of Tylorian theory, not only because of the survival factor, but more profoundly, because the former theory fails to see the essential independence of religious thought from logical thinking.[8] "It is not to be supposed [he writes] that men were inspired to create their first system of the universe by pure speculative curiosity. The practical need for controlling the world around them must have played its part."[9] Freud is not unimpressed by the immense influence that religious ideas have exerted and continue to exert in the world. "This is a fresh psychological problem. We must ask where the *inner force* of those doctrines lies and to what it is that they owe their efficacy, independent as it is of recognition by reason."[10] Durkheim is in substantial agreement, although for him, it is a *sociological* problem: "In fact, it is an essential postulate of sociology [he insists] that a human institution cannot rest upon an error and a lie, without which it could not exist. If it were not founded on the nature of things, it would have encountered in the facts a resistance over which it could never have triumphed" (*EF*, 14). For Durkheim, "it is inadmissible that systems of ideas like religions, which have held such a considerable place in history,

---

7. Durkheim's dependence on Comte appears clearly in an article Durkheim wrote in 1909. W. S. Pickering (*Durkheim on Religion: A Selection of Readings with Bibliographies*, 334) quotes from an abstract of the article as follows: "Religion performs two functions—one is speculative and relates to knowledge about the universe, as such it is now in jeopardy—the other is vital and practical, and for this, science knows no substitute, and because of this religion will continue." Marx and Engels, like Durkheim, were primarily interested in the survival of religion, not in its origin, nor did they contribute anything original to that question (see Delos B. McKown, *The Classical Marxist Critique of Religion*, esp. 65ff.). The persistence of religion and the conditions necessary for its demise give focus to their discussion.

8. Sigmund Freud, *Moses and Monotheism* (1937), 130. Here, he returns to Hume's thesis that religion's sources are affective before they are intellectual.

9. Sigmund Freud, *Totem and Taboo* (1913), 78.

10. Sigmund Freud, *Future of an Illusion* (1927), 29.

and to which, in all times, men have come to receive the energy which they must have to live, should be made up of a tissue of illusions" (*EF*, 87). Together, then, they share a similar view of their task as practitioners of the science of humanity. In Freud's formulation, "we are confronted with the task of finding out how those who have faith in a Divine Being could have acquired it, and whence this belief derives the enormous power that enables it to overwhelm Reason and Science."[11]

The views of our authors converge on the basic premise that some cause other than that presumed by believers must be identified as the hidden but real spring of religious experience. But are they not now yielding again to what Vico called the "conceit of scholars"—that anachronistic practice of the learned interpreters of ancient myth (the "allegorizers") who refused to accept the data at face value? There are, to be sure, some important similarities. Durkheim and Freud do share with the allegorists the attempt to find a deeper truth beneath the "literal sense" of the religious texts and actions to be interpreted. Both seek to unveil something in the myth (or ritual) that is only inchoately intended and pointed to through it. But the allegorists discovered a transcendent metaphysical or religious ground which both explained everything religious and toward which everything intended, and through understanding of which the deepest *religious* aim expressed in the words would be fulfilled; our analysts, on the other hand, reveal systems of natural causes unrecognized by the conscious intentions of believers. These forces, moreover, were not at all what the religious subjects had in mind or could acknowledge as the fulfillment of their own ultimate aim.

By the allegorizers, the literal and religious intention was seen as fundamentally true in its direction and aim; for Freud and Durkheim, that intention, while profoundly human and responsive to real powers operating in experience, could not fulfill its wish by simple extension to and discovery of its own depth; rather, the religious required transformation into a theoretical explanation of hitherto unrecognized natural causes, and a reformulation of intention based on a dis-illusioned understanding of reality.

The crucial difference is this: in the ancient mode of allegorical interpretation, the religious subject and the allegorist agree on the fundamental categorical explanation of religious experience. Both base it and account for it in the same way. But with the new analysis, an explanation quite at odds with that of the religious subjects is postulated, on the theory that their religious language can be accounted for by universally operative psychological and/or social forces. In the causal scheme of things, these forces stand in place of "spiritual beings."

The success of Durkheim and Freud in describing such psychosocial systems marks the completion of a naturalistic paradigm for the study of religion because their allegation that psychosocial causes are at the root of religious

---

11. Sigmund Freud, *Moses and Monotheism*, 157.

experience was subject to testing through scientific methods of observation and correction—a process that continues still. Despite the fact that no final scientific "proof" of their theses can be imagined (a problem shared by the most comprehensive paradigms in the natural sciences as well), the theories were supported by argument and evidence of sufficient power and coherence to support a new generation of specialized studies.

It is important to stress that Durkheim and Freud took the literal or surface sense of their texts more seriously than the allegorists did, as we shall see. They acknowledged to a much greater extent that the believers really meant what they said and did—no doubt in part because our analysts were under no pressure to "save the [dignity of] the appearances" on grounds of piety toward the ancients or their gods.

Moreover, because Durkheim and Freud took with new, "pre-Enlightenment" seriousness the reality of the powers to which believers testified. They began by honoring the conviction of the religious that their ideas and actions are responses to something real—some generative system of forces quite exceeding the critical power of reason either to reproduce or to eradicate. By acknowledging some power or force that lay beneath rational justifications of religion, Durkheim and Freud raised the problem of explaining religion to a level quite beyond that of the Enlightenment. Their acknowledgment that religious actors were not deceived in their conviction that they were in the embrace of powers larger and more profound than reason can control or imagination simply create ex nihilo made the task of explaining religion far more complex than was recognized by earlier analysts.

Despite their concession, however, Durkheim and Freud agreed that believers do not understand the real grounds of their convictions. As Durkheim put it, "[Religion] does not know itself. It knows neither what it is made of, nor what need it satisfies. Far from being able to dictate to science, it is itself the subject of scientific investigation . . . Religion is on the dissecting table awaiting vivisection."[12] This diagnostic metaphor is perhaps even more appropriate to Freud, who pronounced that "in all believers, . . . the motives impelling them to religious practices are unknown, or are replaced in consciousness by others which are advanced in their stead."[13] Both could therefore agree with Durkheim's clear formulation, that to understand religious practice and thought,

> one must know how to go underneath the symbol to the reality which it represents and which gives it its meaning. The most barbarous and the most fantastic rites and the strangest myths translate some human need, some aspect of life, either individual or social. The reasons with which the faithful justify them may be, and

12. Quoted by W. S. F. Pickering, *Durkheim on Religion*, 251.
13. Sigmund Freud, "Obsessive Acts and Religious Practices," 188.

generally are, erroneous; *but the true reasons do not cease to exist, and it is the duty of science to discover them. (EF,* 14–15; my italics)

One is reminded of the classic formula of biblical hermeneutics, that the letter kills, when Durkheim writes: "When only the letter of the formulae is considered, these religious beliefs and practices undoubtedly seem disconcerting. . . . "; the worship of plants and animals, for example, cannot have arisen from their literal impressiveness (*EF,* 14). "Ducks, rabbits, kangaroos, lizards, worms, frogs, etc." can hardly have evoked the feelings directed toward them in the primitive cult; "their objective qualities surely were not the origin of the religious sentiments which they inspired" (*EF,* 105).[14] Behind and beneath these representations, then, must lie some generative force or energy that awaits to be explained (*EF,* 217).

In sum, if the objects of religious veneration are not satisfactory to explain religion, and if one cannot see how to account for the efficacy and persistence of religion by appeal to supernatural power, and if the theories of Tylor et al. are not adequate because the predicted demise of religion is not occurring on evolutionary schedule, then some other explanation has to be offered, one that identifies those forces universally testified to but not correctly identified by believers. Such explanations, Durkheim and Freud understand, cannot be arrived at simply by ignoring what believers say and do; rather, one has to learn how to interpret their words and actions in a new way.

Before proceeding to Durkheim, an item of contrast between him and Freud needs to be noted. Both operated within an evolutionary framework, but in Durkheim's case it was not necessary for the elucidation of an explanation of religion.[15] Freud's theory, on the other hand, is *inherently* developmental. This fact results in some interesting differences when it comes to approaching the problem of the origin of religion, which in their day revolved around the problem of totemism, widely thought of as the earliest (and perhaps the earliest possible) form of religion. Both Durkheim and Freud engaged in the current debate on the subject; both sided with those who held totemism to be religious, or at least immediately prereligious in a decisive way. Unfortunately, they never discussed each other's work.

The diverse nature of their theories caused them to select different items of evidence as significant, and comparison is interesting since they both depended on the same body of ethnological research (both even acknowledged

14. Notice the difference from both Charles de Brosses and the allegorists. De Brosses took the representations of fetish worship literally but concluded that they made no sense at all except as revelations of the infantile state of the savage mind (see his *Du culte des dieux fétiches,* 185, and my discussion in chapter 5). The allegorists took the same representations nonliterally in order to give fetishism a more dignified religious significance.

15. See Steven Lukes (above, n. 4), 456–57, on the residual importance of evolution for Durkheim's theory. This is not to say, however, that Durkheim was uninterested in the process of evolutionary change or that his theory in any way is incompatible with it: see below n. 27.

receiving decisive insight from W. Robertson Smith, a man who understood religion from inside).[16] For instance, Durkheim emphatically did not consider totemism to be universal, or a stage through which all societies must have passed—a point he stresses (EF, 114)—because his theory was sociological, postulating ever-present causes that could be applied to other systems as well. On the other hand, his theory was monocausal in that it sought to explain everything by social causes—a unilateralism that has drawn wide criticism.[17] Freud, on his part, modestly denied that something so complex as religion can be reduced to a single source,[18] but insisted that every society *must* have passed through a totemic phase. The reason is that his theory, springing from a developmental view of individual and species, presupposed the universality of the oedipal mechanism which, at the phylogenetic level, accounted for religion and the possibility of culture itself (of which more in chapter 9).

We may expect, then, some sort of lawlike, developmental theory in connection with Freud's account of the rise of religion, while in Durkheim's case certain perpetual forces will suffice—again, reflecting Comte's first and second theories of religion both in structure and implications: for Freud, religion is obsolete and to be superseded in the name of the inexorable progress of reason and truth; for Durkheim, religion endures in virtue of its social necessity.

I shall now examine each author in terms of his own peculiar theoretical approach; Durkheim first.

With almost maniacal concentration, Durkheim attacks the problem of religion from a new theoretical perspective that, for him, alters the very terms in which the problems are defined. An adversarial relationship with Freud appears inevitable, especially when we begin with Durkheim's sociological approach; for he is at pains to prove that it describes and explains the facts at a deeper and more primal level than that offered by psychology. Freud will claim as much for his view. The issue is joined between collectivism and individualism, for Durkheim believes that one or the other must be chosen as "square one" in the exposition of the religious life.

In a remarkable testimony to the decisive importance of the sociological approach for his own intellectual career, Durkheim pays tribute to W. Robertson Smith:

> it was only in 1895 [he writes in 1907] that I had a clear understanding of the important role played by religion in social life. It was in that year that I found the method of approaching the study of religion sociologically for the first time. It was

16. See T. O. Beidelman, *W. Robertson Smith and the Sociological Study of Religion*, which includes an account of this Christian scholar's troubles with the Scottish church.

17. Lukes (above, n. 4), 481, on the "all-consuming" quality of Durkheim's "sociocentric fixation."

18. Sigmund Freud, *Totem and Taboo*, 100.

a revelation to me. During 1895 a line of demarcation was drawn in the development of my thought, so much so that all my earlier research had to be looked at afresh and made to harmonize with these new views. Wundt's *Ethik*, which I had read eight years previously, had nothing to do with this change in direction. It was entirely the result of the studies of religious history, which I had just undertaken, notably the reading of the work of Robertson Smith and his school.[19]

The sociological approach seems, in Durkheim's mind, to transcend and resolve a debate between two rival alternatives for explaining the "higher" life of human beings—one being materialism (the quotation raises the spectre not only of Tylor, but also of Freud and Marx-Engels), the other theism. Better than either,

> sociology appears destined to open a new way to the science of man. Up to the present, thinkers were placed before this double alternative: either explain the superior and specific faculties of men by connecting them to the inferior forms of his being, the reason to the senses, or the mind to matter, which is equivalent to denying their uniqueness; or else attach them to some superexperimental reality which was postulated, but whose existence could be established by no observation. (*EF*, 495)

The continuation of the quotation, however, shows that Durkheim's target here is not so much materialism or idealism (in Tylor's mind, it will be recalled, the essential issue), but what he sees them to hold in common—individualism: "What put them in this difficulty was the fact that the individual passed as being the *finis naturae*—the ultimate creation of nature; it seemed that there was nothing beyond him, or at least nothing that science could touch." Now comes the essential point: "But from the moment when it is recognized that above the individual there is society, and that this is not a nominal being created by reason, but *a system of active forces, a new manner of explaining men becomes possible (EF, 495; my italics).*"[20]

Anticipating a little, we shall see Durkheim using totemism as a proof that the priority of the collective is supported by evidence from the most primitive form of religion known. From it, he will demonstrate to his own satisfaction

19. Pickering (above, n. 12), 241, quoting from a letter Durkheim wrote in response to a review of the *Elementary Forms*. This is a nice example of the sort of "conversion" experienced by some scientists and described by Thomas Kuhn, *The Structure of Scientific Revolutions*, 122ff. Comparison to Martin Luther's account of his so-called *Turmerlebnis* is irresistible (cf. the autobiographical "Preface to the Complete Edition of Luther's Latin Writings," in *Luther's Works*, 34:336–37).

20. In a review article (1897), Durkheim wrote: "I believe that this idea—that social life must be explained, not by the notions of those who participate in it, but by more profound causes which are unperceived by consciousness—is fruitful; and I think also that these causes must be sought principally in the manner according to which the associated individuals are grouped. In this way—and in this way only—it seems to me, can history become a science, and sociology itself exist" (quoted by John W. Bowker, *The Sense of God: Sociological, Anthropological and Psychological Approaches to the Origin of the Sense of God*, 22).

that "the first form of individual religion met with in history appears, not as the active principle of all public religion, but, on the contrary, as a simple aspect of this latter. The cult which the individual organizes for himself in his own inner conscience, far from being the germ of the collective cult, is only this latter adapted to the personal needs of the individual" (*EF*, 208). Durkheim realizes the advantages of the individualistic approach: not only is it simple, but it has "the advantage of being in harmony with the conception of religion which is currently held; this is quite generally regarded as something intimate and personal" (*EF*, 200).

Sociology shows another way. It begins with the study of social things, regarded as a part of nature in the sense of being subject to the same regularity as physical nature, and reveals causal relationships and other essential features of human life that simply cannot be discovered from study of individuals. Social facts are *sui generis,* and sociological *explanations* are not reducible to psychological ones, because "a combination of units yields new properties which cannot be derived from the study of any one of these units considered in isolation."[21] Durkheim offers an example from metallurgy: "The hardness of bronze is not in the copper, nor the tin, nor the lead, which served to create it and which are soft and malleable bodies; it is in their mixture."[22] From these considerations, Durkheim states as a primary principle that "the determining cause of a social fact must be sought among antecedent social facts and not among states of individual consciousness."[23] He observes that "as far as social facts are concerned, we still have the mentality of primitives," even though we have ceased to believe in miracles. With his method, he promises to usher us into the modern world of social-scientific thinking (*EF*, 42).

Durkheim's achievement rests not merely in applying a new sociological perspective to recognized data, but, by examining the data themselves, in isolating two features that come much closer to the core of distinctly *religious* realities than those which had been recognized by Tylor and others: namely, "*the sacred*" and *community.* He recognizes that something must be said about this first, in order to define the domain of inquiry and to avoid misconstruing religion as "a system of ideas and practices which has nothing at all religious about it, or else of leaving to one side many religious facts, without perceiving their true nature" (*EF*, 37). As we have already noted, by concentrating on the purely mental activity that, while aiming to explain experience in the world, produced first myth and later science, much religious data was simply ignored. To get research on track, it was necessary at the outset to identify what is essentially religious, that is, "to indicate a certain number of external

21. Anthony Giddens, introduction to *Emile Durkheim: Selected Writings,* 34.
22. Ibid., quoting from Durkheim's *Rules of Sociological Method.*
23. Ibid., 74 (part of selection from *Rules of Sociological Method,* and italicized in the text).

and easily recognizable signs, which will enable us to recognize religious phenomena wherever they are met with, and which will deter us from confounding them with others" (*EF*, 37–38).

First, "the sacred." *The* "distinctive trait of religious thought," according to Durkheim, is the "division of the world into two domains, the one containing all that is sacred, the other all that is profane" (*EF*, 52; cf. the formal definition, 62–63). This bifurcation of the world into two realms is characteristic of all known cultures; these two radically heterogeneous spheres embrace all that exists and divide the universe into exclusive departments (*EF*, 53, 56). Attention has now shifted from the realm of thinking and ideas alone and now must also embrace the cult and the whole realm of religious activity, as well as mere "belief in spiritual beings."

Lukes summarizes Durkheim's fundamental distinction between sacred and profane as follows:

> Thus, on the one hand, there is the sacred—"elaborated by a collectivity," hypostasizing collective forces, fusing individual *consciences* "into communion," imposing respect and love, transferring "society into us" and connecting "us with something surpassing us." On the other hand is the profane—expressing "our organisms and the objects to which they are most directly related," and relating to men's ordinary life, which is seen as involving "daily personal preoccupations," "private existence" and "egoistic passions."[24]

While this distinction is too rigid and static to account for all the data and suffers from serious empirical and conceptual difficulties,[25] it advances the discussion by requiring definition of what exactly is to be taken as distinctly "religious" amid the plethora of phenomena ordinarily associated with that term. Moreover, it makes a coherent and challenging proposal regarding what is sui generis about religion by way of a sociological definition and explanation. Such clarification is all too rare in the literature even today.

The second defining characteristic of religion is a functional one that bears no immediately discernible relationship to the first: religious beliefs and practices "unite into one single moral community called a church all those who adhere to them" (*EF*, 62).[26] As we shall see, however, there is a reciprocity between the two elements Durkheim has isolated, for the very origin of the sacred will be linked to effects that can be generated only in the context of the community in its assembly, while the gathered community will in turn

---

24. Lukes's quotations are all cited as from Durkheim's "Le Dualisme de la nature humaine et ses conditions sociales," *Scientia* 15 (1914): 206–21.

25. Lukes (above, n. 4), 24–28. Lukes follows Stanner's criticism: 26–28; cf. 478.

26. It is interesting that Durkheim here combines substantive ("sacred," "church") and functional (to "unite" in a moral community) elements. Such a definition has both the elasticity required for a developmental viewpoint and the stability required for purposes of identification and differentiation from other phenomena. Cf. the quotation from *EF*, 17, which follows in the text. For further discussion of the problem of the definition of religion, see Melford Spiro (above, n. 1) and Martin Southwold, "Buddhism and the Definition of Religion."

be energized and recreated by communion with those beings it regards as sacred. We shall study this intimate relationship more closely when we come to Durkheim's treatment of totemism.

Durkheim's definition of the subject matter to be explained makes the problem of locating its generative forces much more complex than it was before. In a Tylorian framework, "it was enough to demand which forces had, because of their exceptional energy, been able to strike the human imagination forcefully enough to inspire religious sentiments. But if, as we have sought to establish, sacred things differ in nature from profane things, if they have a wholly different essence, then the problem is more complex" (*EF*, 57). And the increased complexity of the phenomena to be explained, Durkheim continues, now requires a new definition of the task ahead—explaining "the sacred": "we must first of all ask what has been able to lead men to see in the world two heterogeneous and incompatible worlds, though nothing in sensible experience seems able to suggest the idea of so radical a duality to them" (*EF*, 57).

In noting the impersonal and categorical nature of the sacred-profane distinction, we already anticipate that Durkheim will not be satisfied with simply explaining the "birth of the gods," in Humean fashion, as an anthropomorphic projection to cover unknown natural causes. The data demanding explanation are simply not covered by that theory. "The fact that religion represents the causes thus imagined, under the form of personal agents, is not enough to explain how they got a sacred character. *A personal agent can be profane, and also, many religious forces are essentially impersonal*" (*EF*, 104–05, n. 39; my italics).

The real question, then, is the birth of the notion that "there are in reality two categories of things" (*EF*, 104)—and not the birth only but the "ever-present causes" of this persistent way of looking at the world (*EF*, 20). For religions of *all* times and places are alike: "They respond to the same needs, they play the same role, they depend on the same causes; they can also well serve to show the nature of the religious life. . . ." (*EF*, 15).

But why is it desirable to study the most primitive possible religion? Not so that we may point with evolutionary pride at how far we have come, or view with alarm the surviving vestiges of superstition, but because those most elementary and necessary springs from which *all* religious life flows are more transparent to analysis in simpler societies than our own. As Durkheim says:

> At the foundation of all systems of beliefs and of all cults there ought necessarily to be a certain number of fundamental representations or conceptions and of ritual attitudes which, in spite of the diversity of form which they have taken, have the same objective significance and fulfill the same functions everywhere. These are the permanent elements which constitute that which is permanent and human in religion. . . . (*EF*, 17)

Neither Durkheim nor Freud seriously entertained the notion that the causes of religion might have fundamentally changed in human history. As

Durkheim makes clear, moreover, the study of contemporary "civilized" religion is much more difficult for explanatory purposes, because its causes are more deeply buried under immemorial layers of interpretive and rationalizing traditions: "the causes which called it into existence, though remaining active, are no longer perceived, except across a vast scheme of interpretations which quite transform them. Popular mythologies and subtile theologies have done their work. . . . The psychological gap between the cause and the effect, between the apparent cause and the effective cause, has become more considerable. . . . " (*EF*, 20).

By going back to the earliest accessible form of religious life, we are in hopes of finding it "reduced to that which is indispensable, to that without which there could be no religion" (*EF*, 18). Such an identification of the "indispensable" allows us to establish, through time, a coherent account of the career of religion. In complete accord with Comte, Durkheim insists that "we cannot arrive at an understanding of the most recent religions except by following the manner in which they have been progressively composed in history. In fact, *historical analysis is the only means of explanation* which it is possible to apply to them" (*EF*, 15; italics mine). Although the *Elementary Forms* does not try to provide such a *history* of religion, Durkheim is vitally interested in development and change, contrary to some of his interpreters.[27] But (as Vico had argued) it is necessary to arrive as closely as possible at beginnings to give an accurate account of the essential nature of religion, as well as of its development:

Every time that we undertake to explain something human, taken at a given moment in history—be it a religious belief, a moral precept, a legal principle . . . —it is necessary to commence by going back to its most primitive and simple form, to try to account for the characteristics by which it was marked at the time, and then to show how it developed and became complicated little by little, and how it became that which it is at the moment in question. One readily understands the importance which the determination of the point of departure has for this series of progressive explanations, for all the others are attached to it. (*EF*, 15–16)

Durkheim warns that no absolute first beginnings of religion can ever be determined; rather, in our search for the "ever-present causes," we shall study "the most simple social condition that is actually known or that beyond which we cannot go at present" (*EF*, 20, n. 1).

27. Anthony Giddens has challenged Talcott Parsons's thesis that Durkheim is mainly preoccupied with the problem of order. "The central issue informing his [Durkheim's] writings," Giddens contends, "was that of change: in common with virtually all the other major social thinkers of his generation he was preoccupied above all with the confrontation between the dissolving 'traditional' society and the emergent 'modern' type" (Giddens [above, n. 21], 41). This conforms with my own perception of Durkheim's continuity with the concerns of Comte; see, e.g., *EF*, 15, quoted in my text just above n. 25, on the importance of history.

Durkheim arrives at the point of initiating a fresh examination of totemism from his critique of the British anthropologists, whose theories he has labeled *animism* and *naturism*.[28] Their failure as explanations of elementary religion has already been noted in the context of the question of survivals: according to their theories, "a whole world of delusive representations has superimposed itself upon the other, denatured it to the point of making it unrecognizable and substituted a pure hallucination for reality" (*EF*, 106–07).

There is a more basic issue to be investigated: we must explain the notion of *the sacred:*

> Both [animists and naturists] undertake to construct the idea of the divine out of the sensations aroused in us by certain natural phenomena, either physical or biological. For the animists it is dreams, for the naturists, certain cosmic phenomena, which served as the point of departure for religious evolution. But for both, it is in the nature, either of man or of the universe, that we must look for the germ of the grand opposition which separates the profane from the sacred. (*EF*, 106)

Now the screws are tightened. The rival theories make the spirits and gods straightforward representations of natural powers behind phenomena, but this will not do (according to the definition of the problem imposed by Durkheim): "A fact of common experience cannot give us the idea of something whose characteristic is to be outside the world of common experience" (*EF*, 106). What we have to find is something else, "some other reality, in relation to which this variety of delirium which all religion is in a sense, has a significance and an objective value" (*EF*, 107). Beneath animism and naturism must lie some other sort of religious complex "more fundamental and more primitive." It must be something capable of having generated that bifurcation of the world into sacred and profane which is the decisive mark of religion. "In fact, this cult does exist: it is the one to which ethnologists have given the name of totemism" (*EF*, 107).

Among ethnologists, there was considerable agreement that "this religion is the most primitive one that is now observable and even, in all probability, that has ever existed" (*EF*, 194). Moreover, Durkheim notes, totemism is inseparably tied to clans, and "social organization on a clan basis is the simplest [and therefore, by definition in an evolutionary view, the oldest] which we know." Thus, "a religion so closely connected to a social system surpassing all others in simplicity may well be regarded as the most elementary religion we can possibly know" (*EF*, 195). Totemism, therefore, holds great promise as a case study in primal religion: "If we succeed in discovering the origins of the [totemic] beliefs . . . we shall very probably discover at the same time the causes leading to the rise of the religious sentiment in humanity" (*EF*, 195).

28. An excellent sense of that discussion can be gotten from Freud's own careful review of the literature in *Totem and Taboo*.

Now the plants and animals that serve as clan totems utterly lack the majesty and dignity which we associate with the sacred, yet sacred they are. This is a proof against the primary significance accorded to the anthropomorphic thesis by Hume, Comte, Tylor, and Freud.

> It is not at all true that man has had such an inclination to impose his own form upon things. More than that, he even commenced by conceiving of himself as participating closely in the animal nature. In fact, it is a belief almost universal in Australia, and very widespread among the Indians of North America, that the ancestors of men were beasts or plants. . . . Thus, far from seeing beings like themselves everywhere, men commenced by believing themselves to be the image of some beings from which they differed radically (*EF*, 85–86).

"Sacredness"—a forbidding otherness that sets certain objects apart, makes them taboo—somehow attaches itself to these humble totems. Moreover, these totems give the clans their names. "The species of things which serves to designate the clan collectively is called its *totem*. The totem of the clan is also that of each of its members" (*EF*, 123). The direction Durkheim is taking is clear: totemism is going to provide the material validation of his definition of religion (with its decisive elements, "the sacred" and "church"), and it is going to give concrete demonstration to his explanation of religion itself *if* he can sort out the web of causal relationships that constitute this most elementary form of the religious life.

In order to highlight the hermeneutical procedure involved in Durkheim's treatment, I return to the distinction between "letter" and theory. Such a procedure will show the extent to which Durkheim attends seriously to what the participants/believers themselves experience, do, say, and know, as distinct from what he as the analyst and explainer makes of it all.[29]

In order to explain the sources of religion, it is not enough for Durkheim to learn to think like the natives or simply to imagine how they "must" think. The religious life involves the whole person and the whole community that participates in it. The believers would agree that their religious activity is energized and sustained by powers they regard as sacred. Even if we are scientific analysts, therefore, we must do what the believers do: "it is not enough that we think of them [these powers]; it is also indispensable that we place ourselves within their sphere of action, and that we set ourselves where we may best feel their influence; in a word, it is necessary that we act, and that we repeat the acts thus necessary every time we feel the need of renewing their effects" (*EF*, 464).

Clan life is characterized by a regular rhythm of dispersal and assembly, and it is in assembly that the constitutive religious "moment" occurs, centering on the mysterious totem. The totem simultaneously and consciously

---

29. See Wayne Proudfoot's analysis of the distinction between identification and explanation, in "Religion and Reduction," and, at greater length, in *Religious Experience*.

represents two different things which are not, however, explicitly connected in the minds of clan members. As already noted, the totem is the clan's "emblem, a veritable coat-of-arms"; its "crest," "sign," "badge," or "ensign" (*EF*, 134).

So essential is the totem to clan life, that it is impossible to define that life at all without it.

> For the members of a single clan are not united to each other either by a common habitat or by common blood.... Their unity comes solely from their having the same name and the same emblem, their believing that they have the same relations with the same categories of things, their practising the same rites, or, in a word, from their participating in the same totemic cult. Thus totemism and the clan mutually imply each other.... (*EF*, 194–95)

The identification of the clan member with his totem is a crucial feature that had been identified by Sir James George Frazer as the essence of totemism (although he came to deny its religious character in the end), and Freud would also pick up that idea as a critical link in his analysis of the meaning of totemism.

For clan members, this first identification and meaning of the totem as its ensign is simple and straightforward. But, independent of that identification, the totem also—in the mind of clan members—takes on a distinctly religious significance. Set apart and sacred under certain circumstances, especially in the context of periodic assemblies of the clan, it becomes "the very type of sacred thing" (*EF*, 140), because it is believed to embody the mysterious, impersonal, divine "force" widely encountered by ethnologists and referred to under different names, such as "mana," "wakan," and "orenda" (cf. *EF*, 229, 232–33).

In this context, the totem becomes the center of a religious cult, "not of such and such animals or men or images, but of an anonymous and impersonal force, found in each of these beings but not to be confounded with any of them. No one possesses it entirely and all participate in it. It is so completely independent of the particular subjects in whom it incarnates itself, that it precedes them and survives them" (*EF*, 217). As the aborigines conceive it, the totem is really "only the material form under which the imagination represents this immaterial substance, this energy diffused through all sorts of heterogeneous things, which alone is the real object of the cult (*EF*, 217).[30]

A final piece of the puzzle is this: it is in the assemblies of the clan alone that the formative experience takes place that can properly be called "religious." When the clan gathers, something extraordinary happens; "a sort of electricity is formed by their collecting which quickly transports them to an

---

30. Cf. Durkheim's discussion of how, through later development, ancestors got attached to the totems via etiological legends (*EF*, 159).

extraordinary degree of exaltation" (*EF*, 247). Once a participant arrives at such a state, he "does not recognize himself any longer. Feeling himself dominated and carried away by some sort of an external power which makes him think and act differently than in normal times, he naturally has the impression of being himself no longer. It seems to him that he has become a new being. . . . " (*EF*, 249; cf. 355, 469).

Now we must go beyond the realm of experienced feelings and conscious beliefs to Durkheim's explanation. In his view, the experience undergone in a group such as the gathered clan explains the origin of religion *as such*, because such psychic experience can be triggered only by a mechanism peculiar to a group: "collective life . . . brings about a state of effervescence which changes the conditions of psychic activity. Vital energies are overexcited, passions more active, sensations stronger; there are even some which are produced only at this moment" (*EF*, 469).

As with Hume, the rise of religion is seen as a two-step process: first, a peculiar sort of experience; second, how its subjects account for and interpret it. But in place of the anthropomorphic thesis Durkheim sees the primal religious thought as the positing of an "ideal world." Thus (continuing the same discussion), "in order to account for the very particular impressions which he receives, he attributes to the things with which he is in most direct contact properties which they have not. . . . In a word, above the real world where his profane life passes he has placed another . . . to which he attributes a higher sort of dignity. . . . " (*EF*, 469–70; cf. 250). This explanation, Durkheim claims, proves that the formation of the ideal reality of the sacred is "not an irreducible fact which escapes science; it depends upon conditions which observation can touch: it is a natural product of social life" (*EF*, 470; cf. 250).[31]

What needs to be explained next is "how it happens that these [sacred] forces are thought of *under the form of totems*"? (*EF*, 251; my italics). We are told that the believers' experience "could not fail to give men the idea that outside themselves there exist one or several powers, both moral and, at the same time, efficacious, upon which they depend. They must think of these powers at least in part, as outside themselves, for these address them in a tone of command and sometimes even order them to do violence to their most natural inclinations" (*EF*, 239).

What the *believers* believe is that the totem is the emblem of their clan and that the totem is a sacred thing, particularly in the context of the assembly; and that its sacredness consists in the fact that it is the incarnation or vehicle

---

31. Lukes (above, n. 4), 462, cites a group of studies on the crowd psychology of the late nineteenth century which "doubtless affected" Durkheim. He asserts, however, that "there is no evidence that he was specifically influenced by any of them," and that "unlike them, he did not see crowd behavior as pathological. . . . " (ibid.).

of remarkable energies that "transform" them in the practice of the cult. Here, the participants' account exhausts its value for the analyst, because the analyst does not believe their explanation that mysterious transcendent powers beyond the realm of natural causation and the reach of scientific analysis really create this experience.

And so we move again to the explanation—from the "letter" to the theory—believing that the participant does not and cannot identify the real forces that are actually moving him. Again, we recall the extent to which Durkheim has taken the believers seriously in what they say about themselves: we can, he notes, affirm that "the believer is not deceived when he believes in the existence of a moral power upon which he depends and from which he receives all that is best in himself" (*EF*, 257). Indeed, "it is an eternal[!] truth that outside of us there exists something greater than us, with which we enter into communion" (*EF*, 257). Nevertheless, the participant/primitive does not know the secret;

> does not . . . see that these impressions [of vitality, dependence, etc.] come to him *from the group*. He does not know that the coming together of a number of men associated in the same life results in disengaging new energies, which transform each of them. All that he knows is that he is raised above himself and that he sees a different life from the one he ordinarily leads. (*EF*, 252; my italics)

To explain *why* primitives think the energy comes to them from a power in the totem, Durkheim invokes "a well-known [psychological] law," to wit, "that the sentiments aroused in us by something spontaneously attach themselves to the symbol which represents them. . . . This transference of sentiments comes simply from the fact that the idea of a thing and the idea of its symbol are closely united in our minds; the result is that the emotions provoked by the one extend contagiously to the other" (*EF*, 251). Now we already know that for clan members the totem represents the clan, so "it is natural that the impressions aroused by the clan in individual minds—impressions of dependence and of increased vitality—should fix themselves on the idea of the totem rather than that of the clan: for the clan is too complex a reality to be represented clearly in all its complex unity by such rudimentary intelligences" (*EF*, 252).

At this point we can see that although Durkheim criticized the animists and naturists, his form of argument is parallel to theirs. For Durkheim, the "mystery" that generates religion is not those inexplicable *natural* occurrences whose personifying explanations are to be replaced by those of physics; the puzzle lies rather in mysterious *social* experiences associated with totems whose symbolic power is now capable of being explained by sociology. In both instances, the analyst replaces the primitives' animistic explanations of the relevant occurrences with his own. This parallelism should not, however, obscure the important difference of what is regarded as relevant data: Durkheim is here focusing on the primitives' collective experience with totemic symbols rather than on their explanations of natural phenomena. In the latter case, the analyst explains (or corrects) a faulty explanation; in the case before us, he explains the real power behind a symbol. Durkheim has noted that the totem is symbol *both* of the "god" (however the power is conceived) and of the clan, or the community. His explanation is now completed by joining them thus: if the totem

> is at once the symbol of the god and of the society, is that *not because the god and the society are only one? How could the emblem of the group have been able to become the figure of this quasi-divinity, if the group and the divinity were two distinct realities?* The god of the clan, the totemic principle, can therefore be nothing else than the clan itself, personified and represented to the imagination under the visible form of the animal or vegetable which serves as totem. (*EF*, 236; my italics)

Durkheim's explanation claims to have located the "living reality" behind the "letter of the symbol": again, Durkheim recognizes without hesitation that the believer is not deceived about being influenced by real "moral power."

> It is true that he is wrong in thinking that this increase of vitality is the work of a power in the form of some animal or plant. But this error is merely in regard to the *letter of the symbol* by which this being is represented to the mind and the external appearance which the imagination has given it, and not in regard to the fact of its existence. *Behind these figures and metaphors,* be they gross or refined, there is a *concrete and living reality.* (*EF*, 257; my italics)

In another formulation, Durkheim notes the considerable conceptual distance that separates society, as a living system with causal power, from the sacred totem which represents it symbolically. Under that symbol, the original force has been rendered "unrecognizable," transformed in the imaginary geography of the "sacred" (*EF*, 426) into a "mythological sociology" (Lukes's phrase).[32] Thus, the myths of the believers do indeed "translate" a "reality," but in doing so they radically "disfigure" it (*EF*, 445; cf. 239–40).

In a summary paragraph, Durkheim condenses his "explanation of why it [the totem] holds the first place in the series of sacred things":

> Since religious force is nothing other than the collective and anonymous force of the clan, and since this can be represented in the mind only in the form of the totem, the totemic emblem is like the visible body of the god. Therefore, it is from it that those kindly or dreadful actions seem to emanate, which the cult seeks to provoke or prevent; consequently, it is to it that the cult is addressed. (*EF*, 253; cf. 239–40)

Since Hume, it had been a commonplace that religious life was a response to power. It is Durkheim's remarkable thesis that this power is originally not that of nature but of society: "everything tends to prove that the first

---

32. Lukes (above, n. 4), 467.

powers of which the human mind had any idea were those which societies have established in organizing themselves" (*EF*, 409). Society is capable of generating and sustaining religious feelings, because "to its members it is what a god is to his worshippers. In fact, a god is, first of all, a being whom men think of as superior to themselves, and upon whom they feel that they depend" (*EF*, 237).[33] In a passage that echoes Comte and sounds very much like Freud's words in *Future of an Illusion* and *Civilization and Its Discontents*, Durkheim elaborates on society's attributes:

> [it] gives us the sensation of a perpetual dependence. . . . It requires that, forgetful of our own interest, we make ourselves its servitors, and it submits us to every sort of inconvenience, privation and sacrifice, without which social life would be impossible. It is because of this that at every instant we are obliged to submit ourselves to rules of conduct and of thought which we have neither made nor desired, and which are sometimes even contrary to our most fundamental inclinations and instincts. (*EF*, 237)

The experience of the collective uniquely creates an intensity of feeling "which no purely private states of consciousness could ever attain, for they have the strength of the innumerable representations which have served to form each of them" (*EF*, 238).

We began with the notion that our author's thought could be entered through the question of survival of religion; we end on the same note. Building on Comte's idea of the "Great Being," Durkheim has provided a powerful answer to the question of why religion has survived: it is a reality interlocked with society itself. Not only does society generate it, but society depends upon religion for its own renewal: " . . . the effect of the cult really is to recreate periodically a moral being upon which we depend as it depends on us. Now this being does exist: it is society" (*EF*, 389). In the collective religious experience, society itself is "born again"; and "this renewal is in no way imaginary. . . . The individual soul is regenerated too, by being dipped again in the sources from which its life comes" (*EF*, 390).

Durkheim has examined the religious symbols, actions, and beliefs of an entire primitive society, has understood their relation to the social structure, and is in the end able to pinpoint his answer to the survival question in briefest fashion: in notions of spirits and gods, there is "something objective at the basis of these conceptions . . . and this is why they have survived . . . up to the present day" (*EF*, 317).

Of all the criticisms of Durkheim's theory of religion, none is more uni-

---

33. An indication of Durkheim's sensitivity to what religious faith is about is the striking similarity between this statement of what it means to have a god and that of Martin Luther in his exposition of the First Commandment: "What is it to have a god? What is God? Answer: A god is that to which we look for all good and in which we find refuge in every time of need . . . the trust and faith of the heart alone make both God and an idol" (*The Large Catechism*, 9).

versal than that it is—in Lukes's phrase—"altogether too unilateral."[34] Among those who agree with this criticism would no doubt be Sigmund Freud, whose psychogenic theory provides a corrective that, if taken as exhaustive, is vulnerable to the same criticism. The concentration of both thinkers on a single causal scheme, each yielding different conclusions about the origin and persistence of religion, will make it clear that the question is not closed, and that each theory has need of the other.

34. Lukes (above, n. 4), 481. Lukes cites with approval Stanner's reference to Durkheim's "all-consuming" "sociological fixation" (ibid.).

Chapter 9

Psychogenic Theory:
Sigmund Freud

Freud's treatment of the origins of religion through his analysis of totemism has to be approached indirectly. Unlike Durkheim's *Elementary Forms*, works like *Totem and Taboo* do not include all the theoretical apparatus necessary for understanding them, even though Freud proposed a powerful theory of religion that filled an important gap in Durkheim's work, and rightly anticipated that the psychoanalytic approach would open up major avenues of research in the science of religion. In this chapter, we shall focus most closely on *Totem and Taboo* (1913) and *Future of an Illusion* (1927), but first we need to fill in some basic theoretical and methodological assumptions from Freud's other works to provide a proper framework.

Throughout, we shall be mindful of three essential differences from the theoretical approach of Durkheim. First, Freud's theory of religion is grounded in an *anthropology*—a description and psychoanalytic explanation of the most fundamental aspects of being a person. Thus, he extends the line of thought that explains religion via analysis of the essential and universal attributes of personhood, but with a critical corrective to the Humean tradition: Freud's theory is constructed so as to take account not only of instincts (like Hume's), but, in the psychodynamics of the family, to include a social dimension to explain the notion of repression. Thus, although Freud will be somewhat more continuous with the British tradition, and will even incorporate a psychoanalytic reading of the venerable anthropomorphic thesis, his theory is irreducibly social as well, signaling the necessity of combining sociological and psychological elements for an adequate theory of religion.

Freud also differs from Durkheim in that his theory is essentially sequential rather than static—a significant difference to be discussed later. Finally, Freud's system of the psyche (unlike Durkheim's sociology) was worked out independently of religion, its primary interest not being to explain religious life. This by no means implies that Freud's studies of religion were a mere excursion to the periphery of his concerns. Freud applied his psychoanalytic theory to religion because the materials of ritual and myth demanded it; their remarkable correspondence to the other critical materials of his analysis, such as dreams and neurotic symptoms, promised fruitful results in the quest to explain religion. In addition, Freud's discussion of religion expressed lifelong cultural and philosophical interests that ranged far beyond the study and cure of individuals.

Freud is justly regarded as a master of interpretation: his revolutionary theories illuminated a whole realm of mental life that had before seemed meaningless—neurotic symptoms, dreams, and what he called the psychopathology of everyday life ("mistakes" such as slips of the tongue). Not only did he reveal that these things have meaning, but he claimed that—as evidences of the unconscious—they provide clues to what is most essential to the human predicament.

This chapter, however, will not focus on the vast range of Freudian interpretation. It has a narrower aim based on one essential fact: Freud's breakthrough in interpretation—the discovery and elaboration of meaning—was made possible by his explanatory theory. His revolutionary theory of the unconscious as the product of repression was what opened up to meaningful interpretation what before had been opaque or ignored. Freud showed that these mental phenomena were motivated by "unconscious ideas"—that people, both individuals and civilizations, and therefore history itself, are mobilized and often controlled by purposes of which the actors are unaware.

I have maintained that interpretation is inseparable from explanation, and this is nowhere more evident than in the work of Freud. Norman O. Brown states the case exactly: "Now in what sense does Freud find *meaningfulness* in neurotic symptoms, dreams, and errors? He means, of course, that these phenomena are determined and *can be given causal explanation.*"[1]

We shall approach Freud's explanation of religion indirectly, not only because a grasp of his general psychoanalytic theory is essential to understanding what he says about religion, but also because Freud on the surface seems vulnerable to a Humean objection that he bases too much of his analysis of religion on two fundamental analogies. Those who have read Hume need not be warned how perilous such a procedure can be, especially if it intends to ground a compelling explanatory argument. Thus, we need to take a preliminary look at the two relevant analogies that inform Freud's exposition: that between *religion and neurosis,* and that between the *child and the primitive.*

With regard to the first, it is crucial to understand that in Freud's usage, "neurosis" is universal to the human species, in the sense that repression and its resulting universal discontent are at the very core of the human predicament, because they are a necessary component of culture itself.[2] Religion is therefore not at all exclusive to those people we ordinarily refer to as neurotics. Neurosis is endemic to the human condition and does not signal the appearance of some new psychic principle absent in "normal" people.

---

1. Norman O. Brown, *Life Against Death,* 3 (italics mine). On the fundamental importance of repression, on which the "whole edifice of psychoanalysis" is built, see pp. 3, 5, 78, 112, etc.

2. For a compressed but penetrating summary, see Brown (preceding note), 3–10.

The psychic structures Freud described, and the dynamics of the mental process, do not undergo qualitative change in the unfortunate condition of being out of whack. Instinctive wishes, the unconscious, and repression are universal psychological mechanisms that shape all of culture, in Freud's view.

The fact that Freud studied the similarities between religion and neurosis, then, is not simply name-calling, as when Hume referred to popular religion as "superstition." Hume's label, it will be recalled, came at the end of his explanatory effort; Freud's designation, by contrast, points toward an explanation of religious data: they betray the persistence—the "survival"—in religious belief and practice, of a normal process of childhood retained overlong by adults. It is as a collective and virtually universal cultural expression of the repressed unconscious, signaling a failure to cope realistically with the external world, that religion is "neurotic."[3]

The fact that Freud took this view has led to criticism that his diagnostic approach relieved him of studying cult or ritual "in terms meaningful to the religious."[4] But this is not entirely true: as we shall see, Freud took very seriously what totemists (or others) said about their religion. His analysis would not have been possible without his doing so. The real crux of a religious objection to Freud is "paradigmatic"; his aim, like Durkheim's, was naturalistic explanation—identification of causes underlying religious belief and activity—and the analytic interpretations that such explanation made possible. The relevant objection, therefore, is that he failed to *explain* religion in terms "meaningful" to religious participants. For both Durkheim and Freud, the explanation differed from that of believers, and for that reason a divergent system of meanings emerged as well.

The second analogy, between the child and the primitive, was an old idea applied in an entirely new way. Customarily, savagery was viewed as the "childhood" of the species (often with a complacent assurance of our evolutionary arrival at maturity). For Freud, however, the clinical analysis of childhood neuroses became directly applicable to the development of primitive as well as of contemporary society.

This is more important than the first analogy, because it provided the basis for the decisive "ray of light" which Freud was able to beam onto the puzzles of totemism (as we shall see below): childhood phobias would provide the key to his discovery of the true nature of the archaic totem and the reality beneath it. *Only* if this analogy was good could Freud claim that "analytic study of the mental life of the child has yielded an unexpectedly rich return by filling up gaps in our knowledge of primeval times."[5] Thus, the indirect

---

3. Sigmund Freud, *The Future of an Illusion* (1927; hereafter *FI*), 53. Cf. Philip Rieff, *Freud, the Mind of the Moralist*, 211: "Freud never doubted that the correct model for understanding religious experience was the neurotic symptoms of the individual." Cf. 212, 266.

4. Rieff (preceding note), 212.

5. Sigmund Freud, *Moses and Monotheism* (1937–39; hereafter *M&M*), 107.

evidence used by Tylor and Durkheim—that of contemporary primitives to throw light on primeval times—was now supplemented by an entirely new procedure: the analysis of modern adults uncovered childhood neuroses, and an analogical application of this analysis revealed its alleged phylogenetic foundations.

The justification of this analogy rested in part on the doctrine of the biologist Ernst Haeckel that ontogeny recapitulates phylogeny, in other words, that "the development of the individual is . . . an abridged repetition, influenced by the fortuitous circumstances of life," of the evolution of the human race.[6] On the basis of that doctrine, Freud was able to announce that

> we are encouraged to expect, from the analysis of dreams a knowledge of the archaic inheritance of man, a knowledge of psychical things in him that are innate. It would seem that dreams and neuroses have preserved for us more of the psychical antiquities than we suspected; so that psychoanalysis may claim a high rank among those sciences which endeavour to reconstruct the oldest and darkest phases of the beginnings of mankind. (*ID*, 404)

In Freud's mind, psychoanalysis thus claimed scientific status alongside the more direct paths to prehistory opened up by geology, archeology, anthropology, and biology. Freud was convinced that the child "has to appropriate the results of a cultural evolution which stretches over thousands of years, including the acquisition of control over his instincts and adaptation to society."[7] But more than that, the individual life history of the contemporary person still bears traces of the remotest past: "There probably exists in the life of the individual [Freud wrote], not only what he has experienced himself, but also what he brought with him at birth, fragments of phylogenetic origin, an archaic heritage" (*M&M*, 125).

Brown provides an insight that connects these two analogies (between neurosis and religion, and between ontogenetic and phylogenetic history), and which also reveals the importance of religion in Freud's analysis of culture. Brown writes: "The empirical fact which compelled Freud to comprehend the whole of human history in the area of psychoanalysis is the appearance in dreams and in neurotic symptoms of themes substantially identical with major themes—both ritualistic and mythical—in the religious

---

6. Sigmund Freud, *The Interpretation of Dreams* (1895; hereafter *ID*), 404. On Haeckel's "biogenetic law," see Stan Draenos, *Freud's Odyssey: Psychoanalysis and the End of Metaphysics*, 90. According to A. Goldenweiser, the notion was invented by the biologist Karl Ernst von Baer, who had observed that "the embryonic individual passes in somewhat abbreviated form through the stages represented by the different species of animals" ("Evolution, Social," 657). But according to Philip Rieff (above, n. 3, 188), Freud derived the idea, mainly from Herder and others, that the individual mind in its development presents a resumé of the stages of human history.

7. Sigmund Freud, *New Introductory Lectures on Psychoanalysis* (1933; hereafter *NIL*), 147. On pp. 160–75, Freud summarizes his views on religion as the only significant rival to a scientific worldview.

history of mankind."[8] Thus, as Brown notes, Freud's theory of religion provides the essential link—or rather bridge—between analysis of individuals to that of culture as a whole. For religious myth and ritual are the cultural or *collective* expression of the same unconscious forces and purposes that produce dreams and neurotic symptoms in individuals: they, too, are the expressions, "distorted by repression, of the immortal desires of the human heart."[9]

For Freud, the doctrine that the individual recapitulates the history of the species illumined the meaning of evolution for the individual organism: evolution takes the place of the traditional religious explanation of the sources of spiritual and mental life, encapsulated in the notion of "the image of God." As Stan Draenos puts it, "the past itself takes the place of the superordinate fixed form which the organism strives to become."[10]

A final contrast: Freud's analysis of totemism refers only in passing to Durkheim,[11] and he would not have regarded the latter's theory as having gotten to the root of the matter (modern analysts agree).[12] Surveying the totemic scene as described by Durkheim, we can imagine Freud asking, "But what are these folks really like; what impels them to gather around the totem in ritual action and aspiration?" Durkheim had ruled out the study of motivations and intentions as too subjective for fruitful scientific study.[13] Freud radically rejects such a restriction: indeed, he believes that sociology can be reduced to applied psychology (*NIL*, 179). His analysis will bring us an alternative to Durkheim's explanation of totemism and the "totemic principle"—the power behind the totem as a religious symbol. Freud will tear away the veil of anonymity and reveal its psychogenic root and true identity. He will resuscitate and reformulate the anthropomorphic thesis of Hume and declare that the totem is the father. The Freudian family will emerge as the generative microcosm and the father as the power behind society. And for Durkheim's clan, Freud will substitute a more generalized "psychological group," defined as "a collection of individuals who have introduced the same person into their superego and, on the basis of this common element, have identified themselves with one another in their ego" (*NIL*, 67).

The explanation of the dynamics of the family requires some prior attention to psychoanalytic theory. Freud grounded his early theory in Darwinian

---

8. Brown (above, n. 1), 12.

9. Ibid., 13.

10. Draenos (above, n. 6), 96; Draenos has this sentence in italics.

11. Sigmund Freud, *Totem and Taboo* (1913; hereafter *T&T*), 113, 120, 124.

12. See, e.g., Melford Spiro, "Collective Representations and Mental Representations in Religious Symbol Systems," 71: Durkheim made a "serious error in ruling out the study of mental representations as irrelevant" to the study of collective representations.

13. Cf. Anthony Giddens, ed., *Emile Durkheim, Selected Writings*, 82 (from *Rules of Sociological Method*).

biology. We pick up the thread with Freud's understanding of evolution as interpreted by Draenos—the notion that psychoanalysis intended to give "meaning to being biological and of making that meaning the basis of self-understanding."[14]

Robert Paul supports Draenos's approach, noting that "psychoanalysis provides us with the only theory available at present by which we may trace in detail how man's animal nature, rooted in the instincts he inherited from his precultural ancestors, becomes transformed through dynamic symbolic processes into culture."[15] The key to revealing the "human meaning of being a biological entity, and . . . finding a way to make that meaning the basis of our self-understanding both as individuals and as species members"[16] was the unconscious. The momentous discovery of its mechanism created for Freud a link between the mental and the physical. Draenos quotes a letter written by Freud in 1917:

> "Let us grant to nature . . . her infinite variety, which rises from the inanimate to the organically animated, from the just physically alive to the spiritual. No doubt the Ucs. [Freud's standard abbreviation for the unconscious] is the right mediator between the mental and the physical, perhaps it is the long sought-for 'missing link.' " In the dark realm of the unconscious inserted between mind and body [Draenos comments], Freud thought he had discovered the epistemic space for the investigation of the mind's bodily ground.[17]

Two essential further points need to be made about the Freudian unconscious: the first is that Freud's discovery was not that we *have* an "unconscious." He granted that it had been discovered long ago by poets and philosophers.[18] His innovation, and the cornerstone of psychoanalytic theory, was the doctrine of repression, which made it the peculiar nature of the unconscious to be *"incapable of consciousness" (ID,* 465). The other essential point is that the dynamic content of this unconscious is *wishes,* a fact that explains their remarkable power despite their being rendered incapable of consciousness by repression. A grasp of these two features is absolutely essential to making sense out of Freud's theory of religion. To anticipate: like dreams and neurotic symptoms, religious activity (especially ritual, for example, totemism) is one devious pathway that unconscious material—material that by definition cannot be understood by the actors—takes to find its way to expression. Unconscious wishes find their (again, devious) means of fulfillment in religious impulses, actions, and beliefs.

14. Draenos (above, n. 6), 100.

15. Robert A. Paul, "Did the Primal Crime Take Place?" 334. Following Clifford Geertz, Paul defines culture as "a system of inherited meanings embodied in symbols"; "inherited" means acquired via "external trafficking in public symbolism, not a genetic event" (317). This meaning, he asserts, is compatible with Freud's position in *Totem and Taboo.*

16. Draenos (above, n. 6), 69.

17. Ibid., 56.

18. Brown (above, n. 1), 62.

The first systematic study of the unconscious wish and its operation was the *Interpretation of Dreams* (1895). Freud's breakthrough in interpretation was based on a new explanation. In this work, Freud defined the wish in the psychic machinery: "a current in the apparatus, issuing from pain [= accumulation of excitation] and striving for pleasure [= diminution of excitation through gratification], we call a wish" (*ID*, 450). Freud argues in this book that every dream is a wish-fulfillment (*ID*, 405), and from that premise that dreams are the key to understanding neurosis: "the theory of all psychoneurotic symtoms culminates in the one proposition *that they, too, must be conceived as wish-fulfillments of the unconscious*" (*ID*, 422). The power of wishes was darkly recognized by the ancients; their great respect for dreams "is based on a just piece of psychological divination. It is an homage paid to the unsubdued and indestructible element in the human soul, to the *daemonic* power which furnishes the dream-wish, and which we have found again *in our unconscious*" (*ID*, 464). Freud contends that the wish (rather than reason) is the generator of all psychic activity (for example, *ID*, 420, 446). It is infantile in origin, charged with "inherent energy," "ever-active," "indestructible and incapable of inhibition," the "motive-power" of dreams (*ID*, 412, 446, 455). Freud's belief in the irrepressible power of these infantile wishes never waned.[19] In 1930, he put it forth as assured knowledge that "man's judgments of value follow directly his wishes for happiness—that, accordingly, they are an attempt to support his illusions with arguments."[20] From all of this, Draenos draws a just conclusion about the foundation of Freud's anthropology as a whole: "that unconscious wishful impulses constitute the core of our being is the definitive insight around which Freud's theory of man crystallizes."[21] The unconscious wish, in fact, becomes a "transcendent" ground of all mental activity. Beyond consciousness, it is a timeless, unchanging, never-resting power. Draenos identifies a decisive feature of Freud's paradigm as he discusses Freud's effort to replace traditional metaphysics with a metapsychology as "the new source of transcent meaning": "The transformation of metaphysics into metapsychology substitutes

---

19. Freud later acknowledged that the most disputed point in his whole dream theory was his assertion that all dreams are the fulfillment of wishes (*NIL*, 27). He tried to meet objections without abandoning the basic thesis, by drawing a distinction between three types of dreams: wishful, anxiety, and punishment dreams (ibid.). Punishment dreams are "not of wishes of the instinctual impulses but of those of the critical, censoring and punishing agency of the mind" (ibid.). Pressed further, he fell back on the claim that every dream is at least an *attempt* at wish-fulfillment, even though it can fail (ibid., 29).

20. Sigmund Freud, *Civilization and Its Discontents* (1930; hereafter *C&D*), 92.

21. Draenos (above, n. 6), 76. Cf. 74: "wishful impulses constitute the core of our being." Cf. *ID*, 455. Cf. also Brown (above, n. 1), 7, 17, 31, and especially 34, against the "insane delusion" of Plato and Descartes that "the true essence of man lies in disembodied mental activity."

an immanent 'within' for a transcendent 'beyond' as the ground of self-understanding."[22]

Before examining the texts, we make some observations about the hermeneutical implications of Freud's approach. Freud frequently uses language indicating that the dream-interpreter is engaged in a hermeneutical process. The dream is to be treated "like a sacred text" (ID, 372), for it involves distinguishing between a literal and theoretical-real sense—"the textual difference between the dream content [= manifest meaning] and the thought content [= latent meaning]" (ID, 199). Not only the dream, but all behavior, is two-layered, with its manifest content and its latent psychological motive. As Rieff emphasizes, that which is causal, definitive, and profound is the latent.[23] A proper analysis of the dream therefore provides "the text of the authentic self" (Draenos).[24] Thus, in the Freudian hermeneutic as in Durkheim's, the new interpretations of religious thought and action are grounded in new explanations of the forces that energize and empower those thoughts and actions.

With regard to theory, it goes without further saying that Freud enters the camp of the totemists heavily armed. As with Durkheim, we shall divide the material so as to reflect Freud's hermeneutical procedures, beginning with his account in Totem and Taboo of what the participants suppose they are doing and why, followed by his own account of what is really going on. Just as the freshness of Durkheim's treatment depended on the theoretical tools he brought from sociology to the discussion, so with Freud, it is "one single ray of light" provided by psychoanalytic theory that justifies his intrusion into the anthropologists' realm.

Freud noted especially the following features of totemism: in the names that they give their totems, and in the ceremonies associated with them, the believers stress their identification with their totem. They take their tribal name from it. It is regarded as ancestor, as kin, as forefather, as primal father (T&T, 104, 106, 131). So strong is the bond between totem and clan that Frazer had designated "identification with the totem" as the "whole essence of totemism" (T&T, 118, 131, n. 1).[25] The relationships between the clan and its totem are reciprocal: the totem is the protector, guide, helper in sickness, warner of trouble—in general, one from whom care and protection

---

22. Draenos (above, n. 6), 80; cf. 100 (quoting Freud): " 'The processes of the system Ucs. are timeless, i.e., they are not ordered temporally, are not altered by the passage of time....' The persistence of desire through time expresses for Freud a will-to-be that transcends all discrete, time-bound manifestations of it."

23. Rieff (above, n. 3), 212.

24. Draenos (above, n. 6), 74.

25. Freud cites J. G. Frazer, Totemism and Exogamy (1910), 4:5 as the source of this insight (T&T, 131, n. 1), as well as of further details given below.

are expected. The clan members, on their part, hedge the totem about with protection and taboo; they do not kill the totem animal (or harvest the plant) except under certain ceremonial circumstances involving the whole group (T&T, 103; cf. 107). Moreover, they obey the two laws which seem virtually universal in totemic systems: no sexual relations between clan members (exogamy) and no killing of the totem animal. Violations of these laws are believed to portend injury or death to someone in the clan (T&T, 71) but can be atoned for by acts of expiation or renunciation (T&T, 35). In some cases, the mythology of the clan holds that the ancestors were allowed to eat the totem animal and to have sex with their kin, violating the taboos now observed by the clan (T&T, 115).

In all, the clan is under sacred, quasi-divine protection and constraint; it lives under mythically grounded care and law. Furthermore—of special interest to Freud—the clan celebrates and expresses its bond with the totem through the totem sacrifice, which was first explained in detail by W. Robertson Smith. Freud reviews the essentials of Smith's theory with care and respect, summarizing the account as follows:

> In the earliest times the sacrificial animal had itself been sacred and its life untouchable; it might only be killed if all the members of the clan participated in the deed and shared their guilt in the presence of the god, so that the sacred substance could be yielded up and consumed by the clansmen and thus ensure their identity with one another and with the deity. The sacrifice was a sacrament and the sacrificial animal was itself a member of the clan. It was in fact the ancient totem animal, the primitive god himself, by the killing and consuming of which the clansmen renewed and assured their likeness to the god. (T&T, 138)[26]

Obviously, the killing of the totem involved a violation of the basic taboo; in addition, these rites were sometimes accompanied by sexual excesses. Excess became routine in the ceremonial context (T&T, 140). The other feature noted by Freud was the ambivalence expressed in the ceremony—a combination of celebration and joy on the one hand, and mourning for and apology to the totem over its death on the other. The final intention of the ceremony was to cement the sacred bond between clan and god through eating the totem meal, thereby partaking of the life of the totem: man and god became "one substance" (T&T, 135).[27]

Freud is not shy about his claim that the participants, despite their elaborate "theologies," do not understand, or better, cannot explain, what is really

26. The quotation is part of Freud's extensive review of Robertson Smith's theory, as related in *Lectures on the Religion of the Semites* (1889; Freud used the 1894 ed.); T&T, 132–39.
27. The contrast between Freud's and Durkheim's debts to Robertson Smith is of interest: Durkheim credited Smith with revealing to him the possibilities of a sociological way of explaining human activity. For Freud, it was Smith's exposition of the details and the meanings of sacrifice to its participants that was important. For Smith's significance, see T. O. Beidelman, *W. Robertson Smith and the Sociological Study of Religion*, esp. 66–68.

going on, or why they do the things they do. "There is no sense in asking savages to tell us the real reason for their prohibitions—the origin of taboo. It follows from our postulates that they cannot answer, since the real reason must be 'unconscious' " (T&T, 31). Freud presupposed this. In fact, totemism had initially attracted his psychoanalytic curiosity for the very reason that its two prohibitions exactly paralleled those issuing from repression of the child's oedipal wishes—prohibitions against incest and murder. These prohibitions also, of course, identify the two crimes of Oedipus.[28]

Through the theory brought from psychoanalysis Freud now offers to explain the strange configurations of totemic belief and action in toto as "a product of the conditions involved in the Oedipus complex" (T&T, 132). Having disposed of the essentials of the "literal" (manifest) sense of totemism, we turn now to the "real"—the (latent) psychoanalytic, theoretical—sense. It rests first on certain relevant external facts and constraints that are universal, with children and with society. The first reality is the helplessness of the infant, and the need for parental (especially the father's) protection. This is relevant because the "root of every form of religion" is "longing for the father" (T&T, 148). "The terrifying impression of helplessness in childhood," Freud writes in Future of an Illusion (1927), "aroused the need for protection—for protection through love—which was provided by the father" (FI, 30). Again, in Civilization and Its Discontents (1930), Freud was still convinced that

> the derivation of religious needs from the infant's helplessness and the longing for the father aroused by it seems to me incontrovertible, especially since the feeling is not simply prolonged from childhood days, but is permanently sustained by fear of the superior power of Fate. I cannot think of any need in childhood as strong as the need for a father's protection. . . . The origin of the religious attitude can be traced back in clear outlines as far as the feeling of infantile helplesses. There may be something further behind that, but for the present it is wrapped in obscurity. (C&D, 19; cf. FI, 23–24)

The relevant realities of childhood, then, are (first) real helplessness and real protection by parents. Second, as the child enters into society, he is faced with the necessity of repressing his aggressive and sexual instincts in order to make living in society possible. The repression of instincts (or childhood wishes), in fact, brings into focus the central problem of civilization, for its unrelenting demands of renunciation condemn persons to lives of permanent discontent. But why? Because of the indestructible power of wishes—especially the oedipal wishes that dominate the awakening of sexuality in the child and complicate the simpler feeling of helplessness and need for protection. In this phase, the initially loving identification with the

28. A well-known item of Freud's early biography is that as a *gymnasium* student he made a translation of *Oedipus Rex* from Greek into German. Cf. Ernest Jones, *The Life and Work of Sigmund Freud*, 1:20.

father "takes on a hostile coloring and changes into a wish to get rid of the father in order to take his place with the mother. Henceforward the relation to the father is ambivalent."[29]

We have moved from outer to inner realities discovered by Freudian theory—from actual helplessness and need for protection to the inner "first and most important identification of all" with the father (*E&I*, 39), subsequently turned aggressive, distorted by sexual wishes directed toward the mother, which feelings then require to be repressed. The pre-oedipal identification with the father, according to Freud, now serves as an inner resource for repression itself:

> Clearly the repression of the Oedipus complex was no easy task . . . so the child's ego brought in a reinforcement to help in carrying out the repression by erecting this same obstacle [to realization of the oedipal wish] within itself. The strength to do this was, so to speak, borrowed from the father, and this loan was an extraordinarily momentous act. (*E&I*, 45)

Taking the father "inside"—internalizing his prohibition against fulfilling the oedipal wish—constitutes the formation of conscience, or superego.

Here, then, is a secondary or social-historical root of religion added to the biological fact of the abysmal helplessness of the infant, which Freud has identified as the basis of religion. In reply to a criticism that psychoanalysis ignored the "higher nature" of man, Freud pointed to this internalization of paternal censorship of instinctual wishes as his way of agreeing with the religionists' claim that we have a "higher nature": "Very true . . . and here we have that higher nature, in this ego-ideal or super-ego, the representative of our relation to our parents. When we were little children we knew these higher natures, we admired them and feared them; and later we took them into ourselves" (*E&I*, 47). Taking the parent inside "contains the germ from which all religions have evolved. The self-judgment which declares that the ego falls short of its ideal [because of the persistent power of forbidden wishes which must be denied again and again] produces the sense of worthlessness with which the religious believer attests his longing" (*E&I*, 49).[30]

But what does all this have to do with totemism? We first remind ourselves that the primeval species history is, according to the evolutionary doctrine of Freud's time, recapitulated in the development of the individual. That doctrine assures Freud that his clinical insights, arrived at through diagnosis of patients and others (himself, especially), may be relevantly applied to phylogenetic issues.

That is why, having reviewed at length the tangle of insoluble puzzles

29. Sigmund Freud, *The Ego and the Id* (1923; hereafter *E&I*), 40–41.

30. Cf. Freud's later summation, *NIL*, 58–67. On p. 67, Freud defines the superego as "the representative for us of every moral restriction, the advocate of a striving towards perfection—it is, in short, as much as we have been able to grasp psychologically of what is described as the higher side of human life."

attending the study of primitive totemism, Freud can say, at the artfully contrived denouement in his treatise: "Into this obscurity one single ray of light is thrown by psycho-analytic observation" (*T&T*, 126).

This "ray" emanates from the psychoanalytic discovery that animal phobias in children result from displaced feelings toward fathers (*T&T*, 127–28). The child's attitude toward the animal is ambivalent—a combination of fear and admiration or identification with the animal to the extent that it can be called his "totem" animal. Recalling Frazer's important insight that the "whole essence of totemism" lies in identification with the totem animal (*T&T*, 131, n. 1), and noting "the boy's complete identification with his totem animal and his ambivalent emotional attitude to it," Freud states his thesis: "These observations justify us, in my opinion, in *substituting the father for the totem animal* in the formula for totemism (in the case of males)" (*T&T*, 131; my italics). The totem represents the father, the progenitor of the clan. Freud here points with satisfaction to the fact that he has accounted for a feature of totemism in its literal sense heretofore not understood:

> It will be observed that there is nothing new or particularly daring in this step forward. Indeed, primitive men say the very same thing themselves, and, where the totemic system is still in force today, they describe the totem as their common ancestor and primal father. All we have done is to *take at its literal value* an expression used by these people, of which the anthropologists have been able to make very little. . . . (*T&T*, 131; italics mine; cf. 141, 148)

Freud's answer to Durkheim's question, then, as to the origin of the sacred, would be the moment in which a cult having as its object a father-substitute was instituted. "What is sacred was originally nothing but the perpetuated will of the primeval father" (*M&M*, 156).

The will of the father is not to kill (him) and not to engage in sexual intercourse with his mate(s). From time immemorial, societies have made the father's laws against murder and incest into the laws of God. Again, on the basis of his identification of the primal father as "the original image of God," Freud can acknowledge, against rationalistic reductions on the deistic model, the literal accuracy of the religious explanation. In its confession that the totem is the father, "the religious explanation is *right*. God actually played a part in the genesis of that prohibition [against murder]; it was His influence, not any insight into social necessity, which created it . . . religious doctrine tells us the *historical truth*—though subject, it is true, to some modification and disguise—whereas our rational account disavows it" (*FI*, 42; italics mine. The omitted portion will be noted shortly).

How does religious doctrine reveal what is "historically" true in terms of actually revealing something about the deep human past? We have seen how it is psychoanalytically/ontogenetically true. The next step is to project this truth back to its phylogenetic grounds, to fill in the historical gaps on the basis of one further clue that accords with the new history to be required by the theory. (Freud here proceeds confidently, for he knows what *must* be.) The decisive clue comes from Darwin—it is his suggestion that the original social organization of the species was the primal horde, in which one powerful male ruled over a group of younger, weaker males and reserved to himself access to the females of the horde (*T&T*, 125). Here, the primal father forces the sons into exogamy by establishing his law: no sex at home. J. J. Atkinson had already taken this proposal a step further: under totemism the same law would rule: no sexual relations within the totem clan (*T&T*, 126). Atkinson also divined that the brothers would at length find this situation intolerable, rise up and dispose of the father (*T&T*, 142, n. 1).[31]

From this, Freud presents, in the climactic paragraph, the "historical truth" which the religions reveal: "One day the brothers who had been driven out came together, killed and devoured their father, and so made an end of the patriarchal horde. United, they had the courage to do and succeeded in doing what would have been impossible for them individually.... They devoured their victim as well as killing him." Behold the primal deed, the primal crime. The effects are now immediately described:

> The violent primal father had doubtless been the feared and envied model of each one of the company of brothers: and in the act of devouring him they accomplished their identification with him, and each one of them acquired a portion of his strength. The totem meal, which is perhaps mankind's earliest festival, would thus be a repetition and a commemoration of this memorable and criminal deed, which was the beginning of so many things—of social organization, of moral restrictions and of religion. (*T&T*, 141–42)

The mechanisms discovered by psychoanalysis thus reveal their archaic historic grounds. The sons' hatred having been satisfied by their act of aggression, a new sense of longing, based on their original identification with the father, now comes to the fore. They set their own rivalry aside and internalize his law and his image (cf. *C&D*, 79). Their totemic religion, exactly as Smith had described it, is a symbolic and truthful representation of this history. It symbolically reenacts the primal crime in the communal killing and eating of the totem animal (*T&T*, 145). Celebrated with both joy and mourning, the rite reflects the essential ambivalence toward the father—joy at the triumph over him, remorse over his murder. It commemorates and reinforces identification with the totem-father by eating him and partaking of his very substance. The community resolves to respect his commands, by the prohibition of murder and sexual relations within the clan. The essential dynamics of civilization—and its discontents—are now under way, and (by analysis) now understood.

In Freud's mind, the two essential generative "moments" of religion are in full view in totemism: fulfillment of irrepressible wishes and the institu-

---

31. In the cited footnote Freud reviews the "highly remarkable theory" of J. J. Atkinson (from his *Primal Law*, 1903).

tionalization of repression. Regarding the first, Freud says that religion fulfills the "oldest, strongest and most urgent wishes of mankind"—one of which is the need for protection in helplessness (*FI*, 30). In the sacrificial meal, moreover, the other, oedipal wish (to be rid of the father at the same time that one identifies with him and takes him inside), is also fulfilled. The second essential constitutive moment of religion, repression of murderous and incestuous wishes in obedience to the father's will, institutes as sacred the laws that *must* prevail for social life to be possible—laws that regulate sexual and aggressive instincts. Thus, Freud's story of the primal crime has this outcome: "Though the brothers had banded together in order to overcome their father, they were all one another's rivals in regard to the women. . . . Thus the brothers had no alternative, if they were to live together . . . but . . . to institute the law against incest. . . . In this way they rescued the organization which had made them strong. . . . " (*T&T*, 144). As Rieff summarizes the meaning of all this: "The act of renunciation is at once the establishment of fellowship in society and of the father as God. The war of the generations ends in the deification of the dead father and in the socializing guilt of the brothers."[32] "God" from now on has an indelibly moral meaning, for he is "the positive projection of the act of renunciation."[33]

We can now understand Freud's willingness to credit religious doctrine with the quality of "historical truth." The omitted part of the quotation given earlier reads: "the displacement of man's will on to God [the father-substitute] is fully justified. For men knew that they had disposed of their father by violence, and in their reaction to that impious deed, they determined to respect his will thenceforward" (*FI*, 42).

The theory presented in *Totem and Taboo* is obviously much more than one of the origin of religion. It sets the stage for Freud's later meditations on the dynamics of civilization, particularly *Future of an Illusion* (1927). In those reflections we see the continuing relevance of the paradox identified a century earlier by Auguste Comte: religion has been surpassed as knowledge but its functions still need to be carried out. Freud poses the problem thus: given religion's powerful hold on the psyche, and granted its role as the most important "physic asset" of civilization, dare we renounce it simply because we know that it is based entirely on wishes (Freud's definition of "illusion")? The very possibility of civilization depends upon repression of instinct, because the indestructibility of these innate, instinctual wishes (sexual and aggressive) pose a powerful and eternal threat to human progress and even

32. Rieff (above, n. 3), 197. In *NIL*, 161–63, Freud makes the point that only his theory has been able to provide a *unified* explanation of the apparently disparate and disconnected functions of religion, i.e., to give knowledge about human origins, to provide comfort and protection, and to lay down the law. All of these functions cohere in the Father as progenitor, protector, and lawgiver.

33. Rieff (above, n. 3), 198.

survival. But the high *cost* of repression is that, although socially necessary, it condemns humans to permanent unhappiness. Hence, some form of compensation is required in order for people to feel that they have a stake in the survival of civilization.

Freud recognizes that religion, because of its effectiveness at being both compensatory and repressive, is the most valuable psychic asset that civilization possesses (*FI*, 14). It underwrites, in the form of commands and promises of God, exactly those repressive and compensatory requirements that make civilization possible and individual existence tolerable. As repression, religion threatens punishment; as compensation, it promises divine protection, consolation, and recompense against all the engines of suffering. "Thus the benevolent rule of a divine Providence allays our fear of the dangers of life; the establishment of a moral world-order ensures the fulfillment of the demands of justice, which have so often remained unfulfilled in human civilization; and the prolongation of earthly existence in a future life provides the local and temporal framework in which these wish-fulfillments shall take place" (*FI*, 30). Freud thus recognizes the reasons for religion's durability: "the store of religious ideas includes not only wish-fulfillments but important historical recollections. This concurrent influence of past and present must give religion a truly incomparable wealth of power" (*FI*, 42).

And yet, despite all this, Freud advocates that the risk of renunciation should be taken—that civilization abandon the illusions of religion, submit to fate, and face up to the ordinary unhappiness of a reasoned, scientific view of reality. Like an obsessional neurosis, religion "comprises a system of wishful illusions together with a disavowal of reality" (*FI*, 43).

> A psychologist who does not deceive himself about the difficulty of finding one's bearings in this world, makes an endeavor to assess the development of man, in the light of the small portion of knowledge he has gained through a study of the mental processes of individuals during their development from child to adult. In so doing, the idea forces itself upon him that religion is comparable to a childhood neurosis, and he is optimistic enough to suppose that mankind will surmount this neurotic phase, just as so many children grow out of their similar neurosis. (*FI*, 53)

Thus, Freud has come down, finally, on Tylor's side, despite considerable theoretical advance. Religion is a "survival" of the childhood of the species, as well as of the childhood of the individual adult.

To what genre may we assign Freud's "One-day. . . . " story of the primal crime? In the face of all his critics, Freud called it history, insisting that the crime was real, that it happened—must have happened—over and over again, so that every human being is descended from one of those rebellious brothers and consequently inherits as an indelible and inescapable part of his makeup this psychohistoric legacy. But as Robert A. Paul has noted, no item in Freud's entire repertoire of ideas has been so unanimously rejected by his critics.[34] Perhaps the story is best understood as the creation of a modern myth, a paradigmatic tale that is much more than a fanciful "just so" story, because it tells how things really are, satisfying the notion of the function and legitimation of myth offered by Jacob Neusner. Questions of literal historical truth aside, "the myths of old live [survival, again!] because no one thinks they are other than accurate and ordinary descriptions of what is true about what happens."[35] The capacity to illuminate and inform contemporary existence is also noted by Frederick J. Streng as an essential attribute of a living myth: in it, "the essential structure of reality manifests itself in particular moments that are remembered and repeated from generation to generation."[36]

Freud's horizon of interpretation ranged over "the history of civilization as a whole";[37] this tale, Paul argues, presents the whole saga of the human predicament in germ, seen from the moment of the decisive evolutionary break from prehuman to human, from nature to culture. The saga unfolds as the struggle of the species to endure, constrained by its permanent embodiment in biological nature, is unleashed from the bonds of animal instinct into a terrible freedom based on the power of its symbolic capacity to produce culture.[38]

But Freud would not rest content with a merely abstract legitimation of the story. Religion, culture, and their discontents have their basis in real history. The primal crime really happened. Its reality, for Freud, was substantiated both by psychoanalytic theory and by history.[39] Freud felt that he was forced to the elements of theory by clinical experience with patients. True, he came to believe that the childhood traumas which made some of his patients ill could be fantasies rather than memories of actual events,[40] but in the case at hand the primal trauma must have issued from a real deed, because in that "first" moment of the birth of culture, the very capacity to fantasize the removal of the father without acting upon it was not yet present. This (according to Paul) is because the state of nature which precedes culture

34. Paul (above, n. 15), 312.

35. Jacob Neusner, *The Way of Torah*, 131. Put in scientific terms, Philip Slater explains that "the primal horde myth portrays a sociological process rather than an historical event" (*Microcosm*, 224; cf. 4, n. 3).

36. Neusner, *The Way of Torah*, 29, quoting Frederick J. Streng, *Understanding Religious Man*, 560.

37. Paul (above, n. 15), 333.

38. Ibid., passim.

39. Ibid., 329.

40. Jeffrey M. Masson accuses Freud of suppressing the truth of his original seduction theory (that adult neurosis is caused by childhood traumas resulting from real sexual abuse on the part of adults) in favor of the inadequate theory that these experiences may have been only fantasized: *The Assault on Truth: Freud's Suppression of the Seduction Theory*. See the critical discussion by Charles Rycroft, "A Case of Hysteria."

is defined by a direct and necessary passage from instinct to action, from impulse to deed.[41]

Perhaps more convincing is the fact that the primal crime kept—keeps—repeating itself,[42] baleful witness to the indestructible power of the oedipal wish. Freud's myth, then, "explains' what happens in people's psyches by exposing the generative forces at work in the actual history of the species. Analysts who disagree with Freud argue that religion can be adequately explained without resort to such a primal history. Spiro, for example, holds that the immediate experience of parents explains the grounds of belief created anew with each generation.[43] Freud insisted, however, that religion must be grounded in concrete experience. With Durkheim, that ground is social. Freud seems to be saying, with his stubborn adherence to the reality of the primal crime, that here is something in history without which the rise and survival of religion and culture, and the persistent unhappiness of humans in civilization, would be simply inexplicable.

The parallel between the above and myths of the Bible, particularly the Genesis stories, is instructive. Neusner's justification and explanation of the vitality of the biblical myths for the Jewish community (which goes also for Christianity, with its radical and extended revision by addition) is that, for Jews, these stories say what is true about what happens to the community in history.

But, more specifically, Freud's account is a psychoanalytic parallel to the Genesis story of the Fall. In both cases, we have accounts that are essential to explain (as well as to interpret) everything that comes after. The first eleven chapters of Genesis stand in the Bible as a universal prelude to the particular history that begins with the call of Abraham. Its function is to explain the human situation in its primal predicaments, so as to make sense of the call of Abraham and the whole "redemption history" that follows. It must have happened (or *something* must have happened). In like manner, Freud's myth unveils the human condition and the ultimate forces involved for the elucidation of the history and vicissitudes of individuals and culture. There is no redemption, but at least there is a kind of deliverance into understanding once the truth of the primal myth is recognized.[44]

The parallel can be extended in the disputed question of both traditions

41. Paul (above, n. 15), 342.

42. Ibid., 329ff.

43. Spiro (above, n. 12), 63: "That these beings are believed to exist independently of the collective, as well as mental, representations which signify them is best explained by the correspondence that exists between these representations and the mental representations that the young child previously forms of those actual powerful beings whose reality he has personally experienced—his parenting figures."

44. But see Brown's brilliant attempt to give Freud's "bleak pessimism" a revisionist and redemptive reading on the basis of Freud's own principles, in above, n. 1, 37, 98 et passim.

(religious and psychoanalytic) about whether or to what extent the primal stories are to be taken literally. Was there "the Fall"? Did the primal murder really take place? The middle ground occupied by most people in both traditions is that there is a profound air of truth *in* these myths, as in all great poetry. The myths are not literally and historically true, but they accurately describe the way things are and enable us to see how they must be. They allow us to interpret the relevant and paradoxical data of present history, whether the religious experience of Jewish or Christian people, or the clinical expe ience of analysts, or the human struggle toward civilization.

Despite these parallels, there is a difference which suggests a perhaps unbridgeable gap between the two perspectives, religious and scientific, raising again the issue of the commensurability of paradigms. This difference goes beyond the fact that Freud and Durkheim were atheistic; it is not altogether clear anymore how much theoretical meaning that has, in its traditional-referential sense, among Christian and Jewish intellectuals. It also goes beyond the allegation that myth is obsolete.[45] The critical difference is that the vitality and fruitfulness of the Freudian-Durkheimian approaches is due to the reciprocal relation that holds between theory and data, and the progressive and self-correcting results for research enabled by that reciprocity. The theories of the power of wishes, of repression, and of social forces, and so on, can be, and continually are being, tested and revised over time. Freud and Durkheim are pioneers, "classics," but their texts are not canonical; they do not function as *norma normans* over tradition, to which the tradition in obedience constantly returns. Over the objections of its own fundamentalists, the critical tradition continues to go beyond the classics in response to progress in relating theory to newly studied data.[46]

In the days of traditional theology, the incommensurability of naturalistic versus supernaturalistic paradigms was striking; today, it is much less clear. Theological theory undergoes continual revision (including campaigns against "supernaturalism"), but today, aside from dogmatically defined communities (for example, Roman Catholic, fundamentalist), no one—no licensed group of authorities—speaks normatively for "theology." The options seem unlimited; for, unlike science, theology is controlled (to adopt Freud's language) by no reality principle. Even the question of whether theological language is

45. For one interesting discussion, see E. O. Wilson, *On Human Nature*. Although this champion of sociobiology claims that religion can be explained (cf. esp. 200–01), his essentially Durkheimian understanding of religion, reinforced by his suspicion that we may be genetically wired for religion, leads him to the same paradox (stemming from Comte) with which we have been dealing, viz., that despite the demise of theology, religion is necessary. Wilson goes on to affirm scientific materialism as the new and "more powerful mythology" of our time (214).

46. One not entirely frivolous example: a recent discovery of importance to the theory of religion can be fruitfully applied to the revision of Freud's theory, viz., the "discovery" of women as data for a corrective to his heavily androcentric theory. Cf. Richard L. Rubenstein, *The Religious Imagination*, 14. This discovery is having considerable impact on theology as well.

referential at all is now debated, because no norms are universally recognized to control competing claims about what religious language means. Revision of theological theories is based in part on the internal dynamics of the theological disciplines as they examine "experience," but one wonders whether that experience is "religious experience" as much as it is the experience of implausibility and the demand for apologetic projects aimed at legitimating religion itself in the modern world. Apologetics, moreover, exacts its price by increasing the distance between religious theory and ordinarily lived religious life, thus increasing the gap between theology and the study of religion. As Rieff remarked upon Freud's disdain for philosophers of religion, their refined and rationalistic concepts of God were pitiful remnants of the mighty Father of tradition, only a clever way of leaving the scene of the old God's death.[47]

I began chapter 8 by looking at Durkheim and Freud together as reaching a new plateau from which most subsequent explanation of religion still commences, either from a sociological or psychoanalytic/anthropological base. In conclusion, let us return to some common and comparative considerations; first, the completion of a paradigm shift constituted by naturalistic ways of explaining religion.

In the naturalistic tradition, especially since Hume, the theistic principle had been abandoned, but through Tylor this tradition in its British forms had not reached substantially beyond an intellectual critique of theology. Regarding it as more or less illusory, their analysis had been unable to account adequately for the *survival* of the religious paradigm.

Following the more promising lead of Comte's sociological and functional line of thought, however, Durkheim and Freud were able to offer detailed descriptions of forces and processes sufficient, not only to generate the "original" religious response, but persistent and powerful enough to *sustain* that response in face of rational criticism. "Explaining religion" now emphasized not its original rise but its persistence and vitality in spite of its irretrievable intellectual obsolescence. That achievement is what allows us to credit them with completing the naturalistic paradigm for the study of religion. The importance of their achievement is testified to by its continued vitality and the continuing reexamination of their ideas among researchers today.

As a result of their new forms of explanation, Durkheim and Freud represent a qualitative hermeneutical advance in comparison to Tylor and those who preceded him. After de Brosses's daring exposé of fetishism, the natu-

---

47. Rieff (above, n. 3), 264. Cf. *NIL*, 172, where Freud notes the distance between the religious philosophers and the believing masses, for whom religious truth must correspond with external reality to be meaningful. Here, for once, Freud is on the side of the masses. Wayne Proudfoot refutes the recent claim by D. Z. Phillips that religious language is nonreferential: see Proudfoot, *Religious Experience*, 200ff.

ralist tradition had insisted that primitive texts had to be taken literally because they represented in their literal sense the real intentions of their authors, and these intentions were regarded as sufficient to interpret the evidence in its true historical meaning. Thus, pictures of Egyptians in poses of adoration before images of plants and animals had to be taken in their obvious if shocking meaning, despite the near reverence in which the high Egyptian culture was held in Europe. To allegorize these representations by making the adored plants and animals symbols of deep spiritual realities was to indulge the "conceit of scholars" (Vico), which was to misrepresent and misdescribe the available evidence.

This new literalism accorded perfectly with emerging evolutionary doctrine. It allowed theorists to place fetishism at the beginning of the long upward struggle of intellect toward perfection—exactly as done by Comte. Ethnographic research brought masses of data to the task, but the literalistic approach generated a new problem: it now became impossible to do anything further with it but regard it with contempt (however polite) and self-congratulation regarding the distance that had been put between savage and contemporary religion. Stripped of its cosmetic politeness, Tylor's doctrine of survivals amounted to substantially the same thing.[48]

Durkheim and Freud, in their critique of the British anthropologists, rejected the mere "letter" on the basis of which Tylor et al. had interpreted the ancient texts. They had not read them with full understanding, because they did not explain the real forces that generated the archaic forms of thought—forces deeper than those recognized consciously by the ancient actors themselves, and deeper than the mere curiosity attributed to them by the British anthropologists.[49] Beneath the letter and the surface data worked the unseen and universal forces of the psychic and social systems.

What raised hermeneutical technique to a new level was the paradigmatic (naturalistic) and theoretical (sociological, psychoanalytic) achievements that could now be brought to bear to reveal the realities hidden beneath the letter. Instead of reading the old data only literally and dismissing it as simply false, they read it literally *and* symbolically; as superficially false but deeply "true."

48. The parallel with what happened in the most momentous debate of second-century Christianity—the Marcionite controversy—is instructive (I see Tylor as parallel to Marcion, and Durkheim-Freud to the orthodox solution of the crisis). For Marcion, Judaism amounted now to nothing more than a "survival"—a once-vital relic of an earlier time—which was evident if one read the Hebrew Bible literally. Orthodoxy claimed that there was more in the Hebrew text than appeared on its surface, more even than in the conscious intentions and understandings of the biblical authors: the literal sense remained as the foundation for interpretation, but Christian theory (a new explanation of biblical history) provided the foundation for a new hermeneutic. This is not so dissimilar to the outcome of the Durkheim-Freud shift, in which decisive theoretical advances play the same role in the study of religion that the event of Christ's life played in Christian historiography.

49. Frazer, for example, had understood that the identification with the totem was essential but had no theoretical basis for explaining why this was so.

As Durkheim had protested against earlier critics, no human institution is founded on sheer error; religion, like the others, is based on reality. But that reality—as it happens—is not sufficiently understood by believers themselves.

By tracing this hermeneutical development historically, and by limiting our attention to writers intent on explaining religion, we now encounter, coming from the opposite direction, scholars of religion who identify with the so-called hermeneutical tradition. That tradition, associated with the names of Schleiermacher and Dilthey, has typically been seen as an *alternative* to explanation, explanation being rejected as a procedure inappropriate to, or unworthy of, religion. Without entering fully into the contemporary discussion of hermeneutics, which I confess I have difficulty understanding, I simply note that Paul Ricoeur, who is sympathetic to a religious perspective, echoes Melford Spiro's criticism of the "false dichotomy" between interpretation and explanation, and is critical of the impact of Dilthey's famous distinction (we explain nature, but interpret culture). Thereby, Ricoeur observes, hermeneutics has been "severed from naturalistic explanation and thrown back into the sphere of psychological intuition."[50]

Indeed, the language of Dilthey's own essay, "The Rise of Hermeneutics," left the door open to Freudian inquiry. Dilthey there defined *Verstehen* as "that process by which we intuit, behind the sign given to our senses, that psychic reality of which it is the expression."[51] Describing how a text comes into being, he wrote: "a unified and creative *power, unconscious of its own shaping force*, is seen as receiving the first impulses toward the creation of the work and as forming them."[52] The issue of explanation, far from being closed, is opened wide by such suggestive remarks. As Spiro argues, "valid, rather than just any kind of interpretation, . . . must be no less concerned with 'laws' than [explanation is], because . . . the cogency, if not the validity, of the idiographic interpretation is dependent on the nomothetic theory from which it is implicitly or explicitly deduced."[53] In other words, interpretation implies and is constrained by explanation, whether the interpreter deals with the issue or not. Freud would no doubt still be unhappy, as he was in his

---

50. Paul Ricoeur, *Hermeneutics and the Human Sciences*, 49. A negative example of the importance of the Durkheim-Freud approach is what happens without it: see the essay by David Bidney, "Myth, Symbolism, and Truth." Ignoring Durkheim and Freud, he ends up seeing the alternatives for a proper scientific study of myth in essentially pre-twentieth-century terms— between "literal" and "allegorical" possibilities. This seems to be the result of focusing on problems of interpretation without attending to the explanations which are implicit behind interpretation. Especially, he does not consider that Durkheim and Freud offer a way *both* to honor the truth of the allegorical approaches (there really *is* a hidden sense in myths), *and* at the same time to correct the nonempirical abstractness of modern idealistic allegorization (as represented by Cassirer) by grounding interpretation of myth in psychosocial systems of causation and meaning.

51. Wilhelm Dilthey, "The Rise of Hermeneutics," 232.

52. Ibid., 241; my italics.

53. Spiro (above, n. 12), 64, n. 2.

own day, about the eclectic use of his ideas by people who denied the validity of the theories on which they were based: "Though the structure of psychoanalysis is unfinished [he wrote], it nevertheless presents, even today, a unity from which elements cannot be broken off at the caprice of whoever comes along: but these eclectics seem to disregard this" (*NIL*, 138).

Norman Brown's comments on the use of Freud's theory by art critics implies a similar criticism. Because no complete theory of art is available, critics borrow on Freud to get the meanings they want without reference to (much less mastery of) the theoretical basis involved. Brown writes: "We are free to recognize a psychoanalytic theme in art, but we are not compelled to; and if we do recognize a psychoanalytic theme, we need not be disturbed, because we are free to drown it in a rich orchestration of multiple meanings. . . . Business can go on as usual for professional critics. The ego remains the master in the house of art."[54] And so also in the house of theology and religious studies.

It is unfortunate that in the university this separation of interpretation from explanation tends to be reinforced by institutional separation of departments of religious studies (mainly the home of interpretation) from those of anthropology, sociology, and psychology (the locus of scientific explanation). Such departmental apartheid creates an artificial division in what, ideally, would be a unified effort.

In profound agreement with Durkheim, Freud seems to see religion and morality as inseparable in their original institution. Focusing on the child in *The Ego and the Id* (1923), Freud writes:

> Social feelings rest on the foundation of identifications with others, on the basis of an ego-ideal in common with them. Religion, morality and a social sense—the chief elements of what is highest in man—*were originally one and the same thing*. According to the hypothesis which I have put forward in *Totem und Tabu* they were acquired phylogenetically out of the father-complex: religion and moral restraint by the actual process of mastering the Oedipus complex itself, and social feeling from the necessity for overcoming the rivalry that then remained between the members of the younger generation. (*E&I*, 49–50; italics mine)

But if we look more closely at both of the constitutive elements of religion identified by Freud (wish-fulfillment as well as repression), we see a profound and paradoxical tension. *Wishes* are by nature amoral (cf. *ID*, 450), wholly driven by the pleasure principle,[55] which is precisely why they *must* be repressed and are at the profoundest level elements of the unconscious. Repression, on the other hand, is essentially "moral," an action of the superego impressing the external requirements of parents and society on the ego. Freud thus reveals to us how religion can work at cross-purposes in the psyche and

54. Brown (above, n. 1), 56.
55. Cf. Draenos (above, n. 6), 119.

in society: on the one hand, potentially subverting psychic order by both indulging and repressing the pleasure principle; on the other hand, both subverting and upholding social order by encouraging potentially dangerous illusions even while denying instincts and sanctioning social constraints.

This divergence between Durkheim and Freud poses an interesting problem for students of religious ethics. Durkheim sees the relation between religion and morality as smooth and unbroken. But with Freud we find a basic paradox—a psychoanalytic return to Hume's thesis that a fundamental conflict of interest (not merely a difference) divides religion and morality. Hume, it will be recalled, put an absolute split between them by showing the antagonism between their entirely separate motivations and intents. But he did not see Freud's paradox because he recognized only the negative social functions of religion, failing to see either the sociological elements in its genesis or its integrative social role.

The relationship between religion and morality has been debated in theological circles as well as in the critical tradition examined here. In reaction to the eighteenth-century habit of reducing ("true") religion to morality, Schleiermacher and Otto (*Das Heilige*, 1911), fixed a theological notion of "the sacred" that has been very durable and popular until now:[56] essential religion (which strongly implies "authentic" religion), rooted in an apprehension of "the holy," is utterly prior to either conceptual or moral formulation and elaboration. But opposed to this high-level theoretical legitimation of a specifically religious experience, and of a basic division between religion and ethics, has been the dominant commonsense understanding of the entire Judeo-Christian tradition, that religion and morality are, or at least *ought* to be, inseparable.

Whatever the outcome of this discussion, Freud and Durkheim add a new dimension to the debate, showing that it can be advanced beyond conflicting interpretations only by a deeper probing of theoretical explanations of the tension. Our authors offered testable theories about how best to understand the relationship between religion and morality. Like Hume, Freud discovered a deep tension between them that cannot be overlooked and invites further discussion. Religious doctrine may be the rationalization of social necessities (Durkheim) or the result of instinctual pressures that require moral control (Freud). Whichever of these is nearer the mark, both make a powerful case that morality cannot be regarded simply as straightforward and unambiguous application of "religious experience" to action.

Among further contrasts and comparisons that might be drawn between the theories of Durkheim and Freud, a formal difference exists whose im-

---

56. Mircea Eliade's perennially popular *The Sacred and the Profane* pays handsome tribute, in its introduction, to the contribution of Rudolf Otto's *Idea of the Holy*; see pp. 8–18 of Eliade's book.

portance goes beyond what can be discussed here. Both of them strove to identify the universal and indestructible systems of forces that could account for religion. For Freud the wish, for Durkheim society is forever operative, always the same—powerful, inexorable, generative.

But this should not obscure an important difference: Durkheim's theory tends to be static, while Freud's is sequential. This is not to deny Durkheim's substantial interest in development and change (as Giddens has insisted). But in the explanation of religion according to Durkheim, no sequence is required. His model is the social system, whose forces are perpetually the same. Although history evolves continual changes in social systems, so that for instance there is a steady movement from collectivism toward individualism and freedom, no historical sequence of events is required for his theory of religion to work as an explanation. Religion will surely arise in a different guises from one place and age to the next, but the essential dynamics are systematically rather than sequentially ordered. Although Durkheim was an evolutionist (with qualifications), his theory does not require evolutionary theory for it to work, as Lukes has pointed out.[57] Durkheim presupposed evolutionary ideas in his project of isolating the "elementary" forms, because these were more readily detectable in the simplest and earliest possible society one could study. Finding this in totemism, he nevertheless did not require totemism to be universal, because no sequential imperatives were operative, except that, against the type of explanations offered by the psychologists, Durkheim insisted that the social *must* come first in the causal scheme of things (therefore, totemism and the impersonal totemic principle come before animism and anthropomorphism). But he had no decisive evidence to back up this theoretical order, which was grounded in a prior and ultimately philosophical decision.[58]

That Freud finally embodied his theory in a story alerts us to the difference. His life-cycle model posits a necessary sequential matrix for both the species and the individual: helplessness, oedipal complex, repression, latency, return, maturation, and so on. No individual life history, no theory. Further, the ontogeny/phylogeny analogy was required to project the individual life history onto the phylogenetic level: from primal myth to future of an illusion, religion has such and such a history. The sequence must be universal. Therefore, he thought, totemism must be universal, and all societies must go through it.

Freud's sequence suggests an area for further inquiry untouched by Durkheim—the momentous passage from nature to culture, and the attempt to discover its meaning through the theory of the unconscious. His evolutionary framework also informs the issue of the future of religion: a "mature" hu-

---

57. Steven Lukes, *Emile Durkheim: His Life and Work*, 456–57.

58. See *EF*, 21–33, where Durkheim argues that even the Kantian categories are derived from social experience—a fundamental step in the invention of sociology of knowledge.

manity would learn to get along without it, but the indestructible power of primitive desire, along with social necessity, may insure its survival.[59]

The sequential character of Freud's theory, embodied in his primal myth, seems, in light of contemporary discussion of the evolution of culture and religion, to be more correct than his earlier critics thought. C. W. M. Hart has charged that Tylor, Spencer et al. betrayed the Darwinian advance in evolutionary theory by opening an unbridgeable gap (or rather, reopening it) between man and nature. Hart argues that Spencer and Tylor "substituted a new dualism for the older one, and . . . opened up as big a gap between man and the rest of nature as had been there in pre-Darwinian days."[60] Culture constituted a decisive break from his animal ancestry, and evolutionary theory then flowed into two separate streams, biological and cultural. Tylor's classic definition of culture was in terms of man alone: "capabilities and habits acquired by man as a member of society." Hart's thesis is that this approach "led most anthropologists astray, and perhaps it is that definition more than any other single sentence that is responsible for the present gap between biological and social studies."[61] That was written almost a half-century ago. There is some indication that his call for a replacement of pseudo-evolutionary Spencerian thinking (where evolution is discussed at all) by the Darwinian conception will have to be heeded due to recent discoveries. At issue is the interaction between biological constraints and protocultural activity, especially in that period, established by the discovery of the australopithecenes, between the achievement of bipedalism and of the larger-than-ape-sized brain. W. W. Howells, reflecting on the new situation, wrote in 1950:

> Heretofore we have been given to talking about "the appearance of man"—the tyranny of terminology—as if he had suddenly been promoted from colonel to brigadier general, and had a date of rank. It is now evident that the first hominids were small-brained, newly bipedal, proto-Australopith hominoids, and that what we have always meant by "man" represents later forms of this group with secondary adaptations in the direction of large brains and modified skeletons of the same form.[62]

Clifford Geertz has argued strongly for attention to the overlap between biological and cultural evolution. He takes Howells's observation a step further, noting that "the greater part of human cortical expansion has followed, not preceded, the 'beginning' of culture."[63] For Geertz, "culture" includes

---

59. Cf. Rieff (above, n. 3), esp. 291–94.

60. C. W. M. Hart, "Social Evolution and Modern Anthropology," 108.

61. Ibid., 112.

62. Howells is quoted by A. Irving Hallowell, "Behavioral Evolution and the Emergence of the Self," 44 (from W. W. Howells, *Origin of the Human Stock* [1950], 89).

63. Clifford Geertz, "The Transition to Humanity," 26.

only "post-toolmaking symbolic patterns."[64] The startling implication of this is a point "of fundamental significance for our view of the nature of man. He becomes now, not just the producer of culture but, in a specifically biological sense, *its product.*"[65]

This line of thought is striking with reference to Freud's myth. One much criticized feature of it is that the rebellious brothers had weapons (Freud had written that "some cultural advance, perhaps command over some new weapon, had given them a sense of superior strength"; *T&T*, 141–42). If that is so, how could the murder itself then be seen as the *beginning* of culture?[66] Geertz's breakdown of the sharp line thus seems to be anticipated by Freud. Moreover, we have already discussed the extent to which Freud's whole project, especially in describing the unconscious, was a means of realizing the human meaning of being biological.

Recent paleoanthropological findings, from the Afar region of Ethiopia to El Juyo, Spain,[67] seem to provide grist for the mill in the evolutionary study of religion that has yet to be exploited. And Freud's commitment to anchoring the evolution of culture in the biological heritage seems to be on target. As Draenos observed (repeating a quote given above), If we take evolution seriously as embracing the phenomenon of "man, which in some sense we must, then mind ceases to represent an independent ontological substance that realizes itself in the act of reflection, but instead must be understood to have emerged from matter as the actualization of some potentiality inherent therein."[68]

This poses an unanswered challenge to the standard shibboleth of theologians and philosophers of religion who argue that the "autonomy" of religion insulates it from explanation by anything other than itself, and that it will be violated or misunderstood if it is dealt with on any but "its own terms." The human sciences, of which study of religion is a part, aspire to a "unified science of man" (Ernest Becker), and every element of human culture belongs to a single web of relationships, none of which is autonomous with respect to the others. Religion is no more autonomous when it comes to analysis than literature or political theory.

Clearly, the plea for autonomy in fact can be reduced to one thing: religion's refusal to submit to any explanation other than its own, a claim as time-honored as it is self-serving. Autonomy means being a law unto itself, to be entirely self-determined and determining, or, in sociological jargon, to claim

64. Clifford Geertz, "The Growth of Culture and the Evolution of Mind," 736, n. 10 (this is a longer version of the essay cited in the preceding note).

65. Geertz (above, n. 63), 26.

66. Paul (above, n. 15), 314–15, citing Malinowski's criticism.

67. Cf. Donald C. Johanson and Maitland A. Edey, *Lucy;* L. G. Freeman and J. Gonzalez Echegaray, "El Juyo: A 14,000-Year-Old Sanctuary from Northern Spain."

68. Draenos (above, n. 6), 84–85.

"transcendence" as an "independent variable."[69] Such status means that religion can be an instrument for explaining other social and psychological phenomena but is not itself subject to explanation. The tradition reviewed in this book would have little patience with such pleadings or with those who add, with more directness and less sophistication, that religion is a response to transcendence, and that transcendence is undefinable and inexplicable, else it would not transcend; and therefore questions of its definition and explanation are inappropriate. As Freud said long ago to the theologians who ruled out investigation of the origins of religion because it came from God, "the matter is certainly not decided by saying that this question cannot be asked" (*NIL*, 169–70).

---

69. William R. Garrett, "Troublesome Transcendence: The Supernatural in the Scientific Study of Religion," who argues for scientifically handling "transcendence" by treating it as an "independent interpretive variable" (179).

Conclusion

"Explaining religion" has a cosmic ring to it, but it has not always meant the same thing or had the same scope in the period studied here. The endeavor to explain began narrowly and critically, then gradually extended, following lines determined by the specific problems confronted by our authors. I have tried to illuminate the development of that mode of inquiry which approaches all explanatory problems on naturalistic grounds, arguing that such an approach is the decisive feature which distinguishes the study of religion from theology. I have tried to show how that approach emerged over time, as pursuit of specific problems drew investigators increasingly away from the traditional commitments and concerns that shape theology and the religious traditions. The new approach justified itself by its compatibility with emerging modern perceptions of the world and its ability to solve problems that seemed insoluble under the reigning assumptions of their times. It finally established itself as an element of the "science of man." In what follows, I shall briefly review the problems, solutions, and advances that broke the path for this modern research tradition.

Bodin and Herbert were confronted with the mortal conflict among the European religions (rival forms of Christianity, extended by Bodin to include Jews and Muslims), whose mutually exclusive explanations canceled each other out because each claimed to be based on divine revelation. They could not explain each other except dogmatically or deal with each other except by anathema. Bodin explained this rivalry as a tragic primeval departure from aboriginal religion given to Adam; Herbert saw it as a history of error and fraud obscuring the sure and steady light of the "common notions."

Their achievement is measured by their ability to abstract themselves from the confessional fray and to view religion itself as a critical problem demanding solution, not only for the sake of rationality and conscience, but as a presupposition for a return to political sanity and peace. Despite a Eurocentric orientation that looks parochial from a contemporary perspective, they intended an evenhanded universalism: in doing so, they dared to put Christianity on the same level as the other religions, subjecting it to the same critical and rational standards. Both believed in a universal providence that was only made disreputable by the dogmatic claims of the rival traditions. "True religion," they argued, must consist either in a basic and minimal list of truths (Herbert's common notions; Bodin/Toralba's original religion) or in sincerity of heart (Bodin/Senamus). Their work represented a major theoretical advance—a paradigm shift—for although they stayed firmly within a religious mode of explaining religion, and did not categorically reject the notion of particular revelation, they put reason above the alleged revelations as the norm for religious truth, and they rejected the authority of confessional groups.

Fontenelle and Vico took another tack, more "conservative" in that both professed to be Catholic Christians; and so—prudently—they exempted Christianity from their analyses. More important, however, both approached religion with the intent to explain it historically and, because of their very exemption of Christianity from their analyses, broke free to give critical-historical reason free reign.

Fontenelle asked: Why is it that every people's primal history takes mythic form? What causes primitive peoples to think in this way? Fontenelle sketched a "natural history" of myths that accounted for them as erroneous explanations of natural phenomena, thus formulating an approach and method that would be universalized, without exemptions, and developed further by Hume, Comte, and Tylor. Fontenelle added to this explanation the idea (from Herbert) that the history of religion is replete with fraud as well as honest error. Then, studying a specific case—the beginning of a religious tradition (Christianity)—he provided an exemplar of how critical method could be applied to purge historical explanations of their mythic elements. His achievement was to envisage and to begin to practice a scientific history of religions, tracing them from their origins.

Vico's approach can be framed theologically, given his professed intent to write a theodicy of divine providence—specifically, to account theologically for the universality and utility of religion in light of the particularity of the Christian claim of divine revelation. But even while protesting pious intent, he succeeded in showing how the *entire* history of religions could be construed within the larger framework of a history of institutions—of human society as such. He divined a way of penetrating the ancient myths (which Fontenelle was unable to do) as invaluable historical sources that revealed universal structural principles for the study of culture, identifying those necessities and utilities of social order that characterize all human communities. Furthermore, his conception of a "new science" of humanity was predicated on the conviction that institutions really *can* be explained because they were created by men. The first of these human creations was religion itself. Informed by ancient myths, he was able to imagine humanity in its most primitive state, emerging from brutish existence to found the first human institutions. He proposed to show how, whether divine revelation is given or not, religion *must* come into being. His explanation was naturalistic except for one remaining theological residue—a divinely implanted, universal religious sense.

This theological residue came into focus with Hume, stimulated by the apologetic arguments of his day: how, he asked, can we better explain the religionists' most fundamental legitimating claim that all humans are endowed with an innate sense of the divine? The traditional theological explanation did not satisfy him because of two pieces of anomalous counterevidence: the immense and seemingly irreducible variety of religious forms and the non-universality of religion itself. If religion is grounded in human nature at all, he argued, it would have to show some capacity to determine the form that religion takes and exhibit such forms universally. But religion fails to do this. Therefore, the hypothesis of a universal, innate religious sense analogous to the instincts, which are both universal and regular in their operation, is untenable.

Hume then undertook to explain the "religious sense" on the basis of a psychohistorical analysis of what happens when persons attempt to cope with life, especially the fears and hopes engendered in the encounter with the most disturbing phenomena of the external world: superior and unknown powers that determine one's fate and future. Everyone encounters such things; most people construct religions to cope with them. These religions explain unknown forces, assuage anxiety, and nurture hope through a thought-process that is, Hume claimed, both universal and primordial—construing the system of the world anthropomorphically. In proposing this explanation, Hume disposed (to his satisfaction) of the last remaining *religious* explanation and legitimation of religion—the claim that religion is innate.

For this reason, we credit Hume with the intellectual completion of the paradigm-shift from a religious to a naturalistic framework for the study of religion. What followed him were further advances in theory, but these remained within the same intellectual paradigm. Hume's approach not only separated the study of religion from apologetics but was also able to make sense of the virtually limitless varieties of religious forms, even though his theory could not accommodate the discovery that primitive religion was not universally anthropomorphic—a fact Durkheim would emphasize. Hume agreed that religion required an intellectual component for its construction, but he rooted religion ultimately in the operation of the affections ("passions") rather than in reason, advancing not only the explanatory effort, but finding agreement among religious as well as naturalistic thinkers (for example, Schleiermacher and Freud).

Hume also advanced the study of religion by completing, in his own fashion, Vico's project of defining a comprehensive human science that included religion in it, thus promising to rescue the study of religion from intellectual isolation and neglect by giving it a permanent location on the intellectual map of human studies.

Comte continued the project of constructing a science of humanity by inventing sociology as its core domain of inquiry. In an attempt to identify the natural laws that govern social dynamics, Comte adapted the Humean explanation of the rise of religion but in a more intellectualistic mode than Hume's, because his interest in religion was subordinated to an account of the progress of reason.

Also, unlike Hume, Comte was obsessed by a sense of social and intellectual crisis: the very progress of reason and civilization were being undermined by the anarchy of rival worldviews whose destructive tendencies could not, he thought, be solved by the inadequate social doctrine of the Enlightenment's critical philosophy. So he invented sociology and depended upon it, not only to explain society and religion's role in it, but to save society itself by providing a basis for social reconstruction and unity. To accomplish this task, Comte volunteered to invent a religion, having already explained it.

For Comte, religion was in the paradoxical position of being both an essential part of the problem (as an obstructive survival of archaic ways of explaining the world) and a key to the solution (in providing the unity of thought and loyalty without which society could not survive). The latter led him to new depths in analyzing the historical and social functions of religion, preparing the way for Durkheim's sociology. He shared Vico's profound understanding and appreciation of history as the chief component of any human science, a component without which the present could not be understood nor the future intelligently envisaged. His conviction that the laws governing society were historical led him to lay down an evolutionary scheme that not only organized and explained previous history but also provided the proper instrument for organizing the future. Debatable though Comte's scheme is, new discoveries of the nineteenth century seemed to vindicate the construction of such evolutionary schemes as an obvious task.

Those discoveries—in geology, archeology, and biology—revealed under the very armchairs of European scholars hard evidence of an unimaginably archaic form of life which presented an urgent new problem for solution: how are we to account for the rise of civilization from the Stone Age? Tylor was among the first to attempt a comprehensive solution, although he was by no means the first to abandon altogether the traditional biblical framework of history that had so cramped Vico's style. Tylor's explanation of progress sprang from his belief in the innate and irrepressible curiosity that human beings bring to their experiences of the world. The first great human thought regarding puzzling phenomena, he explained, was animistic, and Tylor regarded this sort of thought as the explanation for the beginning of religion as well.

Tylor's animism was a refinement of Hume's anthropomorphic thesis but, like Comte's theory, was placed in an evolutionary framework so as to explain the whole progress of mind to his own day. In that framework, religion (belief in spiritual beings) found itself consigned to the dustbin of "survivals." The definition still serves to inform some inquiry into preliterate as well as "civilized" religion. The fatal flaw in Tylor's approach, however, was that it could not satisfactorily explain *why* religion not only survives but thrives, in

modern as well as in archaic times. Tylor rightly saw religious explanations
of the world as relics but had no way to explain religions (including modern
ones) as vital and living systems meeting persistent and contemporary needs.

To this question came Durkheim and Freud, armed with superior theoretical perspectives. Both of them challenged the basic thesis that religion
began, survived, or could be explained merely as a form of conscious thinking.
The springs of religion lay deeper, impelled by forces within and without
believers that they did not fully understand themselves, but which they named
in their myths and expressed in their rituals. Recognizing truth embedded
in such materials, Durkheim and Freud proposed new ways to explain them.
Their solutions differed, but together they covered the naturalistic ground—
in other words, the sociological and psychological causes that could give rise
to religion and account for its peculiar phenomena, including its remarkable
power to persist and revitalize itself. Especially in Freud's case, the means
of explanation opened up new avenues of interpetation unavailable before;
the contents of religious myth and ritual could be studied alongside comparable psychic, cultural, and historical phenomena.

Overall, then, we have seen how the endeavor to deal with a series of
discrete problems finally precipitated a new paradigm for the study of religion
that combined critical-historical, psychological, and sociological tools.

Whatever one thinks of the whole enterprise, it is indisputable that this
tradition raised and dealt with questions that fell outside the interests and
capacity of theology to deal with, or even to raise, and that it provided a
whole body of new theory and studies based on those theories—in all, a body
of work that otherwise would not even exist. Questions were formulated and
addressed that were not being asked by theology because they lay outside
the religious paradigm—that is, outside its perception of legitimate, interesting, or appropriate concerns.

Oriented to religious communities, theology has its own integrity and
continues to develop its questions and answers out if its own paradigm. Insofar
as it uses the naturalistic tradition at all, it does so eclectically, often for
apologetic purposes, rather than with the aim of furthering the sort of inquiry
typical of social-scientific students of religion. Such concerns remain at the
periphery for scholars working from a religious perspective. At bottom, the
reason is that the claim to be able to explain religion as such seems out of
bounds, since each religious perspective cherishes within itself the justification of its own existence and devotes its energy primarily to the interpretation of religious experience from within.

However, in the setting of a university, where religion departments gather
as conglomerates representing a variety of interests, commitments, and tech-
nical skills, the possibility of addressing problems of religion in a cooperative
way and from a global perspective presents itself. Some critical problems
have been at least mentioned along the way that are of mutual interest to

theology (understood broadly as a perspective of religious commitment) and to the human sciences. For example (and not necessarily in order of importance, or exhaustively), what is the relation between religion and morality? We have seen how the differing theories of Durkheim and Freud suggest quasi-empirical ways in which the problem can be approached, which may be of use in an ethics literature that relies largely on sheer argument about values. Or again, the question of the anthropological roots of religion, of the relative roles of body and soul—dualism versus materialism—resonate not only in anthropology (the relation between biological and cultural factors) but in theology. (In liberation theology, for example, "dualism" is branded as the root of ideologies of oppression.) Or again, the obscure but important question of the relation between explanation and interpretation (hermeneutics) is of mutual interest and importance, as one can discover in reading both anthropological and theological literature.

It is regrettable that the institutional configuration of studies in the contemporary university tends to obstruct the organization of a unified approach to the broad spectrum of problems inherent in a scientific-humanistic understanding of religion. Specialization and institutional apartheid separate students of religion into disparate departments, reinforcing their intellectual isolation from one another. In the days when religion was the exclusive domain of theological faculties (or separate schools), and was carried on in the interest of furthering the several causes of religion, the contribution of other disciplines was barely missed. The present arrangements in many institutions where religion is studied at the graduate level still relegate scientific study of religion to the periphery. But the study of the humanities and human sciences calls for a different configuration of skills, in comformity with the different sorts of questions that are being raised. We are still struggling with the question of how to address these problems in a more unified way without creating a new dogmatism that would undermine pluralism.

Theology, whether in its confessional or generic modes, fails as a unifying paradigm because its peculiar insistence that religions are "manifestations of the sacred" isolates it from the presuppositions that are otherwise operative in the humanities and human sciences. The claim that religions can be studied and understood *only* from a religious perspective excludes fruitful intellectual interaction with people in other disciplines by staking out its own privileged universe of discourse and, so far, failing to show how that universe intersects with the one constituted by the rough consensus of the academy at large. The issue is not whether "transcendence" refers to something extramentally real, but whether the study of religion wishes to enter as a full partner in the study of culture.

The distinctive feature of the tradition studied here is that it pushes explanation to the limit. Those who operate from a Western religious perspective and find this irreverent could do worse than adapt Vico's view, which was a daring extension of, but not a qualitative departure from, the traditional doctrine that God does *everything* through secondary causes. This approach has—in a university context—a distinct advantage over the contemporary version of the deistic alternative, wherein all religious phenomena are regarded as manifestations of a universal sense of transcendence and/or of its archetypal expressions. Vico's approach concentrates on "secondary causes" and therefore commits itself to historical and psychosocial study of discrete cases. It does not demand to find "transcendence" everywhere so as to order religions hierarchically, to the distinct advantage of the so-called "higher" religions. A determined theological intent has shown its capacity to maintain itself using the former approach even while giving attention to naturalistic theories. John Bowker provides one example of such a view in operation. Near the end of his discussion of Freud in the context of an inquiry into the "sense of God," Bowker assures his readers that

> it would be impossible on psychoanalytic grounds alone to exclude the possibility that God is the source of the sense of God: however much a sense of God may be constructed through, and as a consequence of, the replication of infantile experience, and however much the characterization of God may replicate parental relationships, the possibility cannot be excluded that there may be an *x* in reality which has in the past sustained those replications and which has reinforced the continuity of such terms as "god". (*The Sense of God*, 131)

But possibilities come cheap and are no alternative to well-argued theories such as Freud's. Thus, for all the sophistication of Bowker's work, his manner of argument lacks bite, since any "*x*" is possible. It is equally possible, for example, that the Big Bang theory is nothing more than science's waking up to the truth of the Genesis account of creation, as in "Let there be light." The question, however, is: what kinds of evidence might be adduced by religious apologists to challenge naturalistic theories so as to advance beyond these gratuitous proposals of possibilities?

Meanwhile, the naturalistic approach developed here takes theological interpretations seriously as part of the religious data but not of their explanation; for, as Occam held, explanatory entities (such as "transcendence" or innate religious instincts) must not be multiplied beyond necessity. The naturalistic approach is at once more modest and more ambitious than the religious one: more modest because it is content to investigate the causes, motivations, meanings, and impact of religious phenomena without pronouncing on their cosmic significance for human destiny; ambituous, in that the study of religion strives to explain religion and to integrate its understanding into the other elements of culture to which it is related.

Bibliography

This bibliography lists all works referred to in the footnotes, plus a few additional works that were used in preparation of this book but to which no specific reference is made.

PRIMARY SOURCES

Jean Bodin

Colloquium heptaplomeres de rerum sublimium arcanis abditis.
    Edited by Ludovicus Noack. Paris, London, 1857. Reprint. Stuttgart, 1966.
Colloquium of the Seven about Secrets of the Sublime. Translated by Marion Kuntz.
    Princeton: Princeton University Press, 1975.
De la demonomanie des sorciers. Paris: Iacques du Puys, 1581.
Method for the Easy Comprehension of History. Translated by Beatrice Reynolds. New
    York: Columbia University Press, 1945.
The Six Bookes of a Commonweale. English translation, 1606. Reprint ed. Kenneth
    D. McRae. Cambridge: Harvard University Press, 1962.

Auguste Comte

"Considerations on the Spiritual Power" (1826). In Ronald Fletcher, ed., *The Crisis
    of Industrial Civilization: The Early Essays of Auguste Comte.* English translation by
    H. D. Hutton, 1877. London, Heinemann, 1974, 214–45.
"Philosophical Considerations on the Sciences and Savants" (1825). In Ronald
    Fletcher (see preceding entry), 182–213.
"Plan for the Scientific Operations Necessary for Reorganizing Society" (1822). In
    Ronald Fletcher (see first Comte entry), 111–81.
The Positive Philosophy (1830). English translation and condensation by Harriet Mar-
    tineau (1855). Reprint. New York: AMS Press, 1974.
System of Positive Polity, or Treatise on Sociology: Instituting the Religion of Humanity
    (1851–54). Vol. 1 (1851), trans. J. H. Bridges. London, 1875. Vol. 2 (1852), trans.
    Frederic Harrison (1875); reprint New York, 1968. Vol. 4 (1854), trans. Richard
    Congreve (1877); reprint New York, 1968.

Emile Durkheim

W. S. F. Pickering, ed. *Durkheim on Religion: A Selection of Readings with Bibliog-
    raphies.* London: Routledge & Kegan Paul, 1975.

The Elementary Forms of the Religious Life. Translated by J. W. Swain. New York:
   Free Press, 1965.
Anthony Giddens, ed. and trans. *Emile Durkheim: Selected Writings.* Cambridge:
   Cambridge University Press, 1972.
Steven Lukes, ed. *The Rules of Sociological Method.* Translated by W. D. Halls. New
   York: Free Press, 1982.

Bernard le Bouvier de Fontenelle

Fontenelle's Dialogues of the Dead. Translated from the French. London, 1708.
Histoire des oracles (1686). Critical edition Louis Maigron. Paris, 1908.
The History of Oracles and the Cheats of the Pagan Priests. English translation, 1688.
   Reprinted in L. M. Marsak, ed. *The Achievement of Bernard le Bovier de Fontenelle.*
   New York, 1970.
De l'origine des fables (1724?). Critical edition J.-R. Carré. Paris: Alcan, 1932.
The Origin of Myths. Partial English translation in L. M. Marsak (see preceding
   entry).

Sigmund Freud

Civilization and Its Discontents (1930). Translated by James Strachey. New York:
   Norton, 1961.
The Ego and the Id (1923). Translated by John Riviere. London: Hogarth, 1927.
The Future of an Illusion (1927). Translated by James Strachey. New York: Norton,
   1961.
The Interpretation of Dreams (1895). 1910 ed. translated by A. A. Brill. New York:
   Modern Library, 1950.
Moses and Monotheism (1939). Translated by Katherine Jones. New York: Vintage,
   1967.
New Introductory Lectures on Psychoanalysis (1933). Translated by James Strachey.
   New York: Norton, 1964.
"Obsessive Acts and Religious Practices" (1907). In W. A. Lessa and E. Z. Voght,
   Reader in Comparative Religion: An Anthropological Approach. 1st ed. Evanston,
   Ill., 1958, 185–90.
*Totem and Taboo: Some Points of Agreement between the Mental Lives of Savages and
   Neurotics* (1913). Translated by James Strachey. New York: Norton, 1950.

Herbert of Cherbury

The Antient Religion of the Gentiles and Causes of their Errors Considered. . . . London,
   1705.
The Life of Edward, First Lord Herbert of Cherbury, written by himself. Edited by J. M.
   Shuttleworth. London: Oxford University Press, 1976.
Lord Herbert of Cherbury's De Religione Laici (1645). Edited and translated by Harold
   L. Hutcheson. New Haven: Yale University Press, 1944.
De religione gentilium errorumque apud eos causis (1663). Reprint. Edited by Günter
   Gawlick. Stuttgart-Bad Cannstatt: Fromman, 1967.
De veritate, . . . 3d ed. London, 1645. Reprint. Edited by Günter Gawlick. Stuttgart-
   Bad Cannstatt: Fromman, 1966.
De veritate, by Edward, Lord Herbert of Cherbury (1624). 3d ed. 1645. Translated with
   introduction by Meyrick H. Carré. Bristol, 1937.

David Hume

Dialogues Concerning Natural Religion (1779). Edited by Norman Kemp Smith. Indianapolis: Bobbs-Merrill, 1947.

A Dissertation on the Passions (1739). In *Essays Moral, Political and Literary*, edited by T. H. Green and T. H. Grose. Vol. 2 (London, 1875), 139–66.

"Of Miracles," in *Enquiry Concerning Human Understanding*. Chapter X, *Enquiries Concerning Human Understanding and Concerning the Principles of Morals*, edited by L. A. Selby-Bigge. 3d ed. Revised by P. H. Nidditch. Oxford: Clarendon, 1975.

Natural History of Religion (1757). Edited by H. E. Root. Stanford: Stanford University Press, 1957.

A Treatise of Human Nature (1739). Edited by L. A. Selby-Bigge. Oxford: Clarendon, 1888.

Edward Burnett Tylor

Anthropology. New York: Appleton, 1906.

"On a Method of Investigating the Development of Institutions; Applied to Laws of Marriage and Descent." *Journal of the Royal Anthropological Institute* 18 (1889): 245–69.

Primitive Culture. Researches into the Development of Mythology, Philosophy, Religion, Language, Art and Customs. 3d American from 2d English ed. 2 vols. New York: H. Holt & Co., 1883.

Researches into the Early History of Mankind and the Development of Civilization. New York: H. Holt & Co., 1865.

Giambattista Vico

The Autobiography of Giambattista Vico. Translated by Max H. Fisch and Thomas G. Bergin. Ithaca: Cornell University Press, 1944.

The New Science (1725, 1744). Translated by Thomas G. Bergin and Max H. Fisch. Rev. ed. Ithaca: Cornell University Press, 1968.

Principi di Scienza Nuova. In *Opere*, edited by Fausto Nicolini. Milan: Riccardo Ricciardi, 1953, 365–905.

STUDIES

Allen, J. W. "Jean Bodin." In F. J. C. Hearnshaw, ed., *The Social and Political Ideas of Some Great Thinkers of the Sixteenth and Seventeenth Centuries*. New York, 1926; reprint 1967, 42–62.

Arendt, Hannah. *The Human Condition*. Garden City, N.Y.: Doubleday, 1959.

Aron, Raymond. *Main Currents in Sociological Thought*. Translated by R. Howard and H. Weaver. New York: Basic Books, 1965.

Atkinson, J. J. *Primal Law*. London: Longmans, Green, 1903.

Baxter, Christopher R. "Jean Bodin's Daemon and His Conversion to Judaism." In Horst Denzer, ed. (q.v.), 1–21.

Bedford, R. D. *The Defense of Truth. Herbert of Cherbury and the Seventeenth Century*. Manchester: Manchester University Press, 1979.

Beidelman, T. O. *W. Robertson Smith and the Sociological Study of Religion*. Chicago: University of Chicago Press, 1974.

Bellah, Robert N. "Religious Evolution." *American Sociological Review* 29 (1964): 358–94.

Berger, Peter L. *The Sacred Canopy: Elements of a Sociological Theory of Religion.* Garden City, N.Y.: Anchor, 1969.

Berlin, Isaiah. *Against the Current: Essays in the History of Ideas,* edited by Henry Hardy. New York: Viking, 1980.

———. "Hume and the Sources of German Anti-Rationalism." In George P. Morice (q.v.), 93–116.

———. "A Note on Vico's Concept of Knowledge." In Tagliacozzo and White (q.v.), 371–77.

———. "The Originality of Machiavelli." In Myron P. Gilmore, ed., *Studies in Machiavelli.* Florence: G. C. Sansoni, 1972.

———. *Vico and Herder: Two Studies in the History of Ideas.* New York: Viking, 1976.

von Bezold, Friedrich. "Jean Bodins Colloquium Heptaplomeres und der Atheismus des 16. Jahrhunderts." *Historische Zeitschrift* 113 (1914): 260–315.

Bidney, David. "Myth, Symbolism, and Truth." In Thomas A. Sebeok, ed., *Myth: A Symposium.* Bloomington: Indiana University Press, 1955, 3–24.

———. "Vico's New Science of Myth." in Tagliacozzo and White (q.v.), 259–77.

Bossuet, Jacques-Benigne. *Discourse on Universal History.* Translated by Elborg Forster, edited by Orest Ranum. Chicago: University of Chicago Press, 1976.

Bowker, John. *The Sense of God: Sociological, Anthropological, and Psychological Approaches to the Origin of the Sense of God.* Oxford: Clarendon, 1973.

de Brosses, Charles. *Du Culte des dieux fétiches, ou Parallèle de l'ancienne religion de l'Egypte avec la religion actuelle de Nigritie.* 1760.

Brown, Norman O. *Life Against Death: The Psychoanalytic Meaning of History.* New York: Vintage Books, 1959.

Bryson, Gladys. *Man and Society: The Scottish Inquiry of the Eighteenth Century.* Princeton: Princeton University Press, 1945.

Burke, Peter. *Vico.* Oxford: Oxford University Press, 1985.

Burrow, John W. *Evolution and Society: A Study in Victorian Social Theory.* Cambridge: The University Press, 1966.

Busson, Henri. *Le Rationalisme dans la littérature française de la renaissance (1533–1601).* New ed. Paris: J. Vrin, 1957.

Capaldi, Nicholas. "Hume's Theory of the Passions." In Donald W. Livingston and James T. King (q.v.), 172–90.

Capps, Walter H. "On Religious Studies, in Lieu of an Overview." *Journal of the American Academy of Religion* 42 (1974): 727–33.

Carré, Jean Raoul. *La Philosophie de Fontenelle, ou le sourire de la raison.* Paris: F. Alcan, 1932.

Cassirer, Ernst. *The Individual and the Cosmos in Renaissance Philosophy.* Translated by Mario Domandi. New York: Harper, 1963.

Chauviré, Roger. *Jean Bodin, auteur de la 'République.'* Paris, 1914.

Chitnis, Anand C. *The Scottish Enlightenment: A Social History.* Totawa, N.J.: Rowman & Littlefield, 1976.

Cicero. *On the Nature of the Gods.* Translated by H. C. P. McGregor. Harmondsworth: Penguin, 1972.

Clark, W. E. LeGros *The Antecedents of Man: An Introduction to the Evolution of the Primates*. New York: Quadrangle, 1978.

Collins, J. *The Emergence of Philosophy of Religion*. New Haven: Yale University Press, 1967.

Croce, Benedetto. *The Philosophy of Giambattista Vico*. Translated by R. G. Collingwood. New York: Macmillan, 1913.

Denzer, Horst, ed. *Jean Bodin: Verhandlungen der Internationalen Bodin Tagung in München*. Munich: Beck, 1973.

Despland, Michel. *La Religion en Occident: Evolution des Idées et du Vécu*. Montreal: Editions Fides, 1979.

de Vries, Jan. *The Study of Religion: A Historical Approach*. Translated by Kees W. Bolle. New York: Harcourt Brace, 1967.

Dilthey, Wilhelm. "The Rise of Hermeneutics." Translated by Fredric Jameson. *New Literary History* 3/2 (1972): 229–44.

Douglas, Mary T. *Purity and Danger: An Analysis of Concepts of Pollution and Taboo*. London: Routledge & Kegan Paul, 1966.

Draenos, Stan. *Freud's Odyssey: Psychoanalysis and the End of Metaphysics*. New Haven: Yale University Press, 1982.

Durkheim, Emile. *The Elementary Forms of the Religion Life*. Translated by J. W. Swain. New York: Free Press, 1965.

———. *Montesquieu and Rousseau, Forerunners of Sociology*. Translated by R. Manheim. Ann Arbor: University of Michigan Press, 1960.

Eliade, Mircea. *History of Religious Ideas*. Translated by W. R. Trask. 2 vols. Vol. 1. Chicago: University of Chicago Press, 1978.

———. "The Quest for the 'Origins' of Religion." In *The Quest: History and Meaning in Religion*. Chicago: University of Chicago Press, 1969, 37–53.

———. *The Sacred and the Profane: The Nature of Religion*. Translated by Willard R. Trask. New York: Harcourt Brace, 1959.

Evans-Pritchard, E. E. *Theories of Primitive Religion*. Oxford: Oxford University Press, 1965.

Finegan, Jack. *The Archeology of World Religions*. Princeton: Princeton University Press, 1952.

Finnegan, Ruth, and Robin Horton, eds. *Modes of Thought: Essays on Thinking in Western and Non-Western Societies*. London: Faber, 1973.

Fletcher, Ronald, ed. *The Crisis of Industrial Civilization: The Early Essays of Auguste Comte*. London: Heinemann, 1974.

Fournol, Etienne-Maurice. *Bodin, prédécesseur de Montesquieu* (1896). Geneva: Slatkine Reprints, 1970.

Fox, Marvin. "Religion and Human Nature in the Philosophy of David Hume." In *Process and Divinity*, edited by William L. Reese and Eugene Freeman. LaSalle, Ill.: Open Court, 1964, 561–77.

Franklin, Julian H. *Jean Bodin and the Rise of Absolutist Theory*. New York: Cambridge University Press, 1973.

Freeman, L. G., and J. Gonzalez Echegaray. "El Juyo: A 14,000-year-old Sanctuary from Northern Spain." *History of Religions* 21 (1981–82): 1–19.

Frei, Hans W. *The Eclipse of Biblical Narrative*. New Haven: Yale University Press, 1974.

Garrett, William. "Troublesome Transcendence: The Supernatural in the Scientific Study of Religion." *Sociological Analysis* 35 (1974): 167–80.

Gaskin, J. C. A. *Hume's Philosophy of Religion*. New York: Barnes & Noble, 1978.

Gay, Peter. *The Enlightenment, An Interpretation*. Vol. 1, *The Rise of Modern Paganism*. New York: Knopf, 1966.

Geertz, Clifford. "The Growth of Culture and the Evolution of Mind." In Jordan M. Scher, ed., *Theories of the Mind*. New York: Free Press, 1962, 713–40.

———. "The Transition to Humanity." In Sol Tax and Leslie G. Freeman, eds., *Horizons of Anthropology* 2d ed. Chicago: Aldine, 1977, 21–32.

———, Robert Bellah, and James Dittes. "Religion." In *International Encyclopedia of the Social Sciences*, edited by David L. Sills. 17 vols. New York: Macmillan, 1968, 13:398–421.

Enno van Gelder, H. A. *The Two Reformations of the Sixteenth Century: A Study of the Religious Aspects and Consequences of Renaissance and Humanism*. The Hague: Nijhoff, 1961.

Glick, Leonard. "The Anthropology of Religion: Malinowski and Beyond." In Charles Y. Glock and Phillip E. Hammond (q.v.), 181–242.

Glock, Charles Y., and Phillip E. Hammond. *Beyond the Classics? Essays in the Scientific Study of Religion*. New York: Harper & Row, 1973.

Goldenweiser, Alexander. "Evolution, Social." In *Encyclopedia of the Social Sciences*. New York, 1931, 5:656–62.

———. "Religion and Society: A Critique of Emile Durkheim's Theory of the Origin and Nature of Religion." *Journal of Philosophy, Psychology and Scientific Methods* 14 (1917): 113–24.

Grene, Marjorie. "Reducibility: Another Side Issue?" In idem, ed., *Interpretations of Life and Mind: Essays around the Problem of Reduction*. New York: Humanities Press, 1971, 14–37.

Gruber, Jacob W. "Brixham Cave and the Antiquity of Man." In Melford E. Spiro, ed. (q.v.), 373–402.

Gusdorf, Georges. "For a History of the Science of Man." *Diogenes* 17 (1957): 74–97.

Gutting, Gary, ed. *Paradigms and Revolutions: Applications and Appraisals of Thomas Kuhn's Philosophy of Science*. Notre Dame, Ind.: Notre Dame Press, 1980.

Güttler, Carl. *Eduard, Lord Herbert von Cherbury: ein kritischer Beitrag zur Geschichte des Psychologismus und der Religionsphilosophie*. Munich, 1897.

Hallowell, A. Irving. "Behavioral Evolution and the Emergence of the Self." In B. J. Meggers, ed. (q.v.), 36–60.

Harris, Marvin. *The Rise of Anthropological Theory*. New York: Crowell, 1968.

Hart, C. W. M. "Social Evolution and Modern Anthropology." In H. A. Innis, ed., *Essays in Political Economy in Honor of E. J. Urwick*. Toronto: University of Toronto Press, 1938, 99–116.

Haydn, Hiram C. *The Counter-Renaissance*. New York: Scribner, 1950.

Hazard, Paul. *The European Mind, 1680–1715*. Translated by J. Lewis May. Cleveland: World, 1963.

Herskovits, Melville J. "A Genealogy of Ethnological Theory." In Melford E. Spiro, ed. (q.v.), 403–15.

Hintikka, Jaakko. "Practical versus Theoretical Reason—an Ambiguous Legacy." In Stephan Koerner, ed., *Practical Reason*. Oxford: Blackwell, 1974, 83–102.

Hodgen, Margaret T. *The Doctrine of Survivals: A Chapter in the History of Scientific Method in the Study of Man*. London: Allenson, 1936.

————. *Early Anthropology in the Sixteenth and Seventeenth Centuries.* Philadelphia: University of Pennsylvania Press, 1964.

Hollinger, David. "Thomas S. Kuhn's Theory of Science and Its Implications for History." In Gary Gutting (q.v.), 195–222.

Homans, Peter. *Theology after Freud: An Interpretive Inquiry.* Indianapolis: Bobbs Merrill, 1970.

Honigmann, John J. *The Development of Anthropological Ideas.* Homewood, Ill.: Dorsey Press, 1976.

Horowitz, Maryanne Cline. "Judaism in Jean Bodin." *Sixteenth Century Journal* 13/3 (1982): 109–13.

————. "The Stoic Synthesis of the Idea of Natural Law in Man: Four Themes." *Journal of the History of Ideas* 35 (1974): 3–16.

Horton, Robin. "African Thought and Western Science." In Bryan R. Wilson, ed., *Rationality.* New York: Harper, 1970, 131–71.

————. "Lévy-Bruhl, Durkheim and the Scientific Revolution." In Ruth H. Finnegan and Robin Horton (q.v.), 249–305.

————. "Paradox and Explanation: A Reply to Mr. Skorupski." *Philosophy of the Social Sciences* 3, nos. 3 and 4 (1973): 231–56, 289–314.

————, and Ruth H. Finnegan. See above, Finnegan, Ruth, and Robin Horton.

Hughes, H. Stuart. *Consciousness and Society: The Reorientation of European Social Thought, 1890–1930.* New York: Vintage Books, 1958.

————. "Vico and Contemporary Social Theory and Social History." In Tagliacozzo and White (q.v.), 319–26.

Hutcheson, Harold R. "Lord Herbert and the Deists." *Journal of Philosophy* 43 (1946): 219–21.

Huxley, Aldous. *Brave New World.* New York: Harper & Row (Perennial Library), 1969.

Johanson, Donald C., and Maitland A. Edey. *Lucy: The Beginnings of Humankind.* New York: Simon & Schuster, 1981.

Johnson, Roger A. et al. *Critical Issues in Modern Religion.* Englewood Cliffs, N.J.: Prentice-Hall, 1973.

Jones, Ernest. *The Life and Work of Sigmund Freud.* 3 vols. New York: Basic Books, 1953–57.

Kearns, Edward John. *Ideas in Seventeenth-Century France.* New York: St. Martin's, 1979.

King, Preston T. *The Ideology of Order: A Comparative Analysis of Jean Bodin and Thomas Hobbes.* London: Allen & Unwin, 1974.

Kluckhohn, Clyde. *Anthropology and the Classics.* Providence: Brown University Press, 1961.

Koenig, René. "Comte, Auguste." In *International Encyclopedia of the Social Sciences*, edited by David L. Sills. N.p.: Macmillan & Free Press, 1968, 201–06.

Kuhn, Thomas S. *The Essential Tension: Selected Studies in Scientific Tradition and Change.* Chicago: University of Chicago Press, 1977.

————. *The Structure of Scientific Revolutions.* 2d ed. Chicago: University of Chicago Press, 1970.

LaBarre, Weston. *The Ghost Dance: Origins of Religion.* New York: Dell, 1970.

————. "The Influence of Freud on Anthropology." *American Imago* 15 (1958): 275–328.

Lang, Andrew. *Myth, Ritual and Religion*. London: Longmans, 1913.

Laudan, Larry. *Progress and Its Problems: Toward a Theory of Scientific Growth*. Berkeley: University of California Press, 1977.

―――. "Towards a Reassessment of Comte's 'Méthode Positive.' " *Philosophy of Science* 38 (1971): 35–53.

Leach, Edmund. "Vico and Lévi-Strauss on the Origins of Humanity." In Tagliacozzo and White (q.v.), 309–18.

Sidney L. Lee. "Herbert, Edward. . . . " In *Dictionary of National Biography*, edited by Leslie Stephen and Sidney L. Lee. London: Oxford, 1949–50, 9:624–32.

Lenzer, Gertrude, ed. *Auguste Comte and Positivism: The Essential Writings*. New York: Harper, 1975.

Leroy, A. L. et al. *Studi su Hume*. Florence: La Nuova Italia, 1968.

Lévy-Bruhl, Lucien. *History of Modern Philosophy in France*. Chicago: Open Court, 1899.

―――. *The Philosophy of Auguste Comte* Translated by K. de Beaumont-Klein. Introduction by Frederic Harrison (1903). New York: A. M. Kelley, 1973.

Livingston, Donald W., and James T. King, eds. *Hume: A Re-evaluation*. New York: Fordham, 1976.

Locke, John. *An Essay Concerning Human Understanding* (1690). Edited by Alexander C. Fraser. New York: Dover, 1959.

Lovejoy, Arthur O. *The Great Chain of Being*. New York: Harper & Row, 1960.

Lowie, Robert H. *The History of Ethnological Theory*. New York: Farrar & Rinehart, 1937.

―――. *Primitive Religion*. New York: Grosset & Dunlap, 1952.

Lukes, Steven. *Emile Durkheim: His Life and Work*. New York: Harper & Row, 1972.

―――. "On the Social Determination of Truth." In Ruth Finnegan and Robin Horton, eds. (q.v.), 230–48.

[Martin Luther]. *The Large Catechism of Martin Luther*. Translated by R. H. Fischer. Philadelphia: Fortress, 1959.

―――. "Preface to the Complete Edition of Luther's Latin Writings." In *Luther's Works*, edited by Jaroslav Pelikan and H. T. Lehmann. Vol. 34. Edited by Lewis W. Spitz. Philadelphia: Muhlenberg, 1960, 323–38.

―――. *To the Christian Nobility of the German Nation Concerning the Reform of the Christian Estate*. Translated by C. M. Jacobs. In *Luther's Works*, vol. 44, edited by James Atkinson. Philadelphia: Fortress, 1966, 115–217.

Lyttle, Charles. "Lord Herbert of Cherbury, Apostle of Ethical Theism." *Church History* 5 (1935): 247–67.

McKown, Delos B. *The Classical Marxist Critiques of Religion: Marx, Engels, Lenin, Kautsky*. The Hague: Nijhoff, 1975.

McRae, Kenneth D. "Bodin and the Development of Empirical Political Science." In Horst Denzer (q.v.), 333–42.

Maigron, Louis. *Fontenelle. L'homme, l'oeuvre, l'influence*. Paris: Plon-Nourrit, 1906.

Manson, Richard. *The Theory of Knowledge of Giambattista Vico*. N.p.: Anchor, 1969.

Manuel, Frank E. *The Eighteenth Century Confronts the Gods*. New York: Atheneum, 1967.

―――. *The Prophets of Paris*. Cambridge: Harvard University Press, 1962.

―――. *Shapes of Philosophical History*. Stanford: Stanford University Press, 1965.

Marett, R. R. *The Threshold of Religion*. 2d ed. London: Methuen, 1914.

―――. *Tylor*. London: Chapman & Hall, 1936.

Marsak, Leonard M. "Bernard de Fontenelle: In Defense of Science." *Journal of the History of Ideas* 20 (1959): 111–22.

―――, ed. *The Achievement of Bernard le Bovier de Fontenelle*. Sources of Science, No. 76. New York: Johnson Reprint, 1970.

Marx, Karl. "Contribution to the Critique of Hegel's Philosophy of Right." In Reinhold Niebuhr, ed., *Marx and Engels on Religion*. New York: Schocken, 1964.

de Mas, Enrico. "Vico's Four Authors." In Giorgio Tagliacozzo, ed., *Giambattista Vico: An International Symposium*. Baltimore: Johns Hopkins University Press, 1969), 3–14.

Masson, Jeffrey Moussaieff. *The Assault on Truth: Freud's Suppression of the Seduction Theory*. New York: Farrar, Straus, & Giroux, 1984.

de Mauro, Tullio. "Giambattista Vico: From Rhetoric to Linguistic Historicism." In Tagliacozzo and White [q.v.], 279–95.

Mazlish, Bruce. *The Riddle of History: The Great Speculators from Vico to Freud*. New York: Harper, 1966.

Meggers, Betty J., ed. *Evolution and Anthropology*. Washington, D.C.: Anthropological Society of Washington, 1959.

Merrill, Kenneth R., and Donald G. Wester. "Hume on the Relation of Religion to Morality." *Journal of Religion* 60 (1980): 272–84.

―――, and Robert W. Shahan, eds. *David Hume, Many-sided Genius*. Norman, Okla.: University of Oklahoma Press, 1976.

Mesnard, Pierre. "La Pensée religieuse de Bodin." *Revue du seizième siècle* 16 (1929): 77–121.

Mill, John Stuart. *Auguste Comte and Positivism*. Ann Arbor: University of Michigan, 1965.

Morice, George P., ed. *David Hume: Bicentenary Papers*. Edinburgh: Edinburgh University Press, 1977.

Morrison, James C. "Vico and Spinoza." *Journal of the History of Ideas* 41 (1980): 49–68.

―――. "Vico's Principle of *Verum* is *Factum* and the Problem of Historicism." *Journal of the History of Ideas* 39 (1978): 579–95.

Mossner, E. C. "The Enlightenment of David Hume." In A. L. Leroy et al. (q.v.), 18–29.

Murphree, Idus L. "The Evolutionary Anthropologists: The Progress of Mankind. The Concepts of Progress and Culture in the Thought of John Lubbock, Edward B. Tylor, and Lewis H. Morgan." *Proceedings of the American Philosophical Society* 105 (1961): 265–300.

Neusner, Jacob. *The Way of Torah*. 3d ed. Belmont, Calif.: Wadsworth, 1979.

Niderst, Alain. *Fontenelle à la recherche de lui-même (1657–1702)*. Paris, 1972.

Niebuhr, Reinhold, ed. *Marx and Engels on Religion*. New York: Schocken, 1964.

Nisbet, Robert A. *The Sociology of Emile Durkheim*. New York: Oxford University Press, 1974.

Norbeck, Edward. "The Study of Religion." In Sol Tax and Leslie G. Freeman, eds., *Horizons of Anthropology*. 2d ed. Chicago: Aldine, 1977.

Opler, Morris E. "Cause, Process and Dynamics in the Evolution of E. B. Tylor." *Southwestern Journal of Anthropology* 20 (1964): 123–44.

Otto, Rudolf. *The Idea of the Holy*. Translated by John W. Harvey. New York: Oxford University Press, 1958.

Paley, William. *Natural Theology, or, Evidence of the Existence and Attributes of the Deity, Collected from the Appearances of Nature*. Philadelphia: J. Morgan, 1802.

Parsons, Talcott. "Durkheim's Contribution to the Theory of Integration of Social Systems." In K. H. Wolff, ed. *Emile Durkheim, 1858–1917: A Collection of Essays* ... Columbus: Ohio University Press, 1960, 118–53.

———. "Evolutionary Universals in Society." *American Sociological Review* 29 (1964): 339–57.

———. "The Theoretical Development of the Sociology of Religion." *Journal of the History of Ideas* 5 (1944): 176–90.

Paul, Robert A. "Did the Primal Crime Take Place?" *Ethos* 4 (1976): 311–52.

Penner Hans H., and Edward A. Yonan. "Is a Science of Religion Possible?" *Journal of Religion* 52 (1972): 107–33.

Pompa, Leon. *Vico: A Study of the 'New Science.'* Cambridge: Cambridge University Press, 1975.

Pons, Alain. "Vico and French Thought." In Tagliacozzo and White (q.v.), 165–85).

Popkin, Richard H. *The History of Scepticism from Erasmus to Spinoza*. Berkeley: University of California Press, 1979.

———. "Hume and Jurieu: Possible Origins of Hume's Theory of Belief." In A. L. Leroy et al. (q.v.), 30–47.

———. "Hume: Philosophical versus Prophetic Historian." In Kenneth R. Merrill and Robert W. Shahan (q.v.), 83–95.

———. "Scepticism and the Counter-Reformation in France." *Archive for Reformation History* 51 (1960): 58–87.

Preus, J. Samuel. "Machiavelli's Functional Analysis of Religion: Context and Object." *Journal of the History of Ideas* 40 (1979): 171–90.

———. "Religion and Bacon's New Learning." In F. F. Church and T. George, eds., *Continuity and Discontinuity in Church History*. Leiden: Brill, 1979, 267–84.

———. Review of Michel Despland (q.v.). In *Religious Studies Review* 12 (1986): 112–15.

———. "Zwingli, Calvin and the Origin of Religion." *Church History* 46 (1977): 186–202.

Price, J. V. "Scepticism in Cicero and Hume." *Journal of the History of Ideas* 25 (1964): 97–106.

Proudfoot, Wayne. "Religion and Reduction." *Union Seminary Quarterly Review* 37 (1981): 13–25.

———. *Religious Experience*. Berkeley: University of California Press, 1985.

Pummer, Reinhard. "*Religionswissenschaft* or Religiology?" *Numen* 19 (1972): 91–127.

Rappaport, Roy A. "Ritual, Sanctity and Cybernetics." *American Anthropologist* 73 (1971): 59–76.

———. "The Sacred in Human Evolution." *Annual Review of Ecology and Systematics* 2 (1971): 23–44.

Reinach, Salomon. *Orpheus: A General History of Religions*. Translated by Florence Simmonds. New York: Putnam, 1909.

Remmling, Günter W. *The Road to Suspicion: A Study of Modern Mentality and the Sociology of Knowledge.* New York: Appleton-Century-Crofts, 1969.

Rice, Eugene R. *The Renaissance Idea of Wisdom.* Cambridge: Harvard University Press, 1958.

Rickman, H. P. "Vico and Dilthey's Methodology of the Human Studies." In Tagliacozzo and White (q.v.), 447–56.

Ricoeur, Paul. *Hermeneutics and the Human Sciences: Essays on Language, Action and Interpretation.* Translated by John B. Thompson. New York: Cambridge University Press, 1981.

Rieff, Philip. *Freud: The Mind of the Moralist.* New York: Viking, 1959.

Robinson, John M. *Introduction to Early Greek Philosophy.* Boston: Houghton Mifflin, 1968.

Roellenbleck, Georg. *Offenbarung, Natur und judische Uberlieferung bei Jean Bodin: Ein Interpretation des Heptaplomeres.* Gütersloher: Verlagshaus Gerd Mohn, 1964.

———. "Der Schluss des 'Heptaplomeres' und die Begründung der Toleranz bei Bodin." In Horst Denzer (q.v.), 53–67.

Rose, Paul L. *Bodin and the Great God of Nature: The Moral and Religious Universe of a Judaizer.* Geneva: Droz, 1980.

Rossi, Mario M. *La vita, le opere, i tempi di Edoardo Herbert di Chirbury.* 3 vols. Florence: G. C. Sansoni, 1947.

Rousseau, Jean-Jacques. *The Social Contract.* Edited by Lester G. Crocker. New York: Washington Square, 1971.

Rubenstein, Richard L. *The Religious Imagination: A Study in Psychoanalysis and Jewish Theology.* Indianapolis: Bobbs-Merrill, 1968.

Rycroft, Charles. "A Case of Hysteria." Review of J. Moussaieff Masson, *The Assault on Truth,* q.v. *New York Review of Books,* 12 April 1984, 3–6.

Sabine, George H. "The Colloquium Heptaplomeres of Jean Bodin." In *Persecution and Liberty: Essays in Honor of G. L. Burr.* New York: Century, 1931, 271–310.

Saliba, John A. *'Homo Religiosus' in Mircea Eliade: An Anthropological Evaluation.* Leiden: Brill, 1976.

Salomon, Albert. "Fontenelle: In Praise of the Enlightenment." In idem, *In Praise of Enlightenment: Essays in the History of Ideas.* Cleveland: Meridian, 1962, 98–116.

Sharpe, Eric J. *Comparative Religion: A History.* London: Duckworth, 1975.

Simon, Lawrence H. "Vico and Marx: Perspectives on Historical Development." *Journal of the History of Ideas* 42 (1981): 317–31.

Skorupski, John. *Symbol and Theory: A Philosophical Study of Theories of Religion in Social Anthropology.* Cambridge: Cambridge University Press, 1976.

Slater, Philip E. *Microcosm: Structural, Psychological and Religious Evolution in Groups.* New York: Wiley & Sons, 1966.

Smart, Ninian. "Religion, Study of." In *New Encyclopedia Britannica.* 15th ed. Chicago: Encyclopedia Britannica, 1980. *Macropedia* 15: 613–28

Smith, Grafton E. *The Diffusion of Culture.* London: Watts, 1933.

Smith, Wilfred Cantwell. *The Meaning and End of Religion.* New York: Mentor, 1962.

———. *Toward a World Theology: Faith and the Comparative History of Religions.* Philadelphia: Westminster, 1981.

Smith, William Robertson. *Lectures on the Religion of the Semites* (1899). 3d ed. New York: Macmillan, 1927.

Southwold, Martin. "Buddhism and the Definition of Religion." *Man* 13 (1978): 362–79.

Spencer, Herbert. "Reasons for Dissenting from the Philosophy of M. Comte. In *Recent Discussions in Science, Philosophy, and Morals.* Rev. ed. (New York: Appleton, 1883), 113–36.

Spinoza, Benedict de. *A Theologico-Political Treatise.* Translated by R. H. M. Elwes. New York: Dover, 1951.

Spiro, Melford E. "Collective Representations and Mental Representations in Religious Symbol Systems." In Jacques J. P. Maquet, ed., *On Symbols in Anthropology: Essays in Honor of Harry Hoijer* (1980). Malibu, Calif.: Udena Publications, 1982, 45–72.

———. "Religion: Problems of Definition and Explanation." In Michael Banton, ed., *Anthropological Approaches to the Study of Religion.* London: Tavistock, 1963.

———, ed. *Context and Meaning in Cultural Anthropology.* New York: Free Press, 1965.

Stocking, George W., Jr. "Matthew Arnold, E. B. Tylor, and the Use of Invention." *American Anthropologist* 65 (1963): 783–99.

Strenski, Ivan. "Our Very Own 'Contras': A Response to the 'St. Louis Project' Report." *Journal of the American Academy of Religion* 54 (1986): 323–35.

Tagliacozzo, Giorgio, and Hayden V. White, eds. *Giambattista Vico: An International Symposium.* Baltimore: Johns Hopkins University Press, 1969.

———, and N. Verene, eds. *Giambattista Vico's Science of Humanity.* Baltimore: Johns Hopkins University Press, 1976.

Tax, Sol, and Leslie G. Freeman, eds. *Horizons of Anthropology.* 2d ed. Chicago: Aldine, 1977.

Thrower, James. *The Alternative Tradition: Religion and the Rejection of Religion in the Ancient World.* The Hague: Mouton, 1980.

Trevor-Roper, H. R. *The European Witch-Craze of the Sixteenth and Seventeenth Centuries, and Other Essays.* New York: Harper, 1969.

Van der Leeuw, G. *Religion in Essence and Manifestation.* Translated by J. E. Turner. 2 vols. New York: Harper & Row, 1963.

Waardenburg, J. J. *Classical Approaches to the Study of Religion.* 2 vols. The Hague: Mouton, 1973–74.

Wade, Ira O. *The Intellectual Origins of the French Enlightenment.* Princeton: Princeton University Press, 1971.

Walker, D. P. *The Ancient Theology: Studies in Christian Platonism from the Fifteenth to the Eighteenth Century.* Ithaca: Cornell University Press, 1972.

Wallace, A. F. C. "Revitalization Movements." *American Anthropologist* 58 (1956): 264–81.

Wallis, Wilson D. "David Hume's Contribution to Social Science." In F. P. Clarke and M. C. Nahm, eds. *Philosophical Essays in Honor of E. A. Singer Jr.* Philadelphia: University of Pennsylvania Press, 1942, 358–71.

Webb, Clement C. J. *Studies in the History of Natural Theology.* Oxford: Clarendon, 1915.

White, Leslie A. *The Evolution of Culture: The Development of Civilization to the Fall of Rome.* New York: McGraw-Hill, 1959.

Wiles, Maurice. *The Making of Christian Doctrine: A Study in the Principles of Early Doctrinal Development.* Cambridge: Cambridge University Press, 1967.

Wilken, Robert L. *The Myth of Christian Beginnings*. Notre Dame, Ind.: University of Notre Dame, 1980.

Willey, Basil. *The Seventeenth Century Background*. New York: Columbia University Press, 1958.

Wilson, Edward O. *On Human Nature*. New York: Bantam, 1978.

Wilson, Peter J. *Man, the Promising Primate*. New Haven: Yale University Press, 1980.

Wolf, Eric R. "The Study of Evolution." In Sol Tax and Leslie G. Freeman (q.v.), 33–45.

Wolin, Sheldon. *Politics and Vision: Continuity and Innovation in Western Political Thought*. Boston: Little, Brown, 1960.

Wood, Forrest. "Hume's Philosophy of Religion as Reflected in the *Dialogues*." *Southwestern Journal of Philosophy* 2 (1971): 185–93.

Yandell, Keith E. "Hume on Religious Belief." In Livingston and King (q.v.), 109–25.

Yates, Frances. "The Mystery of Jean Bodin." *New York Review of Books* 23, no. 16 (14 October 76): 47–50.

Index

Printed in the United States
119453LV00002B/26/A

9 780788 503214